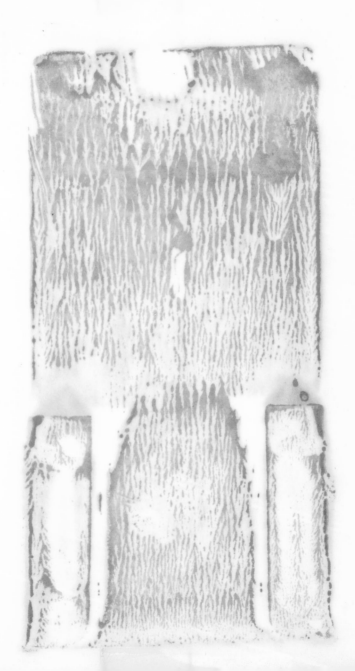

Mark Twain at Large

MARK TWAIN

At Large

Arthur L. Scott

HENRY REGNERY COMPANY · CHICAGO

FOR MY CHILDREN

PATRICIA, LAWRENCE, AND ELIZABETH

106295

ACKNOWLEDGMENTS

I wish to thank the trustees of the Mark Twain Company for permission to quote generously from the unpublished manuscripts of the Mark Twain Papers in the General Library of the University of California at Berkeley and from Mark Twain manuscripts located elsewhere. Special thanks are also due to Frederick Anderson, editor of the Mark Twain Papers, and to his predecessor, Henry Nash Smith, not only for their help and warm hospitality during my four visits to Berkeley, but also for their kindness in reading my manuscript and making valuable suggestions.

Of equal assistance have been Franklin J. Meine and A. Lynn Altenbernd, who also plowed through one of my drafts inch by inch and are responsible for many of the merits which the book may possess. Other scholars and Twainians who have been more helpful than they may realize include Joe Lee Davis, who first sparked and nurtured my interest in this topic many years ago; John T. Flanagan, who helped me to polish and publish my very first article on Mark Twain; and Chester L. Davis and Burney L. Fishback, of the Mark Twain Research Foundation, whose bimonthly *Twainian* and other activities have reawakened the Midwest to its Mark Twain heritage.

The University of Illinois Library in Urbana has, after two decades, ceased to astound me with the extent of its holdings, but its competent staff will never cease to delight me with its readiness to beg, borrow, or buy those odd items I've been unable to locate. To the staff I am most grateful. And surely no book has been inspired by two more beautiful settings than the Henry E. Huntington Botanical Gardens in San Marino and the Grand Teton Mountains of Wyoming.

Once more I add heartfelt thanks to my wife for leaving me strictly alone until those unavoidable days arrive during which she becomes, automatically now, my uncomplaining and indispensable partner in proofreading.

A. L. S.

PREFACE

At the age of thirty Mark Twain was a brash and popular news-paperman on the Pacific Coast. Seeking to broaden his fame, he soon went east, and in 1867 he traveled as a roving reporter on a pleasure cruise around the Mediterranean. His final trip to the continent of Europe came in 1903, when he took his wife back to their beloved Florence to die. Between these two trips, which demarcate his main productive decades, this most American of Americans circled the globe and, as many people fail to realize, passed more than one-third of his life outside the United States.

This book is about Mark Twain's travels and his opinions concerning the entire foreign scene.[1] The fun-loving Westerner of 1867 slowly grew into the international personage of 1897, who was residing with his family in Vienna and being paid court by the great and near-great of many lands. He had not become global in his fame without becoming global in his thinking as well. And because Mark Twain symbolized the American spirit to millions of people the world over, his voice seemed truly to be that of an unofficial Ambassador. With pride, no doubt, he therefore observed in his Vienna notebook, "During 8 years, now, I have filled the post—with some credit, I trust—of self-appointed Ambassador at Large of the U.S. of America—without salary."[2]

How Mark Twain became such an Ambassador-at-Large and finally a kind of oracle and how he served in these capacities are the subjects of the present study. The evidence is abundant. He crossed the ocean more than thirty times, seldom failing to comment on peoples and places. He wrote not only three thick travel books but also several novels set in the European past. Newspapers and magazines printed dozens of his articles about

Europe and elsewhere. Letters, speeches, notebook entries, conversations, interviews, and dictations manifest his lively international curiosity. We now have available for study, moreover, many filing cabinets filled with unpublished manuscripts of vital importance, which are here examined in regard to this subject for the first time. All these things help to fill in the portrait of Mark Twain as an envoy extraordinary.

The United States, as we know, has a long tradition of self-appointed emissaries, many of whom were, like Mark Twain, prominent men of letters. Courageous and democratic Americans had visited the Old World before Mark Twain. Wise men, outspoken men, compassionate men, even funny and irreverent men had traveled and made their reports. Where did Mark Twain fit into the pattern of these other emissaries? That is a question we should keep in mind as we trace his growth from a cocky Westerner into a kind of cosmopolitan conscience.

TABLE OF CONTENTS

Preface   vii

Foreword: A Glance
          at Other Literary Travelers   1

I. Mark Twain: Westerner   14

II. Easterner   71

III. Nationalist   122

IV. Ambassador-at-Large   162

V. Internationalist   224

VI. Oracle   254

Conclusion   301

Notes   308

Index   334

FOREWORD

A Glance at Other Literary Travelers

The unique advantage of America was the opportunity to create a new civilization free from the undemocratic restraints and oppressions of the Old World. Just before and after America won her political independence, such fair-minded gentlemen as Franklin, Jefferson, and John Adams had occasion to reside in Europe, where all three were horrified by the misery of the lower classes. Franklin, although charmed by the "elegant minds" of the upper class, complained that the multitudes were oppressed "below the savage state." Jefferson, like Mark Twain's Connecticut Yankee a century later, placed the blame squarely on the kings, priests, and nobles, whom he called an "abandoned conspiracy against the happiness of the mass of the people." And Adams, particularly shocked by the immoralities and injustices he found in France, deplored the fact that Europe was still shackled to cruel and outmoded gods.

During the early years of the republic few Americans went abroad merely as tourists. They went to study, to visit relatives, to make purchases, to cultivate business contacts. They had little cause to write about their travels. Before long, however, even England began to seem foreign, so that by 1805 guidebooks were appearing, and travelers were beginning to describe the standard sights for their readers.

Prior to the Civil War, American travelers did not deny the superiority of Europe in material progress and the fine arts, but, said Samuel Morse, their blood boiled to hear Englishmen denounce America as a nation of cowardly cheats. As for the aristo-

cratic social structure with its chasm between rich and poor, Noah
Webster voiced the common belief that Europe was "grown old
in folly, corruption, and tyranny" by endeavoring to build upon
the "mouldering pillars of antiquity." In the words of Cushing
Strout, who has recently described the mythology which made
the New World the dialectical antithesis of the Old:

> In this legend America is the land of the Future, where men be-
> long to a society of virtuous simplicity, enjoying liberty, equality,
> and happiness; Europe is the bankrupt Past, where fallen men
> wander without hope in a dark labyrinth, degraded by tyranny,
> injustice, and vice.[1]

Not all travelers believed this growing myth. Many artists,
historians, and men of letters felt a strong attachment to the Old
World. They mourned that America's past was barren and that
her utilitarian climate smothered the imagination. Even the patriotic young poet Philip Freneau complained, "On these bleak
climes . . . Tell me, what has the muse to do?"

Evidence that the muses were more happily pursued abroad
soon appeared in the writings of Washington Irving. With his
Sketch-Book (1819), Irving began a lifetime of glamorizing
Europe. Long residence abroad (1815–32) transformed Irving
from an amorous young dandy into a zealous antiquarian who
constantly strove to share with his plodding countrymen his own
infatuation with the romantic pasts of England, Germany, and
Spain. And so in love did he fall with the decorous high society
of Europe that he bemoaned the motley swarms of Americans
who were beginning to stalk the ancient streets "with all the easy
nonchalance that they would about in their own villages"—the
same easy nonchalance, by the way, with which Mark Twain
would confront Europe in 1867. Irving, with his fastidious
tastes, was what Ferner Nuhn has termed a child of the East
Wind: "West for action, East for status. West for function, East

for ornament. West for democratic color, East for aristocratic form."[2]

An interesting but flighty follower of Irving was Nathaniel Parker Willis, who confessed that his travel books were designed "simply and unambitiously to amuse." Although a good journalist, Willis lacked the antiquarian zeal of Irving. He lived solely for the present. To him pleasure was almost a religion. He seemed to have no sense of outrage at social or economic injustices, and he frankly admitted that the purpose of his travel books was not to demolish illusions but to enhance them. Willis maintained that he was proud to be an American but that he would rather live abroad amid the "ornamental."

Henry Wadsworth Longfellow's years abroad, on the other hand, were animated by none of the airy hedonism of N. P. Willis. The young poet-professor was a true disciple of Irving, whom he journeyed to Madrid to visit in 1835. He was again roving Europe in 1868 and 1869 while Mark Twain was busy writing *The Innocents Abroad*. Longfellow shunned the lighter side of life abroad, because, as he said, the Old World to him was a kind of Holy Land which made his heart swell "with the deep emotions of the pilgrim." As a consequence he viewed all of Europe through a rich and dreamy haze of the past—a haze which obscured the unpleasing aspects of the modern scene before his eyes.

A true scholar, Longfellow learned the languages of the Continent. Adapting and translating, he sought to reveal the glorious world of Europe's poetic lore to his English-speaking readers. His mind became a music box charged with the poetry of the Western world, says Van Wyck Brooks. No matter how we may reproach him for his lack of rugged honesty as a travel reporter, we must be grateful to Longfellow as a cultural ambassador for leading America back to the rich stores of the Old World.

Many Americans, however, did not echo the rhapsodies of

these sentimental travelers. Some were deaf to the siren voice of antiquity and refused to let the romance of the past obscure the coarse realities of the present. John Neal, for example, who went abroad first in the 1820's, was disappointed that he did not find a fortieth part of what he expected to see in Europe after reading Irving's *Sketch-Book*. In his own works, therefore, Neal heaped ridicule upon sentimental American tourists, a generation before Mark Twain popularized such ridicule.

Leading the forces of anti-romanticism in Europe was the great romancer himself, James Fenimore Cooper. When he lived abroad with his family (1826–33), Cooper moved with pleasure among the aristocrats, and yet his aggressive patriotism and his democratic idealism prevented him from yielding to the blandishments of the Old World. No sentimental archaism was able to suppress his deep concern for social justice and individual rights. In his three European novels he denounced tyranny which masqueraded as liberty, and in his five volumes of *Gleanings in Europe* he supported the cause of liberalism everywhere. England in particular he portrayed as a nation oppressed by aristocratic wealth, which dominated army, navy, courts of law, press, church, and even the House of Commons.

Cooper was an observant traveler and a ruggedly honest reporter. Few things escaped his notice. He detested the romantic American travelers—Irving most of all—for their deference to the Old World and for their seeming lack of patriotism. He would have been delighted to find in Europe more of that easy American nonchalance which Irving deplored. Despite his admiration for the titled gentlemen of Europe, Cooper kept his republican principles intact and resolutely set himself in opposition to the uncritical glamorizing of the Old World.

Ralph Waldo Emerson, although he had little in common with the squire of Cooperstown, also told his countrymen that they had "listened too long to the courtly muses of Europe." He shared Cooper's contempt for those tourists who went abroad merely to

cultivate the old graces or to wallow in the atmosphere of antiquity. Emerson himself was a moody tourist, occasionally dazzled,
but more often disappointed and annoyed. In a surprising number
of ways his reactions resemble those of Mark Twain a generation
later. Emerson, too, was something of a Philistine in Europe,
more impressed by good streets, lodgings, and cafés than by art,
music, architecture, and musty ruins. He assaulted the Church in
Italy for contributing to poverty, superstition, ignorance, and the
loosest kind of morals. And he resisted famous sights, saying,
"I won't be imposed upon by a name." In Rome in 1833 he observed:

> One must be thoroughly reinforced with the spirit of antiquity
> to preserve enthusiasm through all the annoyances that await the
> visitor to these ruins . . . What with these truculent fellows
> [guides] and the boys, and the beggars and the coachmen, all
> sentiment is killed in the bud, and most men clap their hands to
> their pockets and run.

Emerson, like Cooper, enjoyed the happy spirit of French
society, and the feudal character of Great Britain shocked his
republican nerves. England, he said, was "still the country of the
rich," while pauperism encrusted and clogged the state. He
seemed to agree with his young friend Thoreau that England was
like an old gentleman encumbered with a great load of ancient
baggage and trumpery which he had not the courage to burn.
"Whence this worship of the past?" Emerson asked. And yet,
like Mark Twain in his later years, he came to the conclusion that
the security of the world resided in the stability of England because England possessed a "national sincerity," was less mutable
than France, and stood for liberty.

Still more ambivalent in his attitude toward the Old World
was Nathaniel Hawthorne, not a tourist like Emerson, but like
Cooper a family man residing abroad for seven years. Hawthorne
began by making fun of the "vaunted scene of Europe." But later

he told a friend, "The United States are fit for many excellent purposes, but they certainly are not fit to live in." Yet he did come back to America to live, having decided that New England, although hardly gay, had less "mischief" in its atmosphere than anywhere else in the world. Henry James, who felt the same two-way pull himself, explained, "At home he [Hawthorne] fingered the musty, but abroad he seemed to pine for freshness."

In England and Italy both, the only foreign countries he knew well, Hawthorne was enchanted by the ingredients of romance: shadow, antiquity, mystery, "picturesque and gloomy wrong." These appealed to the artist in him. On the other hand, he burned with indignation at the social and political atrocities he witnessed. It was one thing to roam happily through crooked lanes, great cathedrals, and rare curiosity shops; it was quite another to follow the Thames, which, he said, cleft open the rotten heart of London, exposing faces distorted with vice and misery. "The whole question of eternity is staked there," he cried. "If a single one of these helpless little ones be lost, the world is lost."

Hawthorne found the human situation in Italy even more pitiable, for there the masses were oppressed by a Church unspeakably corrupt and by a priesthood bloated, pampered, and utterly without conscience; Mark Twain was far from first in attacking the Church in Italy. The Italian nobility, moreover, in contrast to England's, he found to be indolent and seemingly to cultivate a vicious way of life as if it were an art, and the only art worth learning. It is worth noting that Hawthorne's fictional heroes eventually turn their backs on the romantic charms of the Old World, just as Hawthorne, who recognized the relative barrenness of the American scene but unlike Henry James was not thwarted by it, himself did.

In England, in 1856, Hawthorne was visited by his old friend and neighbor Herman Melville, who was embarking on his last long trip. Melville had visited Europe twice before, and his reactions had been much like Hawthorne's, except that he was not much impressed by antiquity. He did envy England her poets and her hearty, robust novelists, but he was repelled by all the ugly by-products of the caste system. France and Germany failed to interest him, and he closed his 1849–50 journal with the cry, "Tomorrow I am *homeward-bound!* Hurrah & three cheers!"

Melville, like Mark Twain, was one of the few early authors also to visit the Pacific Islands, and his observations about them are curiously similar to those of the great humorist. Both men lamented that Christian missionaries were generally the vanguard of a most disagreeable kind of Western culture. Happy and harmless natives, said Melville, were too often "civilized" into draught horses and "evangelized" into beasts of burden. He asked his lecture audiences to pray with him that the gentle Polynesians might be spared all contaminating influences, including annexation by the United States.

Still more curious are the resemblances between Melville's journal of his 1856–57 Mediterranean trip and Mark Twain's observations about the same countries ten years later. Melville was in search of knowledge and truth whereas Mark Twain was interested only in money and pleasure, but both men heartily cursed the wild dogs of the Near East—the flies, the fleas, the footpads, and the beggars. Both were fascinated by the teeming Arab bazaars, but they both had the rough honesty to give disillusioned reports on the Holy Land: "Whitish mildew pervading whole tracts of landscape—" said Melville, "bleached-leprosy-encrustation of curses— . . . mere refuse and rubble of creation." To both men the once elegant façades now looked like spoiled pastry at which mice had been nibbling. And quite in keeping with *The Innocents Abroad* is Melville's tragic observation, "In the emptiness of the lifeless antiquity of Jerusalem the emigrant Jews are like flies that have taken up their abode in a skull."

Only in his final stop in England did Melville's spirits revive, causing him to echo faintly the sentimentalism of Washington Irving. It was while visiting the old colleges at Oxford that he for the first time felt love for his motherland, he confessed, and "hailed her with pride." He wished all of his countrymen could visit Oxford, for "I know of nothing more fitted by a mild & beautiful rebuke to chastize the sophomorean pride of Americans as a new and prosperous country."

Almost forgotten today, despite a rich and varied career, is Bayard Taylor, known in his time as the "great American traveler." Between 1846 and 1874 Taylor ranged widely throughout the world, learned many languages, wrote ten travel books, all very popular, and lectured extensively about his journeys. A vigorous and compulsive sightseer, he had been brought up on Washington Irving and later dazzled by N. P. Willis, whom he took as his model. Like Willis he resolved to be entertained by everything, even the Turkish narghili (water pipe) and his two hashish orgies. Almost invariably he treated illustrious sights with a sentimental awe which endeared him to his genteel readers. Flitting restlessly from continent to continent, Taylor, said Park Benjamin, traveled more and saw less than any other man of his day. In the words of his modern biographer, commenting on Taylor's travel books: "Movement is his deity; variety replaces thoroughness. The result is, most often, confusion and disappointment."[3]

Another traveler of fading reputation was James Russell Lowell, better known as a gentleman scholar and diplomat. Lowell made two extended tours of the Old World in the 1850's before settling down to teach, edit, write, and finally to serve his country as Minister to Spain and England. Ironically, Lowell made his most famous comment about Europe before he went there. In his *Fable for Critics* he cried boldly, echoing the Emersonian plea to his fellow Americans:

> Forget Europe wholly, your veins throb with blood,
> To which the dull current of hers is but mud;
> Let her sneer, let her say your experiment fails,
> In her voice there's a tremble e'en now while she rails.

But as time went on Lowell lost the fiery liberalism of his youth. His travel sketches are tedious, flabby, eager to display his erudition. Fresh, original comments in them are few. Before many years had passed, Lowell became a conservative New England Brahmin. Instead of "forgetting Europe wholly" and instead of hailing the vigorous native voices of Walt Whitman and Mark Twain, he was himself burrowing back with affection into the romantic old lore of Europe.

A decade or two younger than Lowell and Taylor was a new group of writers who were to pass many years abroad. Mark Twain, William Dean Howells, and Henry Adams were born between 1835 and 1838, and Henry James in 1843. All died between 1910 and 1920. The oldest, Mark Twain, got to Europe last, while the least traveled, Howells, wrote the most travel books. The one true expatriate, Henry James, employed Europe mainly for fiction, whereas the most widely traveled, Henry Adams, published the least about the foreign scene.

In his early years abroad Adams got what he termed a sort of "education reversed," in the beer gardens and music halls of Germany. His purpose was to equip himself for a career; to his disgust, however, he was forever getting "drunk on his emotions" and learning nothing useful. German politics he called "a scandal and a nuisance," and, like Mark Twain, he disliked almost everything about France, particularly the "French mind."

During the 1860's Adams lived in England, where his father had been appointed Minister by President Lincoln. To an extreme degree he shared the current hatred of the British, many of whom hoped to see his country divided and crippled by the Civil War. To know the British, he said, was to despise them, a "besotted race." He wanted nothing so much as to "wipe England off the earth." But most Anglo-American wounds quickly healed during the 1870's, and in time Adams lost his bitterness entirely. Indeed, in 1898 he went so far as to make a prophecy, as did Mark Twain at the same time, that in the coming century there would be a "new centralization, of which Russia is one pole, and we the other, with England between. The Anglo-American alliance is almost inevitable."

After his wife's suicide in 1885, Adams voyaged widely in Japan and the South Seas and finally returned to Europe to steep himself in the Middle Ages of the great cathedrals. Like Melville and Mark Twain, he was saddened to discover that Western culture was already ravaging the tropical Edens of the Pacific. Furthermore, also like Mark Twain, he had grown up in an atmosphere of buoyant faith that the power of science would be directed to noble ends, bringing peace and unification to the world. The faith of both men, however—men different in so many ways—collapsed in the swirling disorder near the end of the century. They lost their faith in Western civilization. Mark Twain found solace in nothing. Henry Adams found solace in the thirteenth century unified by the power of Christianity.

William Dean Howells, soon to be Mark Twain's second-best friend, fell in love as a young man with Italy, the only foreign country he really came to know. He had been appointed Consul in Venice as reward for his campaign biography of Abraham Lincoln. Although Howells never again resided in Europe for a prolonged period, in spite of the urgings of Mark Twain, he wrote a number of thoughtful, quite popular books about Italy, and five of his novels are laid in that country. In fact, says James Woodress, more than one-third of Howells' books exploit his Italian experience to some degree.

In his European travel books Howells is sober and objective; he sought to inform rather than to entertain. Venice to him was an enchanted city, but he called the renowned Bridge of Sighs a "pathetic swindle," and, like Mark Twain, he gave a disillusioned report on the dirty canals, the faded Old Masters, and the depressing, comfortless houses. In Rome he was not impressed by St. Peter's; as for the famed Blue Grotto of Capri, he thought it just another cave, dull and clammy. On the other hand, Howells did not join the democratic attack on the Church of Rome. The priests he met were "kind and amiable." Although distressed by the Italian moral code, he begged his readers to remember that Italian women, restricted as they were culturally, had almost no other release than sexual intrigues. Time and again he defended the Italian character, reminding American critics of those "long ages of alien and domestic oppression, in politics and religion, which must account for a vast deal of every kind of evil in Italy."

The travel books of Howells display little originality or humor, but they manage to cut through many a sentimental cliché about the Old World. All things considered, the distinction of Howells' many books about Europe lies in their beautiful blending of history and honest contemporary reporting. One could *read* history at home, he remarked, but one could *realize* it only on the spot where it had been lived. His books were carefully designed to make the reader his partner in the attempt to realize Europe's past and present.

While foreign experience was important to Howells, it was most of life to his friend Henry James, who seems to have been born with a nostalgia for Europe. His sensitive soul was offended by the boisterous United States, which he considered a "huge Rappaccini-garden, rank with each variety of the poison-plant of the money-passion." Consequently, after a disenchanting year in Paris, James took up permanent residence in a quiet retreat in England, visiting France and Italy in the summers.

Henry James was neither a passionate pilgrim nor an analytic traveler, but he did try to cultivate a true sense of the past. The beautiful by itself was not enough for him. It must be suffused, he said, with an aura of historic suggestion, with a "perfume of something done." Consequently, he had none of the common yearning to discover, because the novel and the remote had small attraction for him. In Europe, his artistic and antiquarian eye, he confessed, often subdued his critical senses, almost reconciling him to dirt, mold, and dilapidation even while his stomach rebelled. For example, the battered and slime-covered houses along the Arno would have been just squalid slums to him in America, said James, but in Italy they glowed "in the perfect felicity of picturesqueness."

Henry James was never completely happy in Europe, because his desire to be an urbane cosmopolite was forever at war with an inner yearning to be what he called a "concentrated patriot." The conflict within his soul reflected itself in a long series of international novels and stories, many of which treated the American traveler in the shifting scene of Europe. In his fiction, as in his travel sketches, James subordinated matters of a political, economic, and sociological nature. He loved the old forms and stately offices and pleasant rites of Europe, as had Irving and many others, but underneath them he discerned moral laxity, oppression, snobbery, and servile adoration of rank. Refinements and graces were plentiful on the Continent, but he did not find there the forthright moral virtues possessed by his native land. Consequently, he was torn between the two worlds of America and Europe. In book after book he brought into collision the rich sophistication of the Old World and the simple innocence of the New. And there is no avoiding the fact that, although James himself chose to live in Europe, his most admirable characters are American: Christopher Newman, Bessie Alden, Isabel Archer, Maggie Verver, Milly Theale, Lambert Strether.

Eventually the time came when Henry James confessed to his brother William that he had grown "deadly weary" of the whole international state of mind, partly because Europe always held the outsider at arm's length. He urged William to make his own sons "stick fast and sink up to their necks" in everything America could offer, instead of assimilating halfheartedly, as Henry himself was doing, the "alien splendors—inferior ones, too," of Europe. Long absence, it appears, made the thought of America nearly as romantic to the aging Henry James as the thought of Europe had been in his youth. But for him it was too late. In 1904

he made a trip to the States, where he was appalled by the new-
ness, the teeming masses, the feverish scramble for money. "Monstrous, monstrous!" he cried, retreating once more to England.
In spite of its sturdy moral virtues, America remained for Henry
James a sinister land of commercial barbarism, vulgar and desolate. He continued to live in Europe and to love Europe, accepting
her faults, partly for the romantic associations, but chiefly for
the beautiful and gracious culture he professed to find there.

I

Mark Twain: Westerner

Fʀᴏᴍ Benjamin Franklin through Henry James these early travelers were, all except Howells, men of the East Coast. To most of them travel meant crossing the Atlantic Ocean. Few cared to wander very far west in the United States, and the majority allowed a trip or two to Europe to sate their appetites for foreign travel.

Not so Mark Twain. Born in the Midwest, he sailed the Pacific before the Atlantic. A *Wanderjahr* of his boyhood had taken him east, but it was the great mines of Nevada which beckoned him during the Civil War. From there he crossed the Sierras into California, then the waters to the Sandwich Islands (Hawaii). Before his journeying was ended in the month of his death, there was almost nowhere he had not visited except South America, China, and Japan. He had crossed the ocean more than thirty times, not counting numerous trips to Bermuda and the Caribbean, and had taken up residence with his family in the five major countries of Europe.

Mark Twain's foreign travels began early in 1866. After having prospected and done newspaper work in Nevada for three years, he had been living in the fascinating city of San Francisco for two years. His boyhood in Hannibal, Missouri, seemed far behind him now, as did his four happy years of piloting on the Mississippi. He was doing local reporting for the newspapers, as he had been doing in Virginia City, Nevada, and he was beginning to grow "unspeakably tired" of it, he said. "I wanted another change. The vagabond instinct was strong upon me."[1] He was now thirty.

At this juncture there came an attractive offer from the *Sacramento Union*. The editor, keenly aware of the California-Hawaii trade, thought the time was ripe for some informative and entertaining letters from the Sandwich Islands. Mark Twain was just his man. Not only did Twain want to visit the romantic Islands, but also the *Union* was his kind of paper—a paper which lived up to its pledge to attack wrongs and corruption no matter where they might be and to befriend the common man. Mark Twain had been attacking corruption ever since he had reached the Coast. His attacks became so explicit and so fierce that public officials stood in fear of his pen. A San Francisco editor did not dare to print some of his more savage pieces. Mark Twain, indeed, had become known as a sort of moral censor. In trouble with the corrupt police, he once even had to flee to the hills to escape their wrath. There was a kind of good-natured irascibility to it when Mark Twain waded knee-deep in the blood of watchmakers, barbers, and chambermaids, but the fun went out of it when he turned his cold fury onto those who did injury to the basic human dignity of their fellow men.

The most striking example of this type of wrong on the West Coast was the mistreatment of the Chinese. These were the first foreigners Mark Twain had ever seen in large numbers. They did much of the dirty, menial work, and he liked them. "They are quiet, peaceable, tractable, free from drunkenness," he reported, "and they are as industrious as the day is long. A disorderly Chinaman is rare, and a lazy one does not exist."[2] How different they were from the troublesome Europeans he had encountered in Philadelphia many years before! In those days he had complained about the "abominable foreigners . . . who hate everything American."[3]

One Sunday afternoon a gang of hoodlums stoned a Chinese laundryman while an amused policeman simply looked on. Mark Twain, also a witness, wrote up the incident in such fiery language that his publisher killed the column, fearful of offending his lower-class readers. Only this lower class—and, later, he singled out the Irish immigrants as chief among the offenders —said Mark Twain, abused the Chinese: "they, and, naturally and consistently, the policemen and politicians, likewise, for these are the dust-licking pimps and slaves of the scum, there as well as elsewhere in America."[4] Strong words! And though inspired by the heat of the occasion, they were left unweakened five years later in *Roughing It* (1872). During the winter of 1870– 71 Mark Twain wrote a series of articles for the *Galaxy* magazine, "Goldsmith's Friend Abroad Again," about the persecution of the Chinese in San Francisco. In the *Buffalo Express,* too, of which he was part-owner, he continued his defense of the Chinese. As individuals they were tractable, serene, thrifty, and hardworking, he told his Eastern readers. In the domestic economy, he said, the Chinese were a "natural antidote to the reckless labor-strikes" and were proving to be the "greatest labor-saving machine of the age."[5]

Misled, perhaps, by the serenity of the Chinese, Mark Twain displayed no concern for the state of virtual slavery in which they worked both in Hawaii and on the Pacific Coast. He was in favor of coolie labor. He advocated more of it, especially in the mining regions of California. Coolies were paid only five dollars a month, he said, instead of eighty or a hundred. They were efficient, gave no trouble, and were obliged to complete their working contracts. The Pacific Railroad Company, he said, employed several thousand coolies and considered them the best and most peaceable and most faithful laborers they had ever tried.

Mark Twain's admiration for the Chinese people during these early years may have influenced a number of his actions later in life. Anson Burlingame, American Minister to China, was one of his heroes in those days, and it must have been extremely flattering to Mark Twain to be counseled in 1868 to try for the post upon Burlingame's resignation. Had he not already met Olivia Langdon, his bride-to-be, he might have campaigned. It was a position of honor among people he respected. Livy, however, seemed to need assurances of his stability, so he wrote her, "Wandering is *not* my habit, nor proclivity. Does a man, five years a galley-slave, get a habit of it & yearn to be a galley-slave always?"[6]

One should evaluate with care everything that is said in love letters. The fact remains, however, that Mark Twain did not seek the post in China. His interest in the Chinese, however, remained high, and ten years later he went out of his way to befriend them once more. He persuaded General Grant to intercede with the Peking government in behalf of outstanding Chinese students being educated in America. In the early eighties, moreover, he urged Grant to associate himself with a syndicate to help China to free herself from Tartar rule by constructing a system of railways, and in all probability the high regard which Mark Twain formed for the Chinese people in California in the sixties animated his support of their stand during the Boxer Rebellion at the turn of the century.

After the Chinese, the first foreign group Mark Twain studied was in Hawaii during his trip for the *Sacramento Union*. His intention was to stay for one month, but he stayed for four. He fell in love with the Islands, writing twenty-five travel letters, which total close to eighty-five thousand words—enough for a small book.[7] This was his first challenge in sustained writing. That he met the challenge well is attested by the fact that his reentry into San Francisco turned out to be a triumphal occasion. But if Mark Twain put the Islands on the map, they certainly returned the favor. They opened the lecture platform to him, they paved the way for his first European cruise, and they provided him with sixteen fresh chapters at the end of *Roughing It*.

California readers found Mark Twain's letters from Hawaii

to be entertaining and instructive. The letters were also unexpectedly moving in their descriptions of the natural beauties of the Islands. Interspersed among political, historical, and economic facts were amusing comments about native cigars, markets, donkeys, old legends, and such curious customs as the hula-hula and bathing in the nude.

The Hawaiian Islands provided Mark Twain with an experience both rich and confusing. Even the hula-hula confused him. He seems to have enjoyed it as a skilled and lovely performance, but his Victorian upbringing obliged him to report that it was also lascivious and demoralizing. A like ambivalence colored his thinking upon more important matters, such as the effect of Island living on white people, the influence of the missionaries, and imperialism.

Island living, he thought at first, could have no effects which were not beneficent. In place of the bustle and noisy confusion of San Francisco, the Islands presented him with a summer calm as tranquil as dawn in the Garden of Eden. It was a paradise without rowdies or beggars, a land of soft voices, free and joyous laughter. "No careworn or eager, anxious faces in the land of happy contentment," he said, "God what a contrast with California and the Washoe."[8] Californians, he believed, ought to come to this "Sunday land" of indolence and dreams at least twice a year to soothe their frazzled nerves. They would find a native hospitality which seemed to say:

> the door's always open— . . . come in when you feel like it—take a drink, take a smoke—wash your feet in the water pitcher if you want to—wipe 'em on the bedclothes—break the furniture—spit on the table-cloth—throw the things out doors—make yourself comfortable—make yrself at home.[9]

After four months in Hawaii, Mark Twain was disillusioned to find that the native hospitality and tropical serenity did not seem to rub off onto his countrymen. American residents, he said, always treated him with "considerable politeness," but seldom with true cheer and cordiality. Years in the Islands seemed to have robbed them of impulsiveness, openness, warmth of feeling, and to have made them "calculating, suspicious, reserved, cold and distant."

> They have cased themselves in a shell . . . and are not, if I may be allowed to suggest it—not happy. I thought differently at first. I thought they were the happiest people I had ever seen.[10]

Mark Twain's opinions about missionary work also underwent revision during his visit. He arrived filled with prejudices against the missionaries. His reading had taught him that the native Kanakas used to be simple, happy children of nature, not virtuous, but blissful in their ignorance. Then came the missionaries with their "Shalt-nots." They spoiled the fun and made the natives miserable by describing heaven and the near-impossibility of man's getting there. Before reaching Hawaii, Mark Twain noted: "S. Islanders never intended to work. Worse off now with all religion than ever before. Dying off fast. First white landed there was a curse to them."[11]

This was a view which Mark Twain was quick to amend upon gaining firsthand knowledge. Ivan Benson asserts that "Twain never could make up his mind definitely about the missionaries,"[12] and this is true. The reason is that he was never able to reconcile the three areas of missionary influence—social, doctrinal, and colonial. Even in these early days it angered him to see missionaries try to seduce natives from the religion of their ancestors and to see them used as pawns in the international game of imperialism.

Only for the "social" missionary did Mark Twain have any respect. The "preachers" simply created an atmosphere of hypocrisy and insincerity, he thought. Fortunately, the second wave of missionaries now on the Islands consisted largely of teachers, doctors, nurses, and village social workers. For these dedicated and self-sacrificing missionaries Mark Twain developed an admiration which amounted to awe. Not only did these missionaries establish schools and hospitals, but also they devised a just system of taxation, instituted a parliamentary government, and, in doing these things, actually set the common man free.

In short, Mark Twain forsook the "noble savage" concept in favor of the "blessings of progress" concept which inspired much of his thinking until about 1900. In Hawaii, he believed, the missionaries had reformed a nation of unsanitary, ignorant liars and thieves by teaching them a respect for human rights and a sense of their own dignity.

> The contrast is so strong—the benefit conferred upon the people by the missionaries is so prominent, so palpable, and so unquestionable, that the frankest compliment I can pay them and the best, is simply to point to the condition of the Sandwich Islands of Captain Cook's time, and their condition to-day. Their work speaks for itself.[13]

Mark Twain distinguished between the work of various denominations. Bishop Staley of the Reformed Catholic Church (High Anglican) was anathema to Mark Twain, who spent his best sarcasm on the Bishop and his Mission. On the other hand, and most curiously, in view of his later contempt for the French and the Catholics, he had nothing but praise for the French Roman Catholic Mission in Hawaii. The French Catholics, he believed, were so honest, industrious, devout, and intelligent that even the American Protestants were forced to honor both them and their work.

Political misuse of missionaries as a colonial weapon was hateful to Mark Twain. He said that France had got possession of the Society Islands and the Marquesas by means of the Roman clergy and was now trying the same strategem in Hawaii. At this date, the fact of imperialism did not trouble his conscience as much as the quality of it. His equalitarian spirit was repelled by the arrogance of the French and British nonmissionaries. They abused, humiliated, and bullied the native King, he said, treating him "like a dog." By means of warships, they forced acceptance of terms so degrading that they would "rankle till the end of time." "Metaphorically," he summed it up, "the French nation spit in the face of Hawaii."[14]

Ironically, added Mark Twain, the French and English had been able later to caress and mollify Hawaiian royalty to such a degree that the King now worshiped them. Still worse, the King hated the Americans, the people most responsible for lifting his country up. Mark Twain thought that this hatred stemmed from Americans' being democratic "through & through—no cringing to royalty—free, out-spoken, independent & fearless."[15] It should be pointed out, however, that the King was well treated when visiting England, whereas he ran into racial prejudice in the United States. A Virginia planter, for instance, announced that he would not sit at table with a nigger.

Repugnance for British and French politics in the Islands caused Mark Twain to hope that America could free Hawaii from the grip of the Old World. The American missionaries, more than others, he thought, had really civilized these natives. America, therefore, had special rights. She would be wise to subsidize a line of fast steamers and to populate the Islands with Americans. This would encourage the investment of more capital as well as provide a labor market. The Islands, he urged, could be of great economic importance, because nowhere else were there grown better sugar, cotton, and rice in such generous supply. "The property has got to fall to some heir," he announced, "and why not the United States?"[16] And yet Mark Twain was not a true expansionist in these early days. He was quick to scoff at

suggestions that the United States purchase the Virgin Islands
or Cuba, because he saw no benefits there. In the words of a
modern critic:

> Though willing to make exceptions for his friends he basically
> agreed with the "little America" position that foreign real
> estate, unlike foreign trade, dangerously built up federal over
> state government at home and gave politicians more patronage
> to misuse.[17]

As a good Californian, however, Mark Twain was willing to
argue that annexing Hawaii would be a smart move by the United
States. Seldom, at first, was he troubled by thoughts of what
annexation might mean to the Islands. As time went on, he began
to ponder this. His thoughts were not pleasant because of the
ugly picture presented to him by American behavior in general.
On January 9, 1873, a month before commencing work on his
satirical novel, *The Gilded Age,* he unburdened himself in the
New York Tribune. The letter, rife with irony, serves as a mild
prelude to his more savage papers at the end of the century:

> We *must* annex those people. We can afflict them with our wise
> and beneficent governments. We can introduce the novelty of
> thieves, all the way up from street-car pickpockets to municipal
> robbers and government defaulters. . . . We can give them rail-
> way corporations who will buy their Legislature like old
> clothes.[18]

Jest though he might about waking up "that little bunch of
sleepy islands," Mark Twain became genuinely concerned for
their welfare. But that was in the future. Meanwhile, he considered the Islands well governed by a benevolent monarchy which
had called into service the best educated, the ablest, and the most
enlightened of all the natives. His letters sang the praises of
royalty and nobility, who were far above the ordinary, in his
opinion. The whole nation, he said, was saturated with the spirit

of "democratic Puritanism." "This is a *republic* to the very marrow," he insisted, "and over it sit a King, a dozen Nobles and a dozen ministers."[19]

No tropical island, of course, is an unadulterated paradise, and Mark Twain had his own method of discussing many disagreeable facts. He pretended to have with him a low-minded traveling companion by the name of Brown. Whenever Mark Twain wished to call attention to such things as fleas, spiders, red ants, mosquitoes, and scorpions, Mr. Brown would be allowed to make a crude remark about them. Sometimes Mr. Brown would complain for minutes at a time. Mark Twain, by objecting to the vulgarity and complaints of his companion, protected his own image as a gentleman who looked on the pleasant side of life. Later, he found Mr. Brown useful for his outspoken realism in letters from the East and from the Mediterranean, but he did away with his services in *The Innocents Abroad* and thereafter.

Outspoken realism, however, remained characteristic of Mark Twain's writing. As a born satirist, he had a keen eye for the unpleasant; as a Westerner, he was used to speaking his mind. It bothered him, therefore, not to be sure exactly where he stood on everything. Ambivalence, such as he experienced with the missionaries and with the annexation of Hawaii, made him uncomfortable. He knew that his writing was not at its best when trying to function within that vast gray area of indifference, vacillation, and uncertainty. He liked to pick sides as quickly as possible. Only then could he seat himself with pleasure at his table to write himself into either an immense enthusiasm or a savage fury. He thrived in an atmosphere of superlatives and emotional fervor.

After his return from Hawaii, Mark Twain did not remain long on the West Coast. His sights were set higher. He proposed to take a trip around the world and contracted with the *Daily San Francisco Alta California* for another series of travel letters. The plan was to visit China for a while, then proceed westward,

ending up at the Paris Exposition.* First, however, he wanted
to see his family and old friends again, now that the war was
over and he had achieved a degree of success as a newspaper
reporter and commentator.

On December 15, 1866, therefore, he sailed on the "America"
from San Francisco, bound for Nicaragua and thence to New
York. The twenty-six travel letters which he wrote aboard ship
and from the East form a valuable link between his Hawaiian
correspondence of 1866 and his letters from the Mediterranean
of 1867.

This middle series of travel letters covers almost six months.
Although the travelers were in Nicaragua for only two days, Mark
Twain got off two letters about crossing the isthmus by padding
the second one with facts and statistics. The travelers crossed by
river, lake, and road. The scenery and atmosphere were enchanting, he said, the road was excellent, the native women were pretty,
and the whole affair was a "jolly little scamper."[20]

Even news of a cholera epidemic, which soon became most
serious, could not dampen Mark Twain's high spirits. The weird
procession of four hundred tourists on horseback and muleback
and in four-mule ambulances amused him as it crossed the isthmus
from one steamer to another. And as their riverboat wound
through the splendid jungle with its gorgeously plumed birds
and "dark grottos, fairy harbors—tunnels, temples," he could
only exclaim that it was "paradise itself—the imperial realm of
beauty, nothing to wish for to make it perfect."[21]

At Key West twenty-one passengers deserted the plague-ship,
and seven more were to die of cholera before reaching New York
on January 12. Mark Twain stuck it out. He had things to do. In
New York, C. H. Webb was preparing *The Jumping Frog* for
publication as a book, and Mark Twain earned publicity, but no
money, when he "poured the Sandwich Islands out" on a packed
house at the Cooper Institute. His travel letters continued, but he

* *China beckoned him several times, but he never got there.*

was unable to find a publisher for the book he wanted to write on Hawaii.

Most exciting to Mark Twain was an announcement of the Mediterranean cruise planned by the "Quaker City." This new-fangled type of argosy intrigued him. He wanted to go and began to to pull strings. Finally, on returning to New York from a six-week visit in Missouri, he got the good news. The chief of the *Alta California* bureau in New York met him with a check for the 1,250-dollar cruise fare and a telegram: "Ship Mark Twain in the Holy Land Excursion and pay his passage."

With his immediate future assured, Mark Twain set about re-newing his old acquaintanceship with New York. He had been here when seventeen; he was now thirty-one. The letters which he continued to mail to the *Alta* teemed with the bustle and diversity of the metropolis. He was fascinated, but by no means pleased, with everything about him, and he was frank to say so in his sketches of the city. In their candid criticism of manners and morals these *Alta* letters were of a piece with his earlier news-paper writing in San Francisco. Critics who denounce Mark Twain's first book of foreign travel for its allegedly biased fault-finding should read his domestic sketches of the 1860's. He inveighed not only against the sentimentalism, the ignorance, the brutality, and the corruption of his countrymen, but also against the shocking failures of their most cherished institutions, such as Congress, the church, and the courts of law. In some ways he let Europe off easy. Critical though he was to be of much that he found in the Old World, Mark Twain did not go abroad with a chip on his shoulder, daring the first Frenchman to knock it off.

Nor did Mark Twain look on the trip as a reverent pilgrimage in the fashion of so many shipmates. He was from Missouri, and he was traveling for money and fun. Not accustomed to glancing deferentially over his shoulder at Europe, he prepared himself now to confront her as if she were an elderly stranger about whom he had heard both bad and good. He was also something of an

American Adam, setting out in a state of innocence to new-name
the flowers and trees and the beasts of the field. To the best of his
ability he would give them the names which fit.

After a great deal of publicity and preparation, the "Quaker
City" sailed from New York on June 8, 1867. It touched at
Bermuda, spent several days in the Azores, then proceeded to
Gibraltar, where a number of passengers chose to travel across
Spain to Paris. Mark Twain, with five friends, plus "five bottles
and 75 cigars," crossed to Tangier for a day and a half, then went
up to Paris from Marseilles. They spent more than a week in
Paris, then went back to Marseilles and over to Genoa. Traveling
mostly by train and stagecoach, Mark Twain deliberately followed
the tourist trail from Genoa to Venice and from Lake Como to
Mount Vesuvius. There is little he missed in the picturesque land
of Italy, which was currently in the process of becoming a unified
nation.

From Naples they sailed to Piraeus, the port of Athens, where
Mark Twain and a few other daredevils ran the quarantine one
night to see the Acropolis. Thence to Constantinople, several
Russian ports on the Black Sea, and south to Smyrna. All this
cruising was followed by long, hot donkey-rides inland to Damascus, then south to Jerusalem, and finally out to the port of
Jaffa. There the "Quaker City" picked up the weary travelers and
carried them to Egypt and back to Spain. On November 19 the
cruise ended in New York.

During these months Mark Twain fulfilled his contract of
fifty travel letters to the *Alta,* an average of two letters a week. He
expected to write his final eight letters during the slow homeward
voyage but received the blighting news in Alexandria that fourteen letters had been lost in the mail and must be replaced. Now
pressed for time, he replaced the lost letters with less careful, less
personal, and less detailed material. He padded these last letters
with more legends and guidebook matter than usual, because his
notes were sketchy. Egypt and the last six weeks of the tour were

never described for the *Alta;* they had to be written from scratch a year later for his book. And, unfortunately, Mark Twain never did leave a record of those "seven delightful days" traveling through southern Spain, because the vivacious and likable Miss Julia Newell was one of his three companions and he feared that he might caricature her, or so he said.[22]

One suspects that Mark Twain left out Spain also because he had no material at hand to refresh his memory a year later. He could "smouch" ideas about Egypt from any number of the other pilgrims, but their writings could not help him with Spain. Even his own notebook was bare—or maybe Spain is in a lost notebook and some lost letters—and "Mother" Fairbanks, his new friend and helper, could be of no use to him here.* Sadly, therefore, Spain remains to this day the only country Mark Twain visited without describing.

In addition to his *Alta* letters Mark Twain sent a number of letters to New York papers. It was probably these which convinced Elisha Bliss of the American Publishing Company that there was gold in this material. That winter it was Bliss who packed Mark Twain off on the long trip back to California to pry permission from the *Alta* to make a book of his own letters, which had been copyrighted by the newspaper.

Once permission was granted, Mark Twain set to work to prepare his text for book publication. To lend his account wider appeal, he modified the burlesque, deleted much of the slang and small-town humor, changed allusions that would be wasted east of the Rockies, and made hundreds of stylistic improvements. As Henry IV had banished Falstaff, Mark Twain now banished

---

* *Mrs. A. W. Fairbanks, of Cleveland, was a sort of adopted mother to Mark Twain during the homeward voyage. He valued her advice while writing his newspaper letters and preparing some of his books. She also supplied him with accounts written by others in the party—accounts which, we are told, "coincide almost exactly" with his own.*[23]

Mr. Brown, who took with him much of the broadest humor and crudest burlesque.[24]

When he wrote *The Innocents Abroad* (1869), Mark Twain was less influenced by literary traditions than any other American writer of importance. He found waiting for him, however, a receptive audience prepared by Artemus Ward, Josh Billings, and the other newspaper humorists of the day. From these men he had learned a means of perception, a point of view, a method of evocation. Broad burlesque, lack of reverence, personal anecdote, grotesque exaggeration, juxtaposition of irrelevant ideas, casual shifting from one comic pose to another—all these were in the vein of Southwestern humor. And Mark Twain had learned his lessons well.

At times he feared lest he had learned some of the lessons too well. In Europe, as in America, he laughed at many objects of traditional veneration and was taken to task for want of taste. Shortly after the book was published, he confessed to his publisher, "The irreverence of the volume appears to be a tip-top good feature of it financially diplomatically speaking, though I wish with all my heart there wasn't an irreverent passage in it."[25] And many years later, in the summer of 1905, his secretary tells us, he "railed at *The Innocents Abroad* because it was 'cheap, ungrammatical, & not fit for a gentleman's library.' "[26]

In his late years it is understandable that Mark Twain deplored the lack of polish in his early book, but there is no sign that he regretted its lack of reverence. In 1869, however, he was courting a shy and delicate girl from an Elmira family of wealth. She had even helped him to edit the book. Who can blame him, therefore, for being stung by the book's rather cool reception in high places? The masses devoured the book with joy, but the *literati,* then as later, believed it completely vulgarized the most revered things in the Old World. To these men *The Innocents Abroad* seemed indifferent to cultural values and grossly ignorant. Its author, they thought, must be lacking in any semblance of historical imagination, must be defiantly American, and must be intent on debasing everything which time and affection had honored.[27]

How unfair this cultivated opinion actually was we shall see in a moment. Still, it did upset Mark Twain. Henry Seidel Canby is probably right in assigning the reason; namely, that Mark Twain was trying hard to become respectable and "wanted to be someone like Bayard Taylor, whom he knew very well later."[28] Be this as it may, Mark Twain at the age of thirty-two was too much the product of his Western environment to be able to change his Jacksonian approach to the Old World. Nor did he—deep in his heart—want to change it. Although he would have welcomed the admiration of the Boston Brahmins, it was one of his fundamental convictions that a discriminating irreverence was the creator and protector of human liberty. And nothing was more dear to his heart than human liberty.

Such respectable authors as Cooper, Emerson, Hawthorne, and Melville had shown the groundlessness of America's subservience to Europe. To their sober analyses Mark Twain added a new dimension by deriding, with comic satire, all sentimental homage to the Old World. With a small band of freeborn and fun-loving companions he romped through venerable lands and reported them inferior to America on many counts. And they were inferior on many counts, else the founding of a new nation in America had been all in vain. It has been suggested that Mark Twain's attitude of flippancy may have been caused by disillusion at making a long pilgrimage, as it were, only to find the tomb empty. Not so. Although his eye was sharp and critical, his mood had been always a holiday mood, never that of a pilgrim visiting a sacred tomb.

Even in his dissent from the sober treatment of Europe, Mark Twain was not really breaking new ground. Theodore Witmer had roamed the Continent in a holiday mood and written a popular travel book entitled *Wild Oats Sown Abroad* (1853). This handsome playboy made fun of romantic guidebooks and was not afraid to charge even the Cardinals of Rome with immoral conduct. Near the end he confessed to having "supped full of ruins" and to being "weary of this eternal call for admiration." He even had the temerity to cry, in annoyance frequently echoed by Mark Twain, "Pshaw upon history! It makes heroes of the past only to belittle the present."[29]

Still closer to Mark Twain in spirit was Samuel Fiske, who had written travel letters to the *Springfield* (Mass.) *Republican* and later published them in *Mr. Dunn Browne's Experiences in Foreign Parts* (1857). Fiske's portrait of Europe was utterly disillusioned. The greedy guides, the beggars, the filth and vermin and mangy dogs enraged him. Also he lampooned the rhapsodic travelers, as well as the "tiresome, trumpery, old brick and stucco humbugs of ancient ruins" which "aren't worth an old brick kiln."[30] Fiske had a keen eye and a turn of phrase not unlike Mark Twain's, and he was even quicker to debunk. At the conclusion of his Italian journey he wrote:

> Believe me, there are things in Italian travelling which are not down in the books. If a person has the temper of an angel, the purse of a nabob, the stomach of an ostrich, the skin of a rhinoceros, is not pressed for time and has not the sense of smell, I see no reason why he should not enjoy a leisurely tour over the whole of this most beautiful land.[31]

Not only in Europe, but also in the Holy Land, Mark Twain had forerunners. Best known, perhaps, is John W. De Forest, a realistic novelist of considerable power. His little book entitled *Oriental Acquaintance; or Letters from Syria* (1856) is light, humorous, and disenchanted. He did not mind emphasizing the inescapable fleas whose "vigorous burrowings" time and again destroyed one's appreciation of a splendid scene. Nor did he romantically ignore the beggars, the wild dogs, the incredible poverty and filth. Although he seldom poked fun either at himself or at his fellow travelers, De Forest was at one with Mark Twain in describing the ugly desolation of the Holy Land and the impossibility of achieving a sense of reverence anywhere. "There is such an air of absurdity about most of the sacred localities and traditions which abound at Jerusalem," he said, "that they excite unbelief and irreverence rather than faith and devotion."[32]

Possibly Mark Twain was not acquainted with the anti-romantic travel books of Witmer, Fiske, and De Forest, but he probably read James De Mill's comic novel *The Dodge Club; or, Italy in MDCCCLIX,* because its serialization in *Harper's Monthly* began four months before his own trip started. Although this novel says little about European travel, Mark Twain may have learned several things from it. It is laced with lively talk and humorous anecdotes. It relates several exciting adventures. The text is interlarded with illustrations, mainly comic in nature. Most important of all, De Mill's focus is always on four or five happy-go-lucky Americans who refuse to be overawed by ancient Europe. Their "principle," as they state it, is to "dodge all humbugs and swindles, which make traveling so expensive generally." Moreover, it makes some of them actually angry to see tourists pretend to go into raptures all the time. Pompeii, for example, disgusts the Senator with its small size. The guidebook's description of it, he complains, is an "enormous imposition":

> The fellows who write about it get into the heroics, and what with their descriptions, and pictures, and moralizing, you believe it is a second Babylon. It don't seem possible for any of them to tell the truth. . . . I know I'm supposed to find this here scene very impressive, but I'll be hanged if I'm satisfied.[33]

The Dodge Club, of course, was fiction, and *The Innocents Abroad* itself was a kind of picaresque novel, an adventure story of several fun-loving American realists in strange lands. One wonders whether Mark Twain was familiar with Lowell's early complaint that in ninety-nine books out of a hundred tourists bored the reader by retailing sensations they thought they *should* have experienced, instead of telling him what they *actually* felt.

"There are two kinds of travellers," said Lowell, "those who tell us what they went to see and those who tell us what they saw. The latter class are the only ones whose journals are worth sifting."[34]

Mark Twain felt the same way. He wrote an enthusiastic letter to his publisher about a suggested Frontispiece: "What they *expected* to see—and what they *did* see."[35] Although such an illustration was not used, Mark Twain made the point in his Preface. The purpose of *The Innocents Abroad,* he asserted, was to suggest to readers how they would be likely to see the Old World, if they viewed it with their own eyes, instead of through the eyes of previous travelers. He offered no apology for writing a different kind of book; "for I think I have seen with impartial eyes, and I am sure I have written at least honestly, whether wisely or not."

To write honestly is a fine and brave thing. It enables one to avoid the time-worn clichés, and it exposes one to censure by the traditionalists. Many writers have tried—too many—but, as R. W. B. Lewis points out, no writer who is both honest and truly American has "been able to pretend an authentic initial communion with the European past."[36] Even young Washington Irving had not pretended such a communion. What chance, then, did the untutored Mark Twain have, brought up as he was on Mississippi mud and fresh come from the boisterous, unsanctified life of the Frontier?

This does not imply, however, that the excursion was a failure for Mark Twain. Far from it. Until he became surfeited with sights and bone-weary with travel in Syria and Palestine, he had a magnificent time. It is true, of course, that in general the sixty-seven Innocents on board the "Quaker City" were indeed a "pretty dusty crowd," as Stephen Leacock has observed,[37] but Mark Twain did manage to round up several happy-go-lucky companions to partake in his romp through venerable lands.

The ship was three weeks crossing to Gibraltar, where the fun actually began. Mark Twain's seven chapters on this part of the trip get the book off to a slow start. Twenty years later he confessed that he and the Lord had made the same mistake: "He thinks about the world, now, pretty much as I think about the 'Innocents Abroad.' The fact is, there is a trifle too much water in both."[38]

His initiation into the European world was not auspicious. The shiftless, vermin-ridden island of Fayal in the Azores did not inspire him. His contempt for the "Jesuit humbuggery" which the Portuguese landowners foisted on the impoverished natives presaged his assault on the Church in Italy. Quite a turnabout from his praise of the Catholic missionaries in Hawaii! For the most part, however, he contented himself with lifting dry statistics from guidebooks on the Azores. His private opinion about the ugliness of the native women was not for print: "They say they are not virtuous," he noted, "but I cannot see how the devil they can possibly be otherwise—for fornication with such cattle would come under the head of the crime without a name."[39]

While the "Quaker City" recoaled for two days at Gibraltar, Mark Twain crossed the straits with five friends to Tangier, Morocco. Here he was plunged into an Arab culture. Swarthy men in flowing costumes and women veiled from masculine eyes milled about him. The buildings were different from any he had ever seen, and so were the streets, the foods, the noises, and even the smells. He was entranced: "We wanted something thoroughly and uncompromisingly foreign—foreign from top to bottom . . . nothing to remind us of any other people or any other land under the sun. And lo! in Tangier we have found it."[40]

If he was entranced, he was also disillusioned about certain things. For two chapters he described the exotic Arab world and the overwhelming impression it made upon him. His glimpses of Arabian women, however, probably recalled to him his first glimpses of the "noble Red Man" in 1861. On actually viewing the scrawny, unsavory Goshoot Indians, Mark Twain had felt the paint and tinsel fall away. He had been seeing these creatures before, he said, only "through the mellow moonshine of romance."[41] So it was with the females of Tangier, whose ugliness was wisely hidden by veils.

Making up for this disappointment was the sight of his first ancient ruins. Hasty critics have accused Mark Twain of lacking historical imagination, of being unable to respond to the relics of the past. The truth is that he frequently waxed as romantic as that fervid antiquarian, Washington Irving. Amid the hoary relics of Tangier, for instance, it seemed like profanation to him to laugh or jest. Even the frivolous chat of the day, he said, was unsuited to venerable antiquity of this sort:

> Here is a crumbling wall that was old when Columbus discovered America; was old when Peter the Hermit roused the knightly men of the Middle Ages to arm for the first Crusade; was old when Charlemagne and his paladins beleaguered enchanted castles and battled with giants and genii in the fabled days of the olden time; was old when Christ and his disciples walked the earth; stood where it stands to-day when the lips of Memnon were vocal, and men bought and sold in the streets of ancient Thebes![42]

When not beset by beggars or other vexations, Mark Twain could match historical sentiment with any of his predecessors. This mood, however, was but one of many in his account. It showed itself also in a number of romantic legends which he introduced to enrich the atmosphere of the book, as well as to pad out its content.

In general, however, Mark Twain had the common, not the scholarly, touch. The Innocent was charmed by novelty, whether it was ancient ruins, sacred relics, or gondolas, bearded ladies, emperors, or Turkish baths. He was a young man from the West; to him the Old World was new. Proud, but not arrogantly proud, of being an American, Mark Twain was not afraid of seeming extraneous to the foreign scene. Nor was he embarrassed to show that he was often interested most of all in those very matters which other travelers suppressed in their writings. For one thing, he was more interested in people than he was in things. In Venice it was not the sculptured palaces that he studied, but rather the marvelous skill of the gondoliers. As a sightseer he was determined to miss nothing on his first trip, with the result that he went to bed every night completely tired out. Not always did he even bother to describe the standard sights; he barely mentioned the renowned International Exhibition in Paris:

> It was a wonderful show, but the moving masses of people of all nations we saw there were a still more wonderful show. I discovered that if I were to stay there a month, I should find myself looking at the people instead of the inanimate objects on exhibition.[43]

In a curious fashion Mark Twain's interest in people rather than things colored even his judgment of art. The Old Master "rascalities" he had complained of in New York before the trip now began to confront him at every turn in Europe. Their faded colors did not please his untrained eye as did the brighter copies, but his chief indictment was of the undemocratic social system in which the Old Masters had worked. He was disgusted by the groveling spirit which caused them to "prostitute their noble talents to the adulation of such monsters as the French, Venetian, and Florentine Princes."[44] He could not bear to look at Raphael's picture of the vicious De Medicis seated in heaven, conversing familiarly with the Holy Family. Such "nauseous adulation" of evil patrons could not be excused. At least one critic, V. F. Calverton, considers these strictures by Mark Twain to display the first truly American spirit, except for Walt Whitman's, in the literature of the United States.[45]

The Innocents Abroad actually contains far less abuse of the

Old Masters than criticism leads one to believe. The original newspaper letters had been more outspoken: Brown had grumbled that "The Last Supper" looked like an old fireboard, and Mark Twain had agreed. A letter from Tiberias even compared Titian and Tintoretto with "Syrian frescoes," that is, with outside walls decorated with drying disks of camel dung. But this sort of thing was thought a bit rough for the book. "Blame the fine arts & the Old Masters, mother mine," he wrote Mrs. Fairbanks in 1868, "that is forbidden ground for me—couldn't say a word without abusing the whole tribe and their works like pick-pockets.—Only a wholesome dread of *you* kept me from doing it anyhow."[46] Most of the fun, therefore, that Mark Twain had in the galleries was, as elsewhere, at the expense of guidebooks, sentimental tourists, and native guides, not at the expense of the art itself.

Mark Twain confessed that he had had no training in the fine arts and that, as a result, his capacity for aesthetic appreciation was limited. It is wrong to suggest, however, that the motto of *The Innocents Abroad* was: "If you don't understand it, laugh at it."[47] Stuart Sherman, in general an ardent Twainian, was equally unfair to say that Mark Twain "laughs at art, history, and antiquity from the point of view of one who is ignorant of them and mightily well satisfied with his ignorance."[48] Mark Twain *was* ignorant of the fine arts, but not of history and antiquity. Never, moreover, was he complacent about his ignorance of music and painting. Time and again he expressed an envy of the fortunate few who could honestly appreciate the esoteric beauties of music and art. He himself wanted to enjoy old paintings and Wagnerian opera ("not as bad as it sounds," he said) and was troubled that he could not:

> If I did not so delight in the grand pictures that are spread before me every day of my life by that monarch of all old masters, Nature, I should come to believe, sometimes, that I had in me no appreciation of the beautiful whatsoever.[49]

No one has ever accused Mark Twain of being immune to the
glories of nature, even in Europe. The Bois de Boulogne in Paris
he found beautiful beyond description. The entire countryside
of France, indeed, appeared to him a bewitching scene, a veri-
table garden, where all was lovely and charming: "such glimpses
of Paradise, it seemed to us, such visions of fabled fairy-land!"[50]
The Alps, the lakes of northern Italy, both Venice and Athens
by moonlight, Naples viewed at sunrise from Mount Vesuvius
—these were among the princely splendors he could appreciate
and describe. "Put Mark Twain on to mountain, lake, storm at
sea, a prairie fire, or a volcano," wrote an English critic, "and you
need not pull out your photographic apparatus. His mind is a
retentive lens."[51]

Somewhat to his surprise, Mark Twain could also savor the
art of Europe when the dosage was not too large. Rare indeed is
the traveler who has not grown weary of the miles of paintings
—faded, gloomy, and monotonous. Mark Twain, like Melville,
was no different. His sensibilities became dulled by too remorse-
less a demand for admiration. It pleased him to make this discovery one day while admiring Raphael's "Transfiguration." Set
in a room by itself in the Vatican, it struck him as a miracle of
beauty. Might not other pictures also be beautiful, he wondered,
if removed from the chaos of the galleries? "It begins to dawn
upon me, now," he confessed, "that possibly, what I have been
taking for uniform ugliness in the galleries may be uniform
beauty after all."[52]

Mark Twain delighted in the exquisite bronzes and cameos
and delicate engravings of Pompeii. The cracked and century-
stained sculptures of "Laocoön" and the "Dying Gladiator"
captured his fancy as few pictures had done. They seemed to him
to be mutely mocking at all efforts to rival their perfections. And
what reader can forget his romantic musings on the ancient
tear jug presented to him in Pisa? In a passage marked by a sentimentalism he was quick to deride in others, he told how this

poor little piece of pottery brought the past alive in his imagination:

> It spoke to us in a language of its own; and with a pathos more
> tender than any words might bring, its mute eloquence swept
> down the long roll of the centuries with its tale of a vacant chair,
> a familiar footstep missed from the threshold, a pleasant voice
> gone from the chorus, a vanished form![53]

Before the passage is done, it may become a bit maudlin, but
at least it proves that Mark Twain was not devoid of sympathy
with the past and did not drag everything in Europe down to the
level of a Yankee drummer. This tiny vessel was a private thing,
but he could become just as excited by the historical associations
of a great public building. In Paris he gazed for a long time at
the mutilated statues which cluster thick on the front of the
Cathedral of Notre Dame. They carried him back to the days
when the Patriarch of Jerusalem stood under them preaching the
Third Crusade. In speaking of them, Mark Twain may have been
flippant, but his feeling for the past was genuine:

> These battered and broken-nosed old fellows saw many a caval-
> cade of mail-clad knights come marching home from the Holy
> Land; they heard the bells above them toll the signal for the St.
> Bartholomew's Massacre, and they saw the slaughter that fol-
> lowed; later, they saw the Reign of Terror, the carnage of the
> Revolution, the overthrow of a king, the coronation of two
> Napoleons . . . I wish these old parties could speak. They could
> tell a tale worth the listening to.[54]

Several weeks later he wandered among the "crumbling
wonders" of Rome, brooding over them by day and dreaming
of them at night, until he seemed to be moldering away himself.
He wanted to write a "real guide-book" on Rome, he said, but
"felt all the time like a boy in a candy-shop—there was everything to choose from, and yet no choice."[55] (Perhaps he was
forced to be vague about Rome, since the only letter he wrote

about it had been lost and he was replacing it many weeks later.)
In Pompeii, too, his imagination ran riot among the ruins. Here,
more than elsewhere, he struggled to recreate the past in his
imagination's eye. He poked through shops and dungeons, he sat
alone meditating in the great theater, he inspected what was left
of once splendid mansions. Never did he seem less the irreverent
savage that some have called him, taking malignant joy in deriding the holy objects in the temple of Europe. He was a man who
yearned deeply to know how things really were in those days
gone by. The puzzle fascinated him. It is incredible that anyone
could imagine that in Europe Mark Twain was obviously "confused, a little frightened, and more than a little unhappy."[56]

The truth was that Mark Twain had an unusually strong sense
of the past and was seldom happier than when exercising this
sense. History was his favorite reading. He could not look at
the Bridge of Sighs without musing on the prisoners who had
crossed it. The dungeons of Edmund Dantes and the "Iron Mask"
filled him with gloomy thoughts. A critic whom many have
thoughtlessly echoed once said (and later retracted) that Mark
Twain "turns the Old World into a laughing-stock by shearing it
of its storied humanity—simply because there is nothing in him to
respond to the glory that was Greece, to the grandeur that was
Rome—simply because nothing is holier to him than a joke."[57]
This is nonsense, for "storied humanity" is precisely what stirred
his passions most profoundly. Attempting to understand how
people lived in centuries past became, at times, almost an obses-
sion with Mark Twain. It was all connected with his concern for
people. The owners of the tear jug, the victims of Vesuvius in
Pompeii, the Crusaders and French Revolutionaries, the prisoners
and Old Masters—people always came first. As he strolled around
the Acropolis by moonlight, he dreamed romantically of the illustrious men who had sat in its temples during ages past. He
dreamed of Socrates and Plato and Aristotle wandering through
the Parthenon, of Demosthenes, Euclid, Pindar, especially of old

Diogenes with his lantern and of St. Paul declaiming from the Areopagus. And later, in the Holy Land, it seemed that every town or well or body of water conjured up memories of men and women of the days of Christ and earlier.

Years later, in his last travel book, Mark Twain would explain that certain places held for him such a potent sense of the past because myriads of human lives had blossomed and withered in these places, age after age. Deserts and ice-barrens, on the other hand, had no speech for him, for they were void of human history; they had nothing wherewith to spiritualize their physical ugliness and lend it charm. He loved what Henry James had called the "perfume of something done."

Whereas the poet was likely to view the present through a romantic haze of the past, Mark Twain usually reversed the process and judged the past by the realistic standards of the present. The celebrated love affair of Abelard and Héloïse in the twelfth century did not impress him as a romance at all, judged by modern standards. He retold the story, deliberately robbing it of its traditional glamour. In his hands the whole affair became nothing but the cold-blooded seduction of an innocent girl by a villain too cowardly to share in her disgrace. "Such is history," he concluded, "not as it is usually told, but as it is when stripped of the nauseous sentimentality that would enshrine for our loving worship a dastardly seducer like Pierre Abelard."[58]

The famed romance of Petrarch and Laura in medieval Italy was also morally repugnant to Mark Twain. Sentimentalists took offense when a realist such as Mark Twain rejected beautiful traditions, but it is certain that such reappraisals of history were long overdue. Despite a few puns, Mark Twain retold these romances with a moral earnestness. Not so the performances in the Coliseum of Rome. Here his technique was almost pure burlesque, with slashes at the bloodthirstiness of the spectators. By good fortune, said Mark Twain, he picked up both an advertising poster and a newspaper review of one of the major Coliseum attractions. He quoted both documents in full. The travesty is magnificent, foreshadowing by twenty years the sustained burlesque of olden days in *A Connecticut Yankee in King Arthur's Court*.

There is, of course, a great deal of burlesque in *The Innocents Abroad*. It is employed in various combinations to amuse the reader, to attack wrongs, and to convey information. The Coliseum passages both amuse and inform. Passages which simply amuse, such as the anecdote about his trying on gloves that were too small, are not relevant to our study. But most of the burlesque is concocted as a sort of sugar-coated type of information. We laugh at Mark Twain's attempt to play billiards with cues that are so crooked that they put English on the wrong side of the ball, We scarcely realize that we have learned something about French manufactured products as well as about the Frenchman's indifference to a popular game. In a similar way we learn something from those farcical scenes in which the "boys" suffer agonies under the hide-lifting razors of French and Italian barbers. And who can forget what happened when Mark Twain realized a cherished dream to partake of the "wonders of the Turkish bath"? His tortures were exquisite. The whole thing was a "malignant swindle," he cried. "The man who enjoys it is qualified to enjoy anything that is repulsive to sight or sense."[59]

For the purpose of comic contrast Mark Twain pumped up to heroic proportions both his anticipations and his disappointments. He loved to deal with extremes. His anticipations actually seem to have been quite modest. To a degree one believes his statement that the streetwalkers of Paris were so ugly that "it would be base flattery to call them immoral," but one laughs off his sorrowful, "Thus topples to earth another idol of my infancy."[60]

Behind Mark Twain's disillusionment, actual and feigned, was a desire to poke fun at sentimental guidebooks and at the tourists who reverenced them. In the art galleries he noted that most of the Innocents gauged their enthusiasm very carefully in accordance with the judgments in their guidebooks, even though the alleged beauties might long since have faded. And when tourists went into ecstasies over such things as the Mosque of St. Sophia in Constantinople, he was sure they had got these ecstasies out of their books.

The motif of disenchantment came to a climax in the Holy Land. Every time he thought how he had been swindled by books on Oriental travel, said Mark Twain, he wanted a tourist for breakfast. His tolerance had worn thin by this time. He quoted a number of long guidebook descriptions which seemed to him "well calculated to deceive." But, he added, the pilgrim who had his guidebook all marked up was going to be astonished at certain sights even if it killed him.

If all the poetry and nonsense that had been discharged upon the scenery around the Sea of Galilee were collected in one book, Mark Twain believed, it would make a most valuable volume to burn. He asked why the truth should not be told about those unpeopled deserts and "rusty mounds of barrenness." Was the truth ever so harmful that it needed to hide its face? In particular, Mark Twain attacked J. C. Prime's *Tent Life in the Holy Land,* one of the favorite sentimental guidebooks of the day. Prime, whom he called "William C. Grimes," was responsible for the so-called opinions of many tourists and not a few Innocents:

> Our travelers have brought their verdicts with them. They have shown it in their conversation ever since we left Beirut. I can almost tell, in set phrase, what they will say when they see Tabor, Nazareth, Jericho, and Jerusalem—*because I have the books they will "smouch" their ideas from.* These authors write pictures and frame rhapsodies, and lesser men follow and see with the author's eyes instead of their own, and speak with his tongue.[61]

Although Mark Twain read the guidebooks which his companions read, he refused to see with another man's eyes or speak with his tongue. It did puzzle him, however, when his own eyes received different images of one scene, and that happened with a frequency that surprised him. He should have realized that it was simply a matter of distance or clarity. His long or hazy view was frequently like that of the romantic guidebooks, whereas his close-up was often realistic, harsh, and discrediting. It was in Venice that he first experienced this double vision. By charitable moonlight Venice appeared a magnificent city, but in the glare of day there was little poetry about her: "Her glory is departed," he said one day, "and with her crumbling grandeur of wharves and palaces about her she sits among her stagnant lagoons, forlorn and beggared, forgotten of the world."[62]

At Naples the veil was of distance, not darkness. At dawn from high up the side of Mount Vesuvius the city presented a picture of wonderful beauty, he said. "But do not go within the walls and look at it in detail," he advised. "That takes away some of the romance of the thing. The people are filthy in their habits, and this makes filthy streets and breeds disagreeable sights and smells."[63] So it was also with Constantinople when viewed from the sea, Damascus when viewed from the hilltop, and the Sea of Galilee under the cloak of darkness. Close inspection by daylight proved their splendors to be illusory.

In Florence, Henry James remarked on the picturesqueness, at a distance, of filth and delapidation to the artistic eye. For him it was not difficult to maintain this aesthetic distance; hence, he was happy in his travels. But it was contrary to the nature of Mark Twain to keep any experience at arm's length. He must embrace it, even at the risk of having the embrace prove blighting. He would know the truth. In this way he discovered that the Bedouins, those wild, free sons of the desert, and their beautiful Arabian mares were not quite what they seemed from afar. Seen close up they were just "tatterdemalion vagrants" and "scrawny nags." "To glance at the genuine son of the desert," he warned,

"is to take the romance out of him forever—to behold his steed
is to long in charity to strip his harness off and let him fall to
pieces."[64]

Everything considered, thought Mark Twain, Oriental scenes
looked best in steel engravings. But no longer could he be imposed
upon by that picture of the Queen of Sheba visiting Solomon: "I
shall say to myself, You look fine, madam, but your feet are not
clean, and you smell like a camel."[65] And what a disappointment
it was to his Sunday-school memories to discover that the grapes
of Jerusalem were not the size of apples, nor the Jordan River
thirty-five miles wide! So it was, mused Mark Twain in playful
earnest, that "travel and experience mar the grandest pictures
and rob us of the most cherished traditions of our boyhood."[66]

As a man straight from the American West, Mark Twain
might have been expected to approach the Old World as he did
—frankly and independently, with a sort of brash pragmatism.
He was no "fanatic iconoclast" like the Old Travelers he satirized
in Chapter Twelve of *The Innocents Abroad,* nor did he poke
nearly as much fun at Europe as he did at himself and his fellow
pilgrims. It was not the Jordan's fault that it was less than thirty-
five miles wide. It was a better river, nonetheless, than the Innocents were tourists. Their behavior struck Mark Twain as both
absurd and inexcusable—not just their parroting of guidebooks,
but also their defacing of old monuments in order to chip off
souvenirs.*

This concern for the tangible was of a piece with his materialistic view of Europe and the Holy Land in general. Like so many
American travelers of today, Mark Twain judged foreign nations
in large part by their technological progress, their modern ap-
pointments. The French railway system, for example, impressed

---

* *Although he condemned this vandalism, he seems to have been a
party to it, bringing home chunks of marble and wood and limestone
from celebrated places. He seems to have wanted something tangible to
prove his trip and to keep it in his memory.*[67]

him for its orderliness and precision, as well as for the politeness of its officials. On the other hand, the trains had no sleepers, and Mark Twain hated being locked into compartments with no water, no heat, no place to stretch out for a nap, and no way to escape from drunken bores.

He found French hotel rooms to be as wretched as French barbers and billiard tables. They lacked modern conveniences. In their "luxury" hotel in Paris there was no soap, no carpet, and nothing but candles to read by. As the group traveled south into Italy and then around the Mediterranean, modern comforts grew scarcer and scarcer so that the pilgrims rejoiced whenever they could spend a night on board the "Quaker City." Nowhere could Mark Twain find even good coffee or cigars. And sanitation seemed a mystery to the Latin and Arab nations. He formed a theory, which may have seemed a bit crude for his book, that the Italians learned how to gesticulate when they talk by "practising" after fleas, which in Italy were "reckless to a fault and impossible to catch."[68] Then there were the pickpockets, the wild dogs, the diseased paupers, the unspeakable slums, the beggars; all these things suggested the essence of the Old World to him more forcibly than did works of art, vast cathedrals, mosques, and pyramids.

The farther he traveled, the more convinced Mark Twain became that Europe and Asia lagged far behind America both in material progress and in government. In only a few practical ways did Europe seem to be ahead: the palatial railroad stations of France and Italy, the public works of Napoleon III in Paris, the splendid railbeds and turnpikes of the Continent. Confessing a kind of Philistinism after the fashion of Emerson, Mark Twain said, "These things win me more than Italy's hundred galleries of priceless art treasures, because I can understand the one and am not competent to appreciate the other."[69]

It is hard to overestimate the importance which Mark Twain attached to this sort of progress in the 1860's. Age and experience would disillusion him, but now he was an admirer of modernity, efficiency, scientific progress, durability. Throughout the Near East, he said, Imperial Rome left the sign of her greatness in roads and bridges that endured to this day. He was enormously impressed. The people of Palestine, he said, never even made a trail; the goats made paths, and the people followed them. In one of his original letters from the Holy Land, he lavished praise on Napoleon III and Alexander II for inaugurating highway and railroad systems that would open up their countries:

> Roads are the highways of the arts, the sciences, and commerce. One can tell what a nation is if he can see its roads. Glance at the thing for a moment. France has such magnificent roads!—miserable Spain has none; England has roads—Portugal has not.[70]

This passage was excluded from *The Innocents Abroad,* perhaps because of second thoughts about the two emperors, but more likely because of another reason: it must have occurred to Mark Twain that to judge Italy by her fine roads would be to contradict almost everything else he wrote about that impoverished and wretched land, not yet even a nation. The roads and railways were just means to an end. The end itself, in his estimation, may have been more materialistic than cultural or spiritual, but it was basically a humanitarian end, for all that. The freedom and welfare of the ordinary citizen in each country were what concerned him most of all.

That he thought these ends could best be achieved by modern technology was the result of his training in the West. Doubtless the Philistine bias of *The Innocents Abroad* did flatter the commercial interests of America and help the sales of the book. It does not follow, however, that Mark Twain had any wish to set a slur of commonness upon true splendor and beauty. He grinned sometimes at certain alleged beauties in Europe, but his was far from the *nil admirari* attitude it has been called.[71]

St. Peter's in Rome may have impressed him only for its immensity, St. Mark's in Venice for its hoary traditions, and St. Sophia's in Constantinople for its dust, dinginess, and gloom, but the Milan Cathedral was another matter. He devoted nearly a chapter to it:

> What a wonder it is! So grand, so solemn, so vast! And yet so delicate, so airy, so graceful! . . . It was a vision!—a miracle!—an anthem sung in stone, a poem wrought in marble! . . . Surely, it must be the princeliest creation that ever brain of man conceived.[72]

Versailles also struck him as a "wonderfully beautiful" sight "worth a pilgrimage to see." It thrilled him "like military music."

> You gaze, and stare, and try to understand that it is real, that it is on the earth, that it is not the Garden of Eden—but your brain grows giddy, stupefied by the world of beauty around you, and you half believe you are the dupe of an exquisite dream.[73]

To the traveler, his own freshness and mood are extremely important. It is impossible to be always at the peak of enthusiasm. At Versailles and Milan, Mark Twain was in the proper frame of mind, but in Florence he was not. He scarcely mentioned the Pitti and Uffizzi art galleries there or even the Duomo and the famed campanile. The Arno River he shrugged off as a "great historical creek with four feet in the channel and some scows floating around."[74] The fact is that he was tired and out of sorts when he arrived in Florence, and his experiences there, such as getting lost at night alone in the maze of streets, were chiefly unpleasant. "How the fatigues and annoyances of travel fill one with bitter prejudices sometimes!" he confessed. "I might enter Florence under happier auspices a month hence and find it all beautiful, all attractive."[75] In fact, in his late years Florence became his favorite Italian city, one to which he returned several times for long visits.

Mark Twain's compassion for the well-being of the common

man caused him to take a close look at the ruling forces in the countries he passed through. He judged them by their fruits. Monarchy and the Church of Rome, which he would assault twenty years later in *A Connecticut Yankee,* were of interest to him in 1867 almost solely by virtue of their economic power. As yet he cared little about theory, doctrine, and theology. He was still far from his later conviction that all thrones had been originally founded in crime and were nothing but "perpetuated piracy."

Only the previous year, we recall, Mark Twain had accepted monarchy in Hawaii because the government seemed to be doing a good job. The kings of Europe were also judged by results alone. For George I of Greece he felt an overpowering contempt because the boy monarch was too ignorant, corrupt, and ambitious to understand his role. By indulging in a hundred ridiculous extravagances in imitation of the great monarchies, George had plunged his nation into poverty. The inevitable result, said Mark Twain, was that the manly people who had performed such miracles of valor at Marathon had been reduced to a "tribe of unconsidered slaves."

Abdul Aziz, Sultan of the Ottoman Empire, aroused Mark Twain to a white-hot fury. At a military review in Paris he saw the Sultan riding alongside the Emperor of France. The contrast, said Mark Twain, was striking. Abdul Aziz looked like what he was: "the genius of Ignorance, Bigotry, and Indolence." He was ruler of a people by nature and training filthy, brutish, unprogressive, and superstitious. The three graces of the Sultan's government were tyranny, rapacity, and blood. Stupid and feeble as his meanest slave, Abdul Aziz reclined dully among his concubines, Mark Twain concluded, while his mother and the premier plundered his wretched empire. This was monarchy sunk to its most degenerate level. His own observations in the Near East merely confirmed Mark Twain's opinion about the inhuman tyranny of the Ottoman Empire. The next time Russia was ready to war with Turkey, he hoped that England and France would not interfere again: "I wish Europe would let Russia annihilate Turkey a little—not much, but enough to make it difficult to find the place again without a divining-rod or a diving-bell."[76]

Was the situation in Russia so much better than that in Turkey? In Mark Twain's opinion it was. We must remember that American feeling in general had grown quite friendly toward Russia during the Civil War. Russian officials made every effort to return this feeling by extending extraordinary courtesies to the "Quaker City." Passports were not even required at Sevastopol—fortunately, since Mark Twain had mislaid his. From the moment they landed on Russian soil the American pilgrims were overwhelmed by cordiality.

The city of Odessa, moreover, with its fine wide streets, its neat houses, and its "familiar *new* look" about everything, made Mark Twain feel right at home. Then the redoubtable Czar himself sent the Americans an unprecedented invitation to call at his summer palace in Yalta. They accepted with pride and discovered the Czar to be a pleasant-looking gentleman, dressed simply. Determination shone in his face, reported Mark Twain, but it was easy to see that he was kind and affectionate. It was not possible for Mark Twain to think of this cordial, unassuming, solicitous gentleman as the merciless Autocrat of Russia.

Although he does not say so, it was Mark Twain himself who wrote the address which was read to the Czar. The address praised the Czar for setting the United States a magnificent example by emancipating twenty million serfs. This act, it stated, was "One of the brightest pages that has graced the world's history since written history had birth."[77]

Perhaps Mark Twain was politically naïve in praising the Czar for an act which, after all, was less humanitarian in motive than it was expedient. Liberating the serfs forestalled a rebellion by over one-third of his subjects. On the other hand, it is more likely that Mark Twain felt obliged to produce praise of this sort for the special occasion. He need not have believed it. At any rate, he did not preserve the address in *The Innocents Abroad,* nor did he repeat his original judgment that the Czar was "one of the most responsible men in Europe."[78] It cannot be denied, however, that Mark Twain was influenced by the warmth and apparent sincerity of his Russian welcome. For example, looking back on the French courtesy that had pleased him so much, he perceived that it had been a "mere ceremonious politeness," lacking both heartiness and sincerity. On the other hand, Russian character, he said, was "politeness itself, and the genuine article."[79] As a French critic observed, " . . . the hairs of the Innocent all assumed a tender curl under the grease of the Northern Bear."[80]

Mark Twain never visited Russia again. As the years went by he came to regard Russian civilization as the most bloody and barbarous in the Christian world. But in 1867 he looked on Russia as a powerful and much-needed ally. A month after his return from Europe he strongly supported "Seward's Folly," the purchase of Alaska, referred to comically as Walrussia. Should the Senate refuse to pay for the new acquisition, said Mark Twain, "they would do a very absurd thing."

> To offend so powerful a friend as Russia for the trifle of $7,000,000 would be unwise. Russia, by her simple attitude of friendship, and without lifting a hand, is able to save us from wars with European powers that would eat up the price of Walrussia in four days.[81]

Mark Twain had not yet begun to theorize about hereditary kingship as a form of government, but he was beginning to think in terms of ententes and power politics.

Mark Twain's first impression of Napoleon III was almost as favorable as his impression of the Czar. The nephew of the great Napoleon had been in power for more than fifteen years. He had undertaken a vast program of public works and was posing as champion of the people. Mark Twain had great admiration for this self-made adventurer who had associated with the common herd in America. He extolled him as the "genius of Energy, Persistence, Enterprise" and the "representative of the highest modern civilization, progress, and refinement."[82] In his original letter to the *Alta* he had gone still further: "That he is the greatest man in the world today, I suppose there is no question. . . . There is no element of true greatness which Napoleon does not possess."[83]

Napoleon's diligence in government, commerce, and public works made him an exceedingly attractive figure to the young American. And the results of his efforts seemed happy. No country appeared to offer greater security to life and property than France, said Mark Twain, and its citizens had all the freedom they wanted, short of making someone else uncomfortable.

Within a few years of his visit to France world events caused Mark Twain to reappraise Napoleon III. Under pressure from the United States, Napoleon had been forced to abandon his puppet, Maximilian of Austria, whom he had put on the Mexican throne in 1863. Maximilian was executed in 1867, and agitation in France forced Napoleon to relinquish much of his personal power. In the light of these developments, Mark Twain thought it wise to modify his spontaneous eulogy of the Emperor. In the book, therefore, he described him as having a "deep, crafty, scheming expression," with "cat-eyes" that darted around suspiciously.[84] He still had to admire Napoleon's nerve, however, as well as his calm self-reliance and shrewd good sense.

The Franco-Prussian War seems to have transformed Mark Twain's opinion of France, as if Napoleon III had treacherously let him down. In the fall of 1870 Napoleon was defeated by Bismarck, whereupon a Parisian mob forced an end to the Empire. Perhaps feeling embarrassed by his recent praise of Napoleon, Mark Twain promptly sat down to make fun of him now. The burlesque took the form of an "interview," in which Napoleon was accused of having stolen from the treasury. Napoleon was also satirized for his emotionalism, his personal uncleanliness, his infidelity to his wife, and even for not being sure who his real father was.[85] From this moment on, like a woman scorned, Mark Twain had never a good word to say about France and the French people. Among the peoples of the world they became, indeed, his pet abomination.

This *volte-face* seems also to have ended Mark Twain's interest in the French language. His study of French had begun in St. Louis back in 1855. Part of his first notebook was taken up with French exercises in neatly numbered lessons. During the sixties he continued the study. Not only did he list French words and phrases, but he also copied several pages of Voltaire's *Dialogues*. He even played around with fractured French in comic sketches; for example, Eve to the Serpent, " 'Mons., le serpent, . . . weel you not have ze bonté to peek me some appel. J'ai faim.' "[86] The defeat of France by Prussia in 1870 seems to have been the cue for Mark Twain to turn from French to German. Thereafter his notebooks teemed with German, with only a scattered sentence or two in French. He had been painfully disillusioned.

If Mark Twain had mixed feelings about the institution of monarchy in 1867, depending upon the benevolence of the monarch, he did not have mixed feelings about the Catholic Church in Italy. The Catholic priest in America, he said, was generally a man of intelligence and ability, but in Italy he was "altogether the reverse." At the Duomo in Florence, Mark Twain was appalled and disgusted. In words which echo the contempt of Emerson and Hawthorne, he wrote:

> It takes three hundred flabby, greasy vagabonds in holy orders to run this awful ecclesiastic swindle. And they don't stand a watch worth twenty dollars a month. They begin dinner at noon and gorge till 3; then they smoke, and swill, and sleep till 5, and then they come on watch for just two hours.

He allowed that they *might* have been good men, but the "majority of them looked stupid, and brainless, and sensual beyond anything I have seen for many a day."[87]

Although this attack on the clergy was cut from the book, Mark Twain had no qualms about attacking the Roman Church on other grounds. He believed that what he called the "relic matter" was a little overdone. About this he was able to laugh. In every old church it seemed that the pilgrims were shown a piece of the true cross and some of the nails which held it together. "And as for the bones of St. Denis," he added, "I feel certain that we have seen enough of them to duplicate him, if necessary."[88] The whole population of Italy was superstitious enough, in his opinion, to be completely taken in by these "religious impostures," whose sole design was to raise money for the Church.

In Palestine it amused him to find that the Church pretended that nearly all the tremendous events of Christian history took place in grottoes, since grottoes do not crumble. He felt, however, that the world owed the Catholics its goodwill for these particular "happy rascalities." There was, after all, some satisfaction in looking at a cave where for centuries people had faithfully believed the Virgin had lived.

It was for its immense economic power that Mark Twain attacked the Italian Church most savagely. He saw the Church as casting a black shadow of oppression over the entire land, assuring salvation only to those who paid well for it. For a rich profit it leased its vast landholdings to the poor. Its mendicant priests prowled by the thousands among the people, begging subsistence. For fifteen centuries, he cried, the Church had bled the people, turning all its energies and finances to building up a vast array of church edifices and starving half the citizens to do it. As a result, Italy was at the same time the most wretched and princely land on earth, "one vast museum of magnificence and misery."[89]

Faced with utter ruin, the Italian Parliament had recently confiscated most of the domains and riches of the Church. Mark Twain rejoiced. The wealth hitherto locked up in the "useless trumpery" of churches could now be put to good use in aiding the common people who had been ground to death by taxes. "It

was a rare good fortune for Italy," he observed, "the stress of
weather that drove her to break from this prison-house."[90]

Mark Twain did object to the subordinate position of Jesus in
the hierarchy of Holy Personages in Rome, but he did not assail
any of the doctrines of the Catholic Church at this time. It should
be noted also that he tried to be fair to the Church, despite the
prejudices of his upbringing. He praised, for example, the heroism of the Dominican friars during the recent cholera epidemic
in Italy. Their devotion and noble efforts cost many of them their
lives, which they laid down cheerfully. And weeks later in the
Holy Land he himself benefited from Catholic kindness. His
Alta letter simply mentioned that the tourists spent a certain night
at the Mars Saba Monastery, but he expanded the account to
several pages for his book. He told of their agonizing ride across
the desert around the Dead Sea and of the extraordinary hospitality of the monks who sheltered and refreshed them that night.
Never would he cease to be grateful, he said, for the Christlike
spirit of these monks at Mars Saba:

> I have been educated to enmity towards everything that is Catho-
> lic, and sometimes, in consequence of this, I find it much easier to
> discover Catholic faults than Catholic merits. But there is one
> thing I feel no disposition to overlook, and no disposition to
> forget; and that is, the honest gratitude I and all pilgrims owe
> to the Convent Fathers in Palestine.[91]

In 1867 Mark Twain was oriented toward people and things
rather than toward ideas. Such concepts as the divine right of
kings or the inherent rights of man were not yet of great importance to him. He judged Church and State as he judged railroads
and restaurants—by the way they affected the well-being of the
ordinary man. There was no irreverence in his treatment of the
Catholic Church, because he was not denouncing religion. He
was denouncing, instead, a Church which seemed to have abandoned religion in its lust for wealth and power. An English

clergyman wisely pointed out that Mark Twain's criticism was leveled not at the "value of religion itself" but simply at the sham and hypocrisy surrounding it.[92] Mark Twain believed that the Church in Italy had forfeited its right to be revered, for its worldly ambition had long been crushing the millions of worshipers the Church was intended to uplift.

In short, Mark Twain held the Roman Church largely responsible for the state of filth and degradation in which most Italians lived out their lives. Some of the lower classes, he said, would rather die than wash. He was especially nauseated by the diseased and monstrous human beings who were allowed to beg alms on the streets. How different all this was from America! He drew a contrast between the two lands by causing an imaginary Italian tourist to bring back to his countrymen an account of the strange and wonderful United States. In America, he told his gaping friends, even the poor often owned their own land, which they cultivated with modern implements. Because of public schools to which anyone could go, many of the common people could read and write. The wealthy sinner in America was not able to escape damnation by making gifts to the Church. Priests and soldiers did not clog the streets there. Jews were treated like human beings, instead of like dogs. Most incredible of all, said the returned traveler, " 'The common people there know a great deal; they even have the effrontery to complain if they are not properly governed, and to take hold and conduct the government themselves . . .' "[93]

About the Italians as a people, Mark Twain was of two minds. Three unpleasant encounters with the police persuaded him that Italian officials were both stupid and corrupt. Certain experiences also suggested that the lower classes were every bit as repulsive as their personal habits. As for the upper classes, he found them less objectionable for two reasons only: they did use soap, and they did not charge two cents for picking up a lady's shawl. The Neapolitans he regarded as an especially "bad lot." "They cheat everybody they can," he said, "and they are always expecting to get cheated themselves."[94] At the theater one night he listened to an audience of "high-born knaves" hiss and jeer at an actress long past her prime. This convinced him that the upper classes of Naples possessed "*all* the vile, mean traits there are."[95]

In spite of these opinions, it appears that Mark Twain found a great deal to like in Italy and its people. For one thing, the women impressed him as being uncommonly beautiful, especially in Genoa. For another, he was bewitched by the enchantments of bygone ages. He concluded a letter to an old friend by saying,

> P. S. Italy is a beautiful land, and its daughters are as fair as the moon that holds her silvery course above their heads and its traditions are rich with the poetry and romance of the old crusading days,—happy days! glorious days but destined never to return! I like Italy.[96]

It was while passing through the northern villages between Lake Como and Venice that Mark Twain made a discovery that startled him: the peasants were not as miserable as he had expected them to be. "We were in the heart and home of priest-craft—" he wrote, "of a happy, cheerful, contented ignorance, superstition, degradation, poverty, indolence, and everlasting unaspiring worthlessness." The simple folk ate and slept like other animals, he said. They worked very little and cared not a whit for the world's concerns.

> They were not respectable people—they were not worthy people —they were not learned and wise and brilliant people—but in their breasts, all their stupid lives long, resteth a peace that passeth understanding! How can men, calling themselves men, consent to be so degraded and happy.[97]

Mark Twain did not have much use for the natives of the eastern Mediterranean. Somehow he got the impression, which he put in his journal, that all Greeks and Armenian Christians were thieves. He also described the Galileans of Bible times as being "just as they are now—ignorant, depraved, superstitious, dirty, lousy, thieving vagabonds."[98] His letter to the *Alta* expanded this impression into several hundred words on the people of Palestine, "ignorant, degraded, lazy, unwashed loafers and savages."

> Dirt and rags and squalor; vermin, hunger and wretchedness; savage costumes, savage weapons and looks of hate—these are the things that meet one at every step in Nazareth. Magdala is a miracle of barbarous degradation; Nazareth is worse.[99]

There was a great deal more of this sort of thing in his original letters, but Mark Twain toned it down considerably for his book. No need to offend the genteel and churchly Easterners too much: he did not lie; he simply modified his strongest language. Here he was in the region sanctified by the mission of Christ, yet the land and the people seemed to bear the curse of Cain. To prove that he understood what readers expected him to write, he quoted frequently from the sentimental word-pictures of J. C. Prime and other travel writers. Then he gave his own contrasting view, or at least a part of it. Discretion warned him that it was wiser to hold his tongue at times—discretion plus Mother Fairbanks and genteel Olivia in Elmira. No longer did he refer to the historic well at Bethesda as a "slimy cesspool."

By the time the pilgrims reached Syria in September they had been traveling for three months and were mentally tired. Physically, however, the most trying part of the trip was just beginning: long hours on horseback under the merciless sun. Mark Twain, furthermore, elected to make the "long trip" from Beirut to Jerusalem by way of Damascus and Baalbec. Only seven men made this racking journey. Sometimes they were in the saddle for more than twelve hours a day. But they were free of the women for a change, and they were off the beaten track. Perhaps they even felt a kind of joy of discovery, which adds zest to travel. When it was all over, however, Mark Twain was hardly exhilarated. In his journal he wrote, "I have only one pleasant reminiscence of this Palestine excursion—time I had the cholera in Damascus."[100]

It was in Jerusalem that the pilgrimage was designed to reach its climax. Above all else most of the tourists had dreamed of walking the streets of the Holy City. By September, though, they had passed their emotional peaks as sightseers; a day or two in Jerusalem gave most of them their fill. It was the surfeit of the Italian art galleries all over again, this time in terms of religious history. "The sights are too many," complained Mark Twain. "They swarm about you at every step." For several days, he said, the pilgrims had been drifting about using their eyes and ears chiefly from a sense of duty. "And too often we have been glad when it was time to go home and be distressed no more about illustrious localities."[101]

More distressing still were the beggars. Mark Twain, who spent four pages on the wild dogs of Constantinople, could hardly ignore the human scum which bedeviled tourists in the Near East. In Italy the beggars had been a nuisance, in Turkey they had been a stomach-turning exhibit of freaks and monsters, but in Palestine they were an inescapable, intolerable, infuriating obtrusion. At the Church of the Nativity in Bethlehem, for example, Mark Twain touched with reverent finger the very spot where Jesus was said to have been born, yet his imagination remained blank:

> You *cannot* think in this place any more than you can in any other in Palestine that would be likely to inspire reflection. Beggars, cripples, and monks compass you about, and make you think only of bucksheesh [alms] when you would rather think of something more in keeping with the character of the spot.[102]

Three years later a mention of Endor in Palestine by a newspaper conjured up in Mark Twain's memory his donkey ride through that "squalid hive of human vermin." He described his encounter with a "galvanized scurvy" who appeared to be threatening his life. He let his vocabulary loose on the "black, mangy, nine-tenths naked, ten-tenths filthy, ignorant, bigoted, besotted, hungry, lazy, malignant, screeching, crowding, struggling, wailing, begging, cursing, hateful spawn of the original Witch" who had swarmed from the caves to besiege them.[103]

When the pilgrims got home, said Mark Twain, they would tell the customary lie about tearing themselves away reluctantly from every noted place in Palestine. But not one of the party did he ever hear say such a thing while in Palestine. The importunate swarms of beggars and peddlers hanging on to their clothes and shrieking in their ears and displaying ghastly sores made the pilgrims "*glad* to get away," he said. Then he made an observation to which millions of tourists will say Amen:

> We do not think, in the holy places; we think in bed, afterward, when the glare, and the noise, and the confusion are gone, and in fancy we revisit alone the solemn monuments of the past, and summon the phantom pageants of an age that has passed away.[104]

Guidebook descriptions notwithstanding, Mark Twain, again like Melville, thought Palestine the most dismal place in the world for dull and unpicturesque scenery. To the eye it was a "hopeless, dreary, heart-broken land." Palestine, he said, sat in sackcloth and ashes, while over it brooded a curse that had withered its fields and fettered its energies. Not a single spot retained the aura of ancient splendor. Nothing, of itself, reminded the traveler that once it knew the high honor of the Savior's presence. Even renowned Jerusalem had lost its grandeur, he mourned, and was become merely a "pauper village." Palestine, concluded Mark Twain, was no longer a part of this workaday world. It was sacred to poetry and tradition; it was a dreamland.[105]

Among the Mark Twain Papers is a twelve-page typescript which is considered a deletion from the Holy Land chapters of *The Innocents Abroad*. The beggars and barren landscape are here, but most interesting is a bitter condemnation of imperial conquest and a very early foreshadowing of Mark Twain's later quarrel with God. This fragment hints that scribes must have tampered with ancient manuscripts, because no respectable God would command the extermination of a tribe whose only "crime" was that four hundred years earlier it had had the effrontery to defend its lands from outside aggression. "Those forefathers," said Mark Twain, "had dared to love their country & to resist the invasion of the Israelite hosts." Was this, he wanted to know, a sin?[106]

Time, it is said, cures many things, and distance lends enchantment. "Things I did not like at all yesterday," said Mark Twain the night his cruise ended in New York, "I like very well to-day, now that I am at home . . . "[107] And on Christmas Eve a year later he wrote to his old companion, Mrs. Fairbanks, "And don't the picture mellow in the distance, now that the greasy monks, & the noisy mob, & the leprous beggars are gone . . . ?" He was a hundred times glad, he said, that he had seen Bethlehem, although at the time the sight had swept away every pleasing fancy he had cherished about the place.[108] And at the end of the book, writing as if still in Palestine, he pondered the Innocents' miseries:

> We have full comfort in one reflection, however. Our experiences in Europe have taught us that in time this fatigue will be forgotten; the thirst, the tiresome volubility of the guides, the persecutions of the beggars—and then, all that will be left will be pleasant memories of Jerusalem . . . We can wait. Our reward will come. To us, Jerusalem and to-day's experiences will be an enchanted memory a year hence—a memory which money could not buy from us.[109]

Time and distance, it would seem, made Mark Twain more sympathetic toward what he called the "poetry and nonsense" in guidebooks about Palestine. As many a city had appeared more enchanting when viewed from a distant hillside, and as most Arabs looked more romantic from far off, so did legendary sites of the Old World appear more fascinating when seen through the veil of time.

Nine or ten years after this trip Mark Twain sought to recapture some of the Holy Land mood by reading *Early Travels
in Palestine,* edited by Thomas Wright (1848). The later pages'
being unmarked and largely uncut show that he did not get quite
halfway through the book.[110] Except for a stagy boast in the Conclusion of *The Innocents Abroad,* Mark Twain never expressed
any desire to return to the Near East. Once was enough.

On the other hand, he could hardly wait to get back to Europe.
So many places, even whole countries, had been missed on this
first trip. He was done, however, with organized tours. Europe
had a thousand charms not found in the Arab countries and at
least one extraordinary blessing not found in America. This
blessing, about which he wrote so eloquently, was the calm and
tranquil leisure of European life. He called it "comfort," but it
had nothing to do with soft beds or soap or luxuries. These things
were always important to Mark Twain, and yet he disliked the
throbbing, restless energy which seemed to accompany them in
the United States. He could hardly wait to own a typewriter and
a telephone when they were invented, but he yearned to be free
from the bustle and drudgery associated with them. Robert Fulton
and Edison were heroes of his, but sometimes it seemed that his
spiritual sire was Henry David Thoreau. In America, wrote Mark
Twain, we hurry too much. We even take our business cares to
bed with us. We bestow thoughtful care on inanimate objects, but
none upon ourselves. As a result we burn up our energies. Either
we die early, or we sink into a mean old age at a time of life considered one's prime on the Continent. What a robust, clear-thinking
people we would be, he urged, if we would only lay ourselves on
a shelf occasionally, like a barber's razor, and renew our edges!

> I do envy these Europeans the comfort they take. When the work
> of the day is done, they forget it. Some of them go, with wife
> and children, to a beer hall, and sit quietly and genteelly drink-
> ing a mug or two of ale and listening to music; others walk the
> streets, others drive in the avenues; others assemble in the great
> ornamental squares in the early evening. . . . They go to bed

moderately early, and sleep well. They are always quiet, always orderly, always cheerful, comfortable, and appreciative of life and its manifold blessings. One never sees a drunken man among them. The change that has come over our little party is surprising. Day by day we lose some of our restlessness and absorb some of the spirit of quietude and ease that is in the tranquil atmosphere about us and in the demeanor of the people. We grow wise apace. We begin to comprehend what life is for.[111]

These thoughts, also quite Jamesian, supposedly came to Mark Twain one evening in Milan. Swept away by the power of his fancy, however, Mark Twain exaggerated the tranquilizing and cheering effect of European life upon shipmates. By his own testimony they proved themselves in the months ahead to be just as restless and solemn as ever. On his return to New York, Mark Twain told the *Herald,* "The pleasure ship was a synagogue, and the pleasure trip was a funeral excursion without a corpse."[112]

Mark Twain gave up his reporting before the "Quaker City" reached Alexandria. His last letter to the *Alta* was mailed on October 2. We can imagine his sense of freedom as he roamed Egypt and southern Spain without having to take out his writing tablets at night. As we have seen, he later did manage to make up some Egyptian chapters for his book, but nowhere did he ever leave a record of those seven days he and three friends spent in Seville, Cordova, Cadiz, and the villages of Andalusia. Nor did he trouble to describe at this time Bermuda, where the ship put in again for several days before heading north. And interesting evidence has just been discovered that a "Miss Langdon" boarded the "Quaker City" for the trip back to New York. Was this Mark Twain's Livy, joining her young brother Charlie for the last leg of the cruise?[113] At any rate, Bermuda was to become the favorite resort of his late years.

In the fall of 1900 Mark Twain was in London preparing to sail for home after nearly a solid decade abroad. When a newsman made a comment about his being an indefatigable traveler,

Mark Twain was quick to contradict him. He had made thirty-four long journeys in his life, he said, and thirty-two of them had been made "under the spur of absolute compulsion." There was no man living, he went on, who cared less about seeing new people and places than he did.

> When I started out in 1867, for a six month's tour in the Quaker City I was a voracious sightseer. We went in for seeing everything that was to be seen. . . . If our meals interfered with our seeing any old thing our meals were put aside. . . . My head used to ache, my eyes to swim. . . . What was the result of this insensate sightseeing? Why, that I was so fagged out that I lost the capacity to appreciate most of what I saw or to carry away any coherent idea of it. Since then only hard necessity has ever driven me to travelling. . . . I have never recovered from the Quaker City surfeit of sightseeing, and don't think there is any reasonable prospect of my doing so now.[114]

So said Mark Twain a generation later. Making the customary allowances for exaggeration and for a memory impaired by grief and years, how should we appraise this comment? Mark Twain was only thirty-one when he set out for Europe and was in robust health. The first three months of travel were passed mainly in the comfort of ship and train. During these months he was surely not "fagged out," and he showed a lively appreciation. The evidence suggests that not until the torturing days in the saddle in Syria and his bout with cholera in Damascus did the strain begin to tell on him. Then, in Jerusalem, he was obliged to catch up on his reporting at the very time that he was doing the most intensive sight-seeing and research of the entire trip. And he had to do it in an atmosphere of almost unbelievable filth and tumult. No doubt this latter portion of the tour left a desolate memory in Mark Twain's mind.

On this first trip abroad, Mark Twain's opinions were not always orthodox, and yet he was not, as sometimes charged, obsessed with being different. In the very first issue of the *Overland*

Monthly in 1868, Bret Harte printed "By Rail through France" by Mark Twain. Then he commented on his friend's *Alta* letters and on realistic travel writings which preceded them:

> The days of sentimental journeying are over. . . . A race of good-humored, engaging iconoclasts seem to have precipitated themselves upon the old altars of mankind. . . . It is true, we have lost something. We have lost that which made Irving's *Tales of a Traveler* possible . . . the romance of foreign travel.[115]

Despite the closing words, Bret Harte approved the recent trend. He knew that Mark Twain had not begun it, but he also recognized that he was by far the best of the breed, a writer not only of honesty and comic genius but also of fine rhetoric and unexpected eloquence.

Furthermore, the "romance of foreign travel," as we have seen, is not truly lost in *The Innocents Abroad*. What *is* lost is the self-indulgent romanticism of Irving's followers, who used imagination as an escape from reality rather than as a means of penetration into it. Mark Twain had plenty of romance in his own soul, but he generally kept it under control. Reality was as dear to him as it had been to Cooper and Melville in their travel writings. Seldom did he indulge his sentiment; never did he use the past as an escape from the present. Instinctively he saw the danger which faced the Old World: she had reached the point of having a past which was so interesting that it was taking the place of the present.

With humor and satire Mark Twain exposed this danger. Most travel books dwelt lovingly on the enduring of the old, but his own had a keen eye also for the emerging of the new—modern Paris and Odessa, for example. America, of course, had more of the new than did Europe, just as the college boy has more new things than does his father, because, unlike his father, he has no old things which, although out-of-date, are still of service. This is not to imply that on occasion Mark Twain could not be moved romantically by the associations conjured up by a crumbling old wall, a tear jug, or the mutilated façade of a great cathedral.

More often, however, he was impressed by the size and durability of things—the immensity of St. Peter's Church, the hand-hewn stone blocks at Baalbec, the pyramids, the Roman bridges and aqueducts of two thousand years ago. Born and bred in the West, Mark Twain was equipped with most of what Frederick Jackson Turner in 1893 called the "traits of the frontier":

> That coarseness and strength combined with acuteness and inquisitiveness; that practical, inventive turn of mind, quick to find expedients; that masterful grasp of material things, lacking in the artistic but powerful to effect great ends; that restless, nervous energy; that dominant individualism, working for good and evil, and withal that buoyancy and exuberance which comes with freedom.[116]

As a Western pragmatist, Mark Twain was a natural culmination of a movement which began long before Emerson's declaration of cultural independence from Europe. It was not significant in itself that Parisian hotel rooms were antiquated, that good coffee and tobacco could not be found in Europe, and that swarms of mangy dogs and whining beggars plagued the tourist. Yet these things were indicative of government, taste, and culture. Indeed, they may even have been by-products of that easygoing serenity and repose that Mark Twain wished to import into his fitful homeland, but this fact he did not consider.

In 1869, the year of *The Innocents Abroad,* young Henry James happened to be in Florence, where he found the American travelers to be "vulgar, vulgar, vulgar." He confessed that they seemed to have character, energy, and intelligence, but he could not endure "their stingy, defiant, grudging attitude toward everything European—their perpetual reference of all things to some American standard of precedent which exists only in their own unscrupulous wind-bags." In short, he concluded, the American tourist was "modern man with *culture* quite left out."[117]

The culture had not been left out of Mark Twain; there simply had not yet been an opportunity to put it in. Even so, he was every bit as annoyed as the genteel James at those Americans in Europe who bragged or complained in loud voices and made themselves generally obnoxious to their hosts. And we might also recall Lowell's observation: "If the tone of the uncultivated American has too often the arrogance of the barbarian, is not that of the cultivated as often vulgarly apologetic?"[118]

Living in Italy twenty years before Mark Twain's visit, Margaret Fuller felt "unspeakable contempt" for what she termed "the servile American," the pilgrim who traveled merely to indulge his tastes. She considered him shallow and worthless. The true artists and the "thinking Americans" won her respect. Finally she described "the conceited American," bristling and proud of he knew not what:

> With his great clumsy hands, only fitted to work on a steam engine, he seizes the old Cremona violin, makes it shriek with anguish in his grasp, and then declares he thought it was all humbug before he came and now he knows it; that there was not really any music in the old things; that the frogs in one of our swamps make much finer, for they are young and alive . . . There is Jonathan in the sprawling state, the booby truant, not yet aspiring enough to be a good school-boy. Yet in his folly there is meaning; add thought and culture to his independence and he will be a man of might: he is not a creature without hope.[119]

In this vivid description, contemptuous yet hopeful, we can see the Mark Twain of 1867. Although he made few Cremona violins shriek with anguish, he was a sort of proud "Jonathan in the sprawling state." In his case, however, the state was already one of transition. He was in the very process of adding thought and culture to his independence. Therein, as Margaret Fuller had prophesied, lay his hope. Therein lay his might. No "booby truant," Mark Twain was far from being indifferent to Europe. Nor did he repudiate the entire Old World without a hearing. He did, in a fashion, turn away from it, but, as we have seen, he looked back over his shoulder and observed much there to admire and much to respect.

It is likely that the instant popularity of *The Innocents Abroad* was owing in part to this very ambivalence. The author's madcap cronies on the West Coast could slap their thighs at his irreverence while his decorous young fiancée in Elmira could bask calmly in his romantic legends or sentimental flights of fancy. There seemed to be something for everybody. Mark Twain was determined from the start that the book must sell. For one thing, he wanted to support Olivia Langdon in the luxury she had always known. While editing his letters, therefore, he chose with care from the numerous poses he had assumed in recent years while working for the newspapers. At certain times it seemed appropriate to simulate the Moralist, the Instructor, or the Sentimentalist. At other times he acted the role of the Simpleton or Tenderfoot.[120] But these roles were not wholly make-believe, because Mark Twain actually was all of these things and more, including, as he proved in Europe, a Romantic. Like Walt Whitman, he was large, he contained multitudes.

Unlike Whitman, he also charmed multitudes. Leon Dickinson has tracked down dozens of contemporary reviews and reports that they were almost uniformly favorable, a surprising number of them even praising the nonhumorous values of the book. Our own times have stressed the disillusionment of the book and its horseplay, tending to ignore its sincere reverence for those places which Mark Twain considered to be truly reverend. Anyone who has visited Jerusalem, for example, knows how easy it would have been for Mark Twain to poke fun at the Church of the Holy Sepulchre, with its fantastic conglomeration of chapels and grottoes, and with its pandemonium of competing religious sects.

But Mark Twain believed this to be the place of the Crucifixion and so meriting respect as the "most illustrious edifice in Christendom."

> With all its clap-trap side-shows and unseemly impostures of every kind, it is still grand, reverend, venerable—for a god died there; for fifteen hundred years its shrines have been wet with the tears of pilgrims from the earth's remotest confines; for more than two hundred the most gallant knights that ever wielded sword wasted their lives away in a struggle to seize it and hold it sacred from infidel pollution.[121]

These are scarcely the words of a merry-andrew intent on dragging everything time-honored down to the level of a common joker. Stuart Sherman, who once asserted that nothing in the Old World was as dear to Mark Twain as a joke, came at last to see his own error. In the rough, iconoclastic Don Juan from the West, he confessed, there was also an important strain of Childe Harold.[122]

It should be stressed again, moreover, that the iconoclasm of *The Innocents Abroad* did not reflect any militant patriotism, because both before and after this cruise Mark Twain found more to censure and ridicule at home than he did abroad. And never did he deride venerable objects nearly as much as he derided all veneration which was not sincere. One of Mark Twain's most perceptive early critics even asserted that, so far as *The Innocents Abroad* was "disrespectful," its satire was aimed at the "dishonest American tourist."[123]

In scoffing at sentimental travel books and at absurd homage to things foreign, Mark Twain was following Fenimore Cooper, although he may not have known it. He was not burdened with Cooper's grudges, however, and he was blessed with a sense of humor which prevented his strictures from becoming too contentious. George Bernard Shaw, who admired Mark Twain as by far the greatest writer in America, observed: "He has to put things in such a way as to make people who would otherwise hang him believe he is joking."[124]

In later years, as we know, Mark Twain paid the penalty for having established a reputation first of all as a humorist. Most people refused to take him seriously when he was most serious. But in the 1860's he was not prepared by training or temperament for a more solid, weighty achievement. Already he had shared in the throbbing activity of America more than most authors twice his age, and these years of restlessness had left him too little time to read, to think, to live deliberately. As a frank modernist caught up in the exuberance of the American West, he subconsciously developed the standards by which he lived and by which he judged men and nations. Not sophisticated or cultural, these standards prized most highly such things as progress, utilitarianism, fair play, and material well-being. In the Conclusion to *The Innocents Abroad* he insisted that "broad, wholesome, charitable views of men and things" could not be acquired by vegetating in one's own little corner of the earth. "Travel is fatal to prejudice, bigotry, and narrow-mindedness," he said, "and many of our people need it sorely on these accounts."[125]

This discovery made Mark Twain begin to move away from the position of a Westerner. He was learning to respect values which were less tangible and less practical than those of the Frontier. Europe, he discovered, was something more than a vast museum or amusement park for tourists. All Americans should go abroad, he urged, if only to lose their smug nationalism. They ought to learn, as he had, that the United States had no monopoly on everything that was worthwhile in the world. Time and again in his "American Vandal" lecture of 1868–69 Mark Twain admonished each of his listeners to go abroad. Travel does one good, he said, and makes a better man of him:

> It rubs out a multitude of his old unworthy biases and prejudices. It aids his religion, for it enlarges his charity and his benevolence, it broadens his views of men and things; it deepens his

generosity and his compassion for the failings and the short-comings of his fellow-creatures. Contact with men of various nations and many creeds teaches him that there are *other* people in the world besides his own little clique, and other opinions as worthy of attention and respect as his own. He finds that he and *his* are not the most momentous matters in the universe. Cast into trouble and misfortune in strange lands and being mercifully cared for by those he never saw before, he begins to learn that best lesson of all—that one which culminates in the conviction that God puts *something* good and lovable in every man his hands create—that the world is *not* a cold, harsh, cruel prison-house, stocked with all manner of selfishness and hate and wickedness.[126]

II

Easterner

THE praise of travel which Mark Twain set forth in his "American Vandal" speech was a noble sentiment, and it rang with eloquence. It is easy to recognize his grateful reference to the Catholic monks of Palestine, but, as we review his life to this point, it is hard to find any other "old unworthy biases" which travel had rubbed out in him. Although he did discover a great world apart from his own "little clique," in most instances he was extremely reluctant to let go of his own opinions. It is doubtful that the cruise actually did very much to enlarge his benevolence or aid his religion. His "giant," to use Emerson's expression, was Western bred and was not about to surrender to powers across the sea. More than a single precipitate voyage would be required before this Western giant would learn the tastes and amenities of cultivated society first in the East and then in Europe, and before he could practice the tolerance of a true cosmopolite.

During his early years Mark Twain had been scornful of the culture of the East. In his first published story the dandy fared badly at the hands of the rugged squatter. Many things began to change, however, with the publication of *The Innocents Abroad* in 1869. Henceforth, Mark Twain found himself associating almost entirely with men from the East and enjoying himself in their clubs and homes. He did not cut off his Western friends, as he had cut the low-minded Mr. Brown from his book, but he came

to realize that his destiny lay in the East. Although he spent the
rest of his life roaming the globe, Mark Twain never visited California or Nevada again.

In 1866 Mark Twain had been given some advice which he
later said had governed his life. Anson Burlingame, the states-
man, advised him always to seek comradeship among his superiors
in character and intellect. This he tried to do on the "Quaker
City," with the Fairbankses, the Severances, and the Moses
Beaches—people of fine and prominent families. And the girl he
fell in love with and married was Olivia Langdon, sister of a
shipmate and member of a distinguished upstate New York
family. The degree of influence which this marriage had upon
Mark Twain's genius is still a matter of debate, but one thing is
certain: it was a marvelously happy union to which both husband
and wife made concessions and made them gladly. Although we
may shrink from Van Wyck Brooks's picture of Mark Twain as a
"shorn Samson led about by a little child," we must acknowledge
that with this marriage Mark Twain did become, as Brooks says,
a "candidate for gentility."[1]

For the first time since he had left the river, a steady, respectable vocation made a strong appeal to Mark Twain. Despite the
booming sales of his book, he still considered himself a newspaper man, so he bought into the *Buffalo Express*. His writings
for the *Express,* few of which were in his own name, are of small
interest. One project, however, he began with enthusiasm. This
was a series of around-the-world travel letters. In the fall of 1869,
four months before his marriage, he explained the project to Mrs.
Fairbanks. Charlie Langdon, Livy's wild young brother and his
former shipmate, was being sent around the world with Professor
D. R. Ford, of Elmira College. The following summer Mark
Twain and Livy planned to meet them in Paris. "I feel a sort of
itching in my feet, mother," he confessed, "and if my life were
as aimless as of old, my trunk would be packed now."[2] The idea
was for Mark Twain to write letters on the basis of information

provided by Professor Ford. The letters began appearing in October and struggled through till spring, when Mark Twain finally gave up in disgust. The Professor, he told the Langdons, had sent only two short letters. He himself had had to make up the other ten.

A new novel by Victor Hugo seems to have caught Mark Twain's attention late in 1869, and he had some editorial fun at the expense of Hugo's proposed remedy for war. Hugo seemed naïve. As Mark Twain put it:

> One has nothing to do but merely to "abolish monarchy, with its civil lists, paid idlers, salaried clergy, pensioned magistrates, aristocratic sinecures, gratuities to public edifices, standing armies.". . . The plan looks perfectly charming and easy. It is all done by a simple turn of the wrist. It is exceedingly singular that Mr. Hugo has not done it before now.[3]

Ironically, the plan actually did look charming to Mark Twain before too many years had passed. Was it not, after all, the very plan which his own Connecticut Yankee would undertake?

Although the Ford-Langdon tandem had broken down, the notion of traveling by proxy died hard in Mark Twain. Late in the autumn of 1870 he began to urge his old Washington, D.C., friend J. H. Riley to make a trip to the mining fields of South Africa. Riley would return with his notes and would relate all his adventures to Mark Twain, who would write them up in the first person. *"That book,"* Mark Twain whooped to his publisher, *"will have a perfectly beautiful sale."*[4] Riley made the trip but unfortunately died soon after returning home. His memoranda were never used.

One senses that Mark Twain envied Charlie Langdon and Riley their freedom to travel at will. Being tied down was a new experience to him. Livy was never very strong, and when she gave birth to a premature baby in November, 1870, family travel seemed out of the question for a while. Mark Twain did hit the lecture trail in America the following year, but the best Livy could do was to study German at home.

The baby, Langdon, died before he was two years old, but by that time the first of Mark Twain's three daughters had arrived. This was Susy, a healthy child. That summer, on August 21, 1872, Mark Twain finally saw his way clear to make his second trip abroad. He went alone and stayed three months in England. Ostensibly, he was arranging for a few lectures, authorizing a special British edition of *The Innocents Abroad,* and ensuring copyright protection in Great Britain for his new book, *Roughing It.* In reality, however, he was spying out the land with the purpose of writing a book about England.

Mark Twain was now thinking in terms of writing books, not of working on newspapers. In the spring of 1871 he had sold out his interest in the *Express* and also composed his farewell piece for the *Galaxy* magazine. Editing and conducting a humorous department, he discovered, were not for him. By the autumn of that year, too, he had moved his family to Hartford, Connecticut, where his publisher was urging him to start work on another book. Hartford was closer to Europe, not only in geography, but also in spirit. There was wealth in Hartford. There were education, decorum, creativity, and the vibrancy of progress.[5] As the new concentration of culture enveloped Mark Twain, his old Western superiority as the child of nature began to abate. West and East were moving closer together.

The trip to England was no casual thing. Mark Twain provided himself with special notebooks which allowed him to keep a duplicate of everything he wrote and mailed home to Livy. From the duplicate he would presumably work on his book. His literary executor, Albert B. Paine, tells us that hundreds of pages were filled with notes and daily memoranda, but that the notes were never completed nor the book begun.[6] Whether or not the notes were completed we may never know, because in the Mark Twain Papers only one volume of them is preserved, numbered

pages 100 to 199 and ending in mid-word.[7] We do know, however, that he wrote to his mother-in-law only a week after his
return:

> I went to work on my English book yesterday & turned out 36
> pages of satisfactory manuscript, but the baby kept me awake
> so much last night that today I find the inspiration is vanished
> & gone, right in the middle of my subject.[8]

The inspiration never returned, it seems, and the book was never
completed. In search of new inspiration, Mark Twain even tried
to persuade Thomas Nast to go to England with him the following year, hoping to induce him to illustrate the book.

It was no use. For at least three good reasons Mark Twain
could never write this particular book: (1) the faults he found
in England were not colorful faults, (2) his experiences were
too restricted and un-foreign, and (3) he liked the English too
well to hurt their feelings. At the end of his first week in London
he confessed to Livy that he had not written in his journal for
four days:

> Confound this town, time slips relentlessly away & I accomplish
> next to nothing. Too much company—too much dining—too
> much sociability. (But I would rather live in England than
> America—which is treason.)[9]

His letters extolled everything from English scenery to the
conspicuous attention paid him by great lords and ladies and by
other *"gentlemen."* It was a heady experience. No longer was
he an unknown Westerner picnicking with other tourists in lands
which were completely foreign, even in language. Now he was
accepted by the brains of London as a man of letters who was
making temporary residence by himself in his own mother country. William Dean Howells, fast becoming one of his closest
friends, asserts that it was in London that Mark Twain was first
made to feel that he had come into his literary heritage.[10]

Mark Twain longed to share this alluring country with his loved ones. He hated to leave. He urged Mrs. Fairbanks to come over with Livy in the spring in order to behold this English countryside, "too absolutely beautiful to be left out of doors," and to meet these British men and women who "take a body right into their inner sanctuary, as it were."[11] We can guess that Mark Twain's plan to write a funny book about England was killed in part by the kindness of her citizens. How could he roast the very people who had toasted him?

These people, of course, were not without faults, but the faults struck Mark Twain as lacking the distinctive stuff required of travel literature. They seemed to be more or less universal faults. When a reporter asked him if he intended to poke fun at the British, he replied that he couldn't. Invariably he was reminded of similar abuses in the United States, and a man with a hump-backed uncle must not make fun of another man's cross-eyed aunt.

This first visit, moreover, was confined almost entirely to London. It lacked both the itinerant pattern of his Mediterranean voyage and the fun-loving companions who provided so many adventures. Mark Twain also realized that the British Isles could provide him with little to compare with the antiquities and novelties of the more exotic lands he had written up before. After about seven weeks in England he confessed as much to Livy:

> The truth is, there *are* no sights for me—I have seen them *all* before, in other places. It does seem to me that there is *nothing* under the sun that is not a familiar old friend to my eye. Consequently, I do just as little sight seeing as possible, but try to see as many people as I can.[12]

Writing in London in 1836, N. P. Willis suggested a reason for its being more difficult for an American to write about England than about other foreign countries. "In other countries," he said in the Preface of *Pencillings by the Way,* "the objects of in-

Part of Mark Twain's letter to Livy, October 25, 1872.

terest are classical or physical, and reducible to known standards; in England they are social or moral, and require diligent observation and study."

Despite the loss of most of Mark Twain's notes, however, we can piece together quite a number of his first impressions of the English people. On his return home he was full of praise for their personal spirit of independence, their public spirit, their "truth," and, of course, their hospitality to him. He told Howells many stories in proof of their virtues. At the same time he did consider that most Englishmen were rather blunt with one another and, in general, somewhat callous with strangers. Significantly, he also disliked, even at this early date, the submissiveness with which they accepted the injustices of hereditary castes.

For another thing, Mark Twain could not understand why some action was not taken to curb John Camden Hotten, the unscrupulous literary pirate. Hotten had robbed him of royalties already. "Hottentot" was Mark Twain's name for "this mollusk, this fungus, this bug, this pill, this vertebrated & articulated emetic." Venting his wrath, Mark Twain wrote two savage attacks (unpublished) on Hotten. One of his more gentle observations was, "Ignorance oozes from him like perspiration."[13]

Mark Twain's republican admiration for honest achievement caused him both puzzlement and anger on remarking the devotion of the English to Prince Albert. "The finest monument in the world," he laughed about the Albert Memorial, "erected to glorify—the *Commonplace*. It is the most genuinely humorous idea I have met with in this land." Why, five hundred tradesmen of Albert's own day had done as much for England as he had! Mark Twain wrote nine pages to show that England owed Albert absolutely nothing. It was Albert who owed England everything for the luck of being elevated to prominence by a beautiful young queen. Implicit in Mark Twain's heated comments is contempt for a people who seem to worship mere titles.[14]

For the British Museum he had great admiration. He praised

its matchless facilities, its service, its air of scholarly quiet, and the kindness of its staff. It shocked him to learn that preachers would often tear whole sermons out of the Museum's books. "And vandals of other kinds," he added, "tear leaves out of valuable books for other purposes, although the Museum furnishes every possible convenience for its visitors."[15]

In the extant volume of "Diary Notes" only once does Mark Twain allude to any discomforts in England, and this merely has to do with the lack of gas in the hotel rooms—just like Paris in 1867. "They give you a candle five inches long," he complained, "& so I send out & buy a ton & burn fifteen at a time." The English, however, did provide plenty of coal, whereas in American hotels, "They send it up to you in a spoon." Then he added as an aside to Livy, "I do like these English people—they are perfectly splendid—& so says every American who has staid here any length of time."[16] How unaware he seemed of the animosities described by Henry Adams and others only a few years before!

Only once, in this notebook, moreover, did Mark Twain break into the sort of burlesque which he had sprinkled throughout *The Innocents Abroad*. The passage begins by describing the red tape involved in visiting some of London's historic buildings. Then come pages of absurdly detailed descriptions of the "front yard" and "back yard" of St. Paul's Cathedral. A parody on statistics-loving guidebooks, of course. The parody on tedium, unfortunately, is itself tedious. The whole comic interlude tapers off in four or five pages about a silly misunderstanding with a waiter who insisted that Mark Twain's "soul" (sole) was "tough."[17]

A curiosity of these notes is the twenty pages (about 2250 words) on Gustave Doré. Although he poked fun again at the Old Masters, Mark Twain was enraptured by what he called the *"intense reality"* of Doré's art. He was positive that the twenty-by-thirty-inch canvas, "Christ Leaving the Pretorium," with its hundreds of dramatic lifelike figures, was "the *greatest* picture

extant." "If Doré had lived in the time of those infernal Old
Masters," he exclaimed, "the people would have worshipped
him."[18] With Frontier exaggeration he then wrote a fourteen-page
farce in which he is hounded to distraction by a man peddling
Doré reproductions.[19] Between these two extremes on Doré,
Mark Twain seems to have been seeking an effective point of
view.

Mark Twain published only three sketches from his "Diary
Notes." The longest and best describes a nocturnal visit to Westminster Abbey by lantern light. "A Memorable Midnight Experience" is sometimes light in tone, but its prevailing mood is
reverent. There are no guidebook statistics here. A cat curled
sleeping upon a rich mausoleum suggests to him the transience
of fame, while the myriad tombs and sculptures speak to him out
of forgotten ages. At the end:

> As we turned toward the door, the moonlight was beaming in at
> the windows; and it gave to the sacred place such an air of rest-
> fulness and peace, that Westminster was no longer a grisly mu-
> seum of mouldering vanities, but her better and worthier self
> —the deathless mentor of a great nation, the guide and en-
> courager of right ambitions, the preserver of fame, and the home
> and refuge for the nation's best and bravest when their work is
> done.[20]

The other two sketches are less flattering to the British.
"Rogers" is a humorous satire on an impoverished Englishman
who has an inordinate yearning to be looked upon as a man of
wealth. Among his close friends, Rogers says, are men of title.
And many of their wives, he confides, are romantically attached to
him. With his expensive talk and foolish deceptions, poor Rogers
is the prototype for Colonel Sellers of *The Gilded Age,* a novel
on which Mark Twain began work in February, 1873, only
months after his return from England.

"Property in Opulent London" is the third sketch. Mark Twain
was astonished to learn how much of the tremendously valuable

land of London was owned by just a few great lords. On this land, moreover, the lords paid almost no taxes. Inequitably, taxes on luxuries and on real estate were trifling in England: "The revenues," said Mark Twain, "come from taxes on the manifold things which Tom, Dick and Harry of the great middle and working classes have got to have and cannot do without. This is neither just nor generous."[21]

Despite his sympathy for the working classes, Mark Twain had no democratic desire to level the British caste structure at this time. At teas and banquets in London he was delighted to move easily among people of "ancient family and noble blood," as he put it, because in general "it was their brains that gave them their celebrity."[22] He was captivated by the aristocracy and by its costly trappings. With no hint of ridicule he described the elaborate ceremonies and panoply at the installation of the Lord Mayor. "I would rather be one of these footmen," he said, "than a rainbow."[23]

As a matter of fact, these happy months in England caused Mark Twain's patriotism to run rather low. His notes speak bitterly of the "stupid regulation" which required United States citizens to take an oath and pay a fee at the American consulate when shipping anything home: "All this infernal clog upon business in order to make the dirty Consulate pay for itself. We do hunt up more ways to save at the Spigot & lose at the bung than any other idiotic government afloat."[24]

In the early 1870's, indeed, Mark Twain was quicker to criticize his own country than to criticize England. *The Gilded Age* is further proof. So is his unsigned 1875 *Atlantic Monthly* piece, "The Curious Republic of Gondour," with its basic distrust of universal suffrage. The corrupt Grant administration was currently in power, providing ample cause for disillusion in the democratic system. Howard Baetzhold, in an informative article called "Mark Twain: England's Advocate," sums up Mark Twain's feelings during these years:

> Altogether, Mark Twain had little use for the government of
> the United States as he saw it at this time. . . . Clearly, it was in
> England that the "best" people seemed to occupy the positions of
> authority.[25]

Further evidence that the "best" people ran things in England
was provided shortly after Mark Twain's return home. He had
crossed on the Cunard steamship "Batavia," whose British seamen he had watched perform acts of heroism in rescuing the crew
of a foundering bark in the Atlantic. Impressed, he wrote a report
of the rescue for the Royal Humane Society. To his delight, the
seamen were awarded medals and were given immediate pro-
motions and raises by the British steamship company. On hearing
this, he sent an enthusiastic letter on "British Benevolences" to
the New York Tribune on January 27, 1873. He extolled not
only the Cunard Line but also the British people in general. No
people, he stated, were more generous toward charities or more
modestly so. And nowhere were benevolent societies managed
more admirably than in England. Without much doubt, this
"Anglomania," as Howells termed it, caused Mark Twain to be
doubly critical of American culture and politics.

Although unable to compose his book about England, Mark
Twain took the time to combat the pirating of Hotten by bringing
out a revised authorized edition of The Innocents Abroad. His
introductory note dated Hartford, July, 1872, shows that he prepared the revision before leaving the States. He spoke of weeding
out nearly all of the "most palpable and inexcusable of its blem-
ishes" and of working additions into almost every chapter. In
actuality, his revisions were sporadic, hasty, and brief. He might
have made them in the ample margins of the American edition.
Unaccustomed to the British audience, he became diffident to
the degree that he polished and formalized his prose style. He
was also self-conscious about his broadest humor, toning it down
or cutting it out. And he made his judgments of the foreign
scene less positive.[26] Finally, he composed a deferential Preface

in which he apologized to the British for the inaccuracy of his
vision and for the "chirping complacency" of the book. The
Preface closed with ingratiating remarks about the "mother
country," remarks of the sort which had caused Fenimore Cooper
a half-century before to denounce Washington Irving as a miserable toady and tuft-hunter.[27]

From this first trip to England, Mark Twain arrived home on
November 26, 1872, and immediately made plans to take his
family across as soon as the weather was mild. His letters and
notes had been so enthusiastic about the English "Fairyland"
that Livy needed no further persuasion. On May 23, therefore,
they set out on a trip from which they would not return until
early in November. Livy took a friend with her, little Susy had a
nurse, and Mark Twain had a theological student with him as
secretary. From then on he seldom journeyed without such an
entourage.

The ensuing months in the British Isles saw a continuous round
of entertainment and honors. "If Mark Twain had been a lion on
his first visit, he was little less than royalty now," Paine reports.
"His rooms at the Langham were like a court."[28]

For Mark Twain a happy break in the social activities came
during the latter part of June. The Shah of Persia was coming
to visit England, and Mark Twain agreed to cover the unprecedented event for the *New York Herald*. In order to get color and
background he crossed the Channel to Ostend, the port from
which the Shah's party would sail. He liked Flanders; its citizens
appeared to be a thrifty, industrious, healthy race, "prolific in the
matter of children." From June 18 to June 30 he wrote five letters
to the *Herald* describing the main activities of the Shah and also
many sidelights.[29] He found the Shah to be a handsome, strong-
featured man, very simply clothed. Mark Twain was favorably
impressed. Not until he had observed the Persian party for more
than a week did he express any dissatisfaction with the Shah or
with the mobs who cheered him. Then he complained that people

hardly even glanced at the young English prince, who one day
would rule a mighty empire:

> We have no eyes but for this splendid barbarian, who is lord
> over a few deserts and a modest ten million of ragamuffins—
> a man who has never done anything to win our gratitude or
> excite our admiration, except that he managed to starve a million
> of his subjects to death in twelve months. If he had starved the
> rest I suppose we would set up a monument to him now.[30]

As he watched "the mountains of money" being spent to entertain the Shah, Mark Twain could only hope that they would
persuade him to adopt "some of the mild and merciful ways" of
Christian rulers. The Shah should learn that a throne can rest as
firmly on affection as on fear, and that an "enlarged liberty
granted to the subject need not impair the power of the monarch."[31] Monarchy per se was still acceptable to Mark Twain. In
fact, he delighted in its pageantry and trappings, which he described in colorful detail. The romance in his nature was stirred
when he saw Lord Nelson's grand old ship all beflagged and
heard her historical guns booming. "God knows," he cried, "I
wish we had some of England's reverence for the old & great."[32]

Shortly after the Shah's visit, the social demands of London became too arduous for Livy's frail body. Mark Twain was also
concerned that he could find no time for writing. He had not yet
abandoned completely the idea of writing a British sequel to *The
Innocents Abroad*. He complained that they saw nothing but
social life; they saw no sights: "nothing, in fact, to make a
book of.—However, I mean to go to work presently, collecting
material." So he wrote to Mrs. Fairbanks.[33]

London engagements were canceled, therefore, and the
Clemens party went quietly to Edinburgh for a rest. No doubt,
Mark Twain went to work collecting material as they traveled
north in July, but none of this material has survived. Livy was
with him now, and his letters to his mother, several trunks full

of them, were burned in 1904.[34] From the old city of York, however, he sent Mrs. Jervis Langdon a long letter. Just a portion of one interminable sentence will suffice to show the way his imagination could still be swept along by historical associations:

> For the present we shall remain in this queer old walled town, with its crooked, narrow lanes, that tell us of their old day that knew no wheeled vehicles; . . . the vast Cathedral of York, with its worn carvings and quaintly pictured windows, preaching of still remoter days; the outlandish names of streets and courts and byways that stand as a record and a memorial, all these centuries, of Danish dominion here in still earlier times; the hint here and there of King Arthur and his knights and their bloody fights with Saxon oppressors round about this old city more than thirteen hundred years gone by . . .[35]

The Clemens party soon reached Edinburgh, where Livy recuperated slowly under the care of Dr. John Brown, henceforth a warm family friend. And after a time there began a round of luncheons, teas, and dinners. Mark Twain grew to love the sociable and gentle Scots. Following Edinburgh, there came a brief stay in Glasgow before they sailed across to Ireland for two weeks. Then back to England to sight-see and to visit friends in a beautiful country retreat. Almost before they knew it they were again in London amid the social whirl. This time they escaped by crossing to Paris for two weeks. There they broke the strain of sight-seeing by making a number of purchases for their new home, which was a-building back in Hartford.

Late in October they finally sailed for America, arriving in New York on November 2. They had been gone since May and had covered quite a bit of territory once they broke away from London society. Unfortunately, the happy months passed in Scotland, Ireland, rural England, and France in 1873 seem destined to remain as blank to history as Mark Twain's carefree week in Spain in 1867. Such evidence as we have indicates that Mark Twain's mood during these months, as during his 1872 visit, was less in harmony with his *Innocents Abroad* than it was with *The Sketch-Book* of Washington Irving. There seemed to be so much to admire, so little to astound or repel.

Within a week after depositing his homesick wife and the others safely back in the States, Mark Twain embarked once again for England. This was his third trip in fifteen months. In London he encountered his young California friend Charles Warren Stoddard, who was happy to act as his secretary and companion. It was now the height of the social season in London, and Mark Twain came for a specific purpose—to lecture. Already in October, just before departing, he had given London a sample of what to expect. For five successive nights and a Saturday matinee the spacious Queen's Concert Rooms, Hanover Square, had been packed to hear his old lecture on "Our Fellow Savages of the Sandwich Islands." On the subject of America's annexing Hawaii, however, he seems to have changed his mind. "To speak truly," he wrote to Whitelaw Reid of the *New York Tribune,* "I would rather those islands remained under a native king, if I were there, but can easily see that it won't suit those planters."[36]

At Hanover Square again, Mark Twain lectured steadily for most of December, 1873. It was a personal triumph without precedent, overshadowing even the success of his old friend Artemus Ward in London seven years earlier. To Joseph Twichell, his friend and pastor, he wrote that he would not lecture in the provinces after all, because he could not get halls large enough. Nevertheless, he did appear in Leicester on January 8 and in Liverpool the next two nights. He was sorry when the tour was ended. Never, he said, had he seen audiences that were quicker to see a point or to seize it, "& in this the comfort of lecturing lies. I had always had an idea, before, that the British risibles were hard to move."[37] Mark Twain's chief disappointment seems to have been the failure of government officials and the conservative nobility to attend his lectures; these powerful Tory elements still looked upon Americans with frank distaste.

Two months in England sped by as Mark Twain cultivated a growing circle of friends and brightened many a dinner with his toasts and speeches. For the first time now he complained of the London fog, which hurt his eyes and sometimes made it necessary for men with lanterns to walk in front of the omnibuses. His only other complaint was about the astounding rudeness of Oxford students at the theater and at concerts. They would crash the gates, bring dogs in with them, and disrupt the performance by meandering noisily around, even across the stage.[38] *

Just before Christmas he left London to visit Stonehenge and Salisbury. The ancient Druid stone circle was one of the most mysterious and satisfying ruins he had ever seen. As for the great cathedral, where he attended a Christmas service: "What a fascinating building it is!" he wrote Livy. "It is the loveliest pile of stone that can be imagined—think of comparing it with that solemn barn at York."[39]

At the urging of his wife, Mark Twain tore himself away from England once again on January 13, 1874. There was still much that he wished to see and do there, however, and he told Joe Twichell that he hoped to return to London in twenty days. But so happy and so busy did he find his life at home that his next visit to England was put off until the summer of 1879. The intervening years were those during which he struck his richest vein of literary ore, in memories of his boyhood and of romantic piloting days on the Mississippi. *Tom Sawyer* was written then, also the best chapters of *Life on the Mississippi* and a portion of *Huckleberry Finn*.

These writings, significantly, were an escape from the graceless Gilded Age into a past which Mark Twain was beginning to view through a veil of sentiment and longing. Beneath its gilt, American society, he was convinced, was racked with miseries

* He would learn more about student traditions and prerogatives in 1907, when the Oxford students shouted to him with happy unrestraint on the occasion of his being awarded an honorary degree.

and corruption almost unknown in England. His opinion of the domestic scene became more and more desolate. With envy he looked across the ocean to where the best minds were running the government. In America, he said, it seemed impossible to reward the most illustrious and capable citizens with the presidency. "This beggarly congress of ignorance and frauds," he cried. "The back-pay gang of thieves."[40] It was exactly the sort of Congress we should expect to produce, he thought, under our stupid laws. His opinion of the average intelligence was at low ebb in 1877:

> Mind, I believe this: Republican government, with a sharply restricted suffrage, is just as good as a Constitutional monarchy with a virtuous & powerful aristocracy; but with an unrestricted suffrage it ought to perish because it is founded in wrong & is weak & bad & tyrannical.[41]

It was with such anti-republican thoughts as these that Mark Twain this year sought out British soil again for what he called the first actual pleasure trip he had ever taken. In May he set out for Bermuda with Joe Twichell. They had six days at sea and only four on the island, but those four days, said Mark Twain, were like being in heaven. Rather pointedly his pastor advised him to make the most of it.

He did. This time he left a record of Bermuda, not only in his notebook, the first one to survive since 1868, but also in "Rambling Notes of an Idle Excursion," which ran in four issues of the *Atlantic* that winter. How different it all was from the Mediterranean countries! On stepping ashore they were pestered by no hackmen or porters. There was not a tramp or beggar to be seen anywhere, and no packs of dogs roamed the island to torment a person on his strolls. Bermuda seemed to have "upwards of a million cats," but cats he always loved; they were so quiet, clean, and dignified.

The streets and sidewalks, too, were clean—so clean, he protested, that he and Joe had to step aside to spit, which made con-

versation somewhat disjointed. The roads, one of his touchstones
of progress, were hard and excellent. As for the city of Hamilton,
it made the whitest, tidiest town in New England appear shabby.
Bermuda was also still free from what he termed the triple curse
of railways, telegraphs, and newspapers. And outside the villages
almost every aspect of nature was pleasing to his eye—the exotic
trees and flowers and especially the enchanting views of the sea.
There were several sights in Bermuda, he said, but they could
easily be avoided, unlike those of Europe.

> Bermuda is the right country for a jaded man to "loaf" in. There
> are no harassments; the deep peace and quiet of the country sink
> into one's body and bones, and give his conscience a rest, and
> chloroform the legion of invisible small devils that are always
> trying to whitewash his hair.[42]

Best of all, Bermuda was free from the poverty so evident in
Europe and the Near East. Its natives were handsome and well
dressed, their homes neatly constructed of a sugary-white coral.
Living, said Mark Twain, was cheap. There were potatoes and
onions for all; nobody could starve. There were also plenty of
schools, so everybody was able to read. Not a sign of unrest or
misery met his eye. To a man coming from a land torn with
strikes and violence, this was dumbfounding. "The spectacle of
an entire nation groveling in contentment," he exclaimed, "is an
infuriating thing."[43] He knew where the credit belonged—to
England. As he and Twichell wandered into a dark and lonely
road on the outskirts of town, they chatted cheerfully:

> Presently the chat took this shape:—"How insensibly the char-
> acter of a people and of a government makes its impression upon
> a stranger, and gives him a sense of security or of insecurity
> without his taking deliberate thought upon the matter or asking
> anybody a question. We have been in this land half a day; we
> have seen none but honest faces; we have noticed the British
> flag flying, which means efficient government and good order;
> so without inquiry we plunged unarmed and with perfect con-

fidence into this dismal place, which in any other country would swarm with thugs and garroters . . ."[44]

This was the high point of Mark Twain's "Anglomania" for at least thirty years to come. In spite of the allurements of Bermuda, however, he never took Livy there, and he himself (for what reason?) did not return there until after her death in 1904. Then, during his last four years, he made annual voyages back to the enchanted island.

Oddly enough, it was on his Bermuda holiday in May, 1877, that Mark Twain first noted the idea for a story which was soon to burgeon into an attack on the very thing he admired most at the time, British justice and fair play. "Write Prince & Pauper," says the memo, "in 4 acts & 8 changes."[45] The idea for a play was postponed, but that summer in Elmira he made a good start not only on that story as a novel but also on the story of Tom Sawyer's friend, Huckleberry Finn.

Mark Twain worked well at the farm in New York. Life in Hartford, on the other hand, was too busy and too sociable to permit him free time. That winter he confessed to his mother that business annoyances were giving him such "a badgered, harassed feeling" that he just could not write at home. He had about made up his mind, he confided, to take his "tribe and fly to some little corner of Europe" until at least one of his books was finished.[46]

It is possible, too, that Mark Twain's sense of guilt over his speech at the Whittier Birthday Dinner late in 1877 made him wish to escape New England society for a while. There was also the matter of money. It cost more than he had anticipated to keep up his large house with its staff of servants and continual round of guests. But the desire to write was uppermost. To Mrs. Fairbanks he explained, "I want to find a German village where nobody knows my name or speaks any English, & shut myself up in a closet 2 miles from the hotel, & work every day without interruption until I shall have satisfied my consuming desire in that direction."[47]

He hired a German nurse named Rosina Hay, and the whole family began to study the German language. The atmosphere of the house became Teutonic for several months. Apparently Mark Twain acquired a working knowledge of German in a short time, but he lacked the perseverance to keep up his studies. For a while that spring and later he strewed German words and phrases throughout his notebooks.

In mid-April the family sailed for Europe. The ménage this time consisted of Livy, her friend, Clara Spaulding, his two daughters, Susy and Clara (ages six and four), the German nurse, Rosa, and their butler, George Griffin, who went along to help with the baggage and serve as valet. They reached Heidelberg early in May after brief stays in Hamburg, Hanover, and Frankfurt. Mark Twain chose Germany for this sojourn, because he had never been there and still was hoping to find inspiration for that second travel book.

The family took rooms in the fine Schloss Hotel beside the famous old Heidelberg Castle and high above the city. For two weeks Mark Twain took language lessons, then gave them up, although he did study spasmodically later on. He was not a patient student. Later that summer in Germany he was speaking in English about some rather private matters when Twichell advised: "Speak in German, Mark—some of these people may understand English."[48]

No doubt Mark Twain's German would have improved more rapidly had he not been in the middle of writing two books and had he not discovered that hideaway in which to work on them. He just could not write and study at the same time, so he dropped German. Each morning after breakfast he would hike along up to his working den, smoking and meditating for a couple of hours on the way. There, perched some fifteen hundred feet above the hotel and overlooking the beautiful Neckar River, he would write from noon till four. Then he would stroll easily back down to his family and sociability. It was a pleasant life. And later that summer he privately confessed to Howells that he had some further good news: "It is this: *we've quit feeling poor!*"[49]

These months in Heidelberg were the start of a lifelong love affair between Mark Twain and Germany. In 1871 Mark Twain and Bret Harte had been the first two American authors selected for introduction to the Germans in the Tauchnitz Editions. Nor was the honor an empty one, said Mark Twain, for Baron Tauchnitz was an honorable gentleman who paid honest royalties. That the Germans reciprocated Mark Twain's affection is shown in the statistic that between 1871 and 1913 they read 134 separate editions of his books printed in Germany. This was more than twice the number of any other American author except for Bret Harte, who had 112 editions. And the Germans found Mark Twain, the man, to be every bit as attractive personally as his books.

Germany was to be the Clemens residence for only part of this extended, meandering trip. Joe Twichell was persuaded to come over for a holiday, and Mark Twain met him in Baden-Baden the first of August. For almost two weeks the two men knocked around Bavaria joyously, then roamed Switzerland for a month. Upon Twichell's departure, the Clemens party moved south into Italy for six weeks, residing chiefly in Venice, Florence, and Rome. By mid-November they were back in Germany—Munich this time—where they remained until the latter part of February, 1879. At this time they went to Paris, where they stayed until July 10, then spent ten days traveling slowly through Belgium and Holland before crossing over to London. Here they lived for about a month. On August 23 they finally sailed from Liverpool, arriving in New York on September 3 after an absence of nearly seventeen months.

Mark Twain managed to get a good amount of writing done while abroad, even some sketches to be included in his new travel book. Completing this book, however, was the most miserable literary experience he had suffered so far. He feared lest he had lost his facility. The pages just would not come. Europe, perhaps, had lost its novelty for him. Shepherding five females, moreover, was less inspiring than vagabonding with a few other young bucks. It was fortunate that Joe Twichell had joined him for six weeks, or else *A Tramp Abroad* (1880) might never have been finished. In Twichell's copy of the book the grateful author wrote:

> Hang it, if you had stayed at home it would have taken me fourteen *years* to get the material. You have saved me an intolerable whole world of hated labor, and I'll not forget it, my boy . . .
> We had a mighty good time, Joe, and the six weeks I would dearly love to repeat *any* time; but the rest of the fourteen months —*never*.[50]

Joe Twichell, of course, is the "Harris" of *A Tramp Abroad*. Mark Twain said that he was in 440 of the 531 pages. This may be true, but Harris is not nearly as important to the reader as Twichell's company was to the author. Yet even their "tramp" together encountered difficulties, for in the midst of it Mark Twain wrote his mother from Lucerne that he was lying in bed smoking all day and letting the others do the excursioning. "I loathe all travel except on foot," he explained, "& rheumatism has barred that to a considerable extent."[51]

About two months after Twichell had returned to the States, Mark Twain found himself in Rome with his family. The ancient capital had fascinated him in 1867, but now, he wrote to Twichell, it was able to interest him as much as East Hartford, no more. He had been too long abroad to retain a zest for sightseeing and the pleasure of making initial discoveries was more limited for him now. In the final paragraph of his new book he observed:

On the whole, I think that short visits to Europe are better for us than long ones. The former preserve us from becoming Europeanized; they keep our pride of country intact, and at the same time they intensify our affection for our country and our people; whereas long visits have the effect of dulling those feelings,—at least in the majority of cases. I think that one who mixes much with Americans long resident abroad must arrive at this conclusion.[52]

Mark Twain had been too short a time abroad to become Europeanized, and yet this travel book makes noticeably fewer comparisons with America than did his first one. Lacking also are facts, history, and statistics. The author seems to have written this time without the aid of guidebooks at his elbow. Unfortunately, he seems to have written also without the fresh spontaneity of *The Innocents Abroad,* without that engaging sense of wonder and surprise. Not only did Germany and Switzerland lack the foreignness of the ancient cultures around the Mediterranean, but also Mark Twain himself was no longer the brash young Western bachelor of the sixties.

An apparent effort is made, however, to imitate successful features of the earlier book. There is talk about shopkeepers, elastic prices, guides, foods, houses, the fine arts. There are the expected comments on strange customs, unusual scenery, peculiarities of dress and behavior. There is satire on American tourists and on elegantly written guidebooks. Romantic legends are scattered throughout as before, except that he does not tell the reader that he himself invented the tragic "Legend of Dilsberg Castle." And then the book is padded generously—too generously—with humorous incidents, extravagant burlesque, and anecdotes which are wholly irrelevant to the foreign scene. The final result, as Howells pointed out, was a volume which confirmed the patriotism of American readers without feeding their vanity.

A Tramp Abroad seeks to make too much out of too little material. Except for a satire on French dueling and three weak

chapters on Italy, it is devoted entirely to southern Germany and
the Alpine region. For some reason, Paris, the Low Countries, and
England are not described at all. Stylistically the book is smoother
than its predecessor, but it is neither as informative nor as entertaining.

Wherever he went in Europe, Mark Twain was unable to make
up his mind whether he preferred the aesthetic charm of the
antique or the practical advantages of the modern. Those towns
which were trying to modernize, he protested, were destroying
antiquity and becoming "monstrously & drearily alike. The modern architect has knocked the picturesqueness clear out of them."[53]
On the other hand, the picturesque, he knew, could be odiously
uncomfortable. It depressed him to see the way that Europeans
were forced to live, even the upper classes:

> They live in dark and chilly vast tombs,—costly enough, maybe,
> but without conveniences. To be condemned to live as the
> average European lives would make life a pretty heavy burden
> to the average American family.[54]

This sort of ambivalence marks a great deal of the book. It was
still Mark Twain's manner to make sweeping generalizations
about almost any subject at hand. In private he admitted this:
"You perceive I generalize with intrepidity from single instances.
It is the tourist's custom. When I see a man jump from the
Vendôme column, I say 'They like to do that in France.' "[55]
(Twelve years later he framed the aphorism: "Text. It is permitted to the superficial observer in a foreign land to generalize
broad principles from isolated instances."[56])

In private Mark Twain made quite a few observations about
Europe which did not quite agree with his published opinions.
Some of these observations are contained in the two notebooks
covering July-September, 1878, which he seems to have given to
Joe Twichell,[57] and there is other evidence we shall examine.
Germany in 1878 was under the powerful hand of Bismarck, who

defeated Napoleon III in 1870 and, as a consequence, united the
German states under Wilhelm I. Mark Twain thought the Kaiser,
then in his eighties, a "splendid old fellow." After the Kaiser
was wounded by a would-be assassin, Mark Twain wrote with
emotion, "I have not seen anything like this outburst of affectionate indignation since Mr. Lincoln's assassination gave the common globe a sense of personal injury."[58]

Mark Twain liked the Kaiser partly because his country seemed
like such a paradise, at least at first. After only ten days he raved
to Howells about the good faces he saw everywhere and about the
tranquil contentment. What prosperity there was, what genuine
freedom, what superb government! He wrote spiritedly in praise
of this government, detailing its effectiveness in different areas of
daily life. For some reason, however, he excluded nearly all of
this political talk from his book, perhaps because it might have
led him to make ill-tempered comparisons with the United States.
This was, after all, only a year after his Bermuda holiday with its
anti-republican outbursts. Germany, like Bermuda, he believed,
enjoyed superior administration of laws:

> There are only three persons in any country,—You, Me, & the
> Government. I judge that bad government is government which
> looks chiefly after Your comfort, & leaves Me to shift for myself,
> & that good government makes Me's of all of us, & so takes care
> of us all alike.

Observation convinced him that the fair-minded and intelligent
monarchy of Germany passed this test of good government,
whereas the so-called republican system of the United States
failed it:

> We blab so much about "Republic." When you set aside mere
> *names* & come down to realities, you find that we are ruled by a
> King just as other absolute monarchies are. His name is The
> Majority. He is mighty in bulk & strength . . . He rules by the
> right of possessing less money & less brains & more ignorance

than the other competitor for the throne, The Minority. Ours is
an Absolute Monarchy.[59]

Much more suitable than this sort of thing in a travel book,
Mark Twain realized, was a description of student life in Heidelberg. During the spring of 1878, he was close to this life and
captivated by it. His admiration for the educational system of
Germany ran very high. By the time these young men arrived at
the university, they had worked so hard and learned so much that
they deserved the new freedom open to them. Now they would
simply specialize at will and, as he phrased it, put a sort of roof
on their learning.

The comradeship between students and professors was a surprise to him; they even drank together in the beer halls. Far from
endangering the eminence of the teaching profession, in some
miraculous fashion, said Mark Twain, this informality seemed to
contribute to the profound education of the students. Stranger
still to him were the duels of the student corps. These were bloody,
dangerous combats, despite their formality. Mark Twain deplored the custom, but he made no effort to hide his admiration
for the skill and courage of the duelists. *A Tramp Abroad* contains no chapters more stirring than those which describe in detail
the background, etiquette, and actual fighting of these duels.
Years later these were the chapters which Kaiser Wilhelm II
praised particularly when Mark Twain had dinner with him.

By way of contrast, Mark Twain could not resist the tempta-
tion to describe a French duel. One of his earlier scrapbooks contains many clippings about M. Gambetta's celebrated *affaire
d'honneur,* so he simply burlesqued the details in order to make
fun of the French, whom he considered affected and cowardly.
His own error, he said, was in agreeing to act as Gambetta's second and in standing behind him at the start of the duel. Gambetta
collapsed with fright, crushing him under a mountain of flesh.
Mark Twain reported that he himself thereupon became an object

of national interest and was voted the Legion of Honor as the only man to be hurt in a French duel in forty years.

Balancing his increasing distaste for the French was his increasing regard for the Germans. Even their politeness, he said, was the genuine article. Civil questions always met with civil answers in Germany. Frequently Germans would drop whatever they were doing and guide the questioner to his destination, even though it might be to a rival shop. "One feels so cowed, at home, so unindependent, so deferential to all sorts of clerks & little officials," he noted, "that it is good to go & breathe the free air of Europe & lay in a stock of self-respect & independence."[60]

Mark Twain was pleased to discover that the Teutons had stricter standards of personal hygiene than the Latins and Arabs. Everywhere he saw only clean, neat clothes. Village and city presented a cleanliness to which he thought America could not aspire. There were no filthy tramps or beggars, no packs of dogs. As for the dwellings: "These peasants," he said, "are as cleanly in their houses as the Yankee of romance, and more cleanly than the reality."[61]

This combination of courtesy and cleanliness made the average hotel in Germany a gratifying place to spend the night. In most flattering terms Mark Twain described his experiences at a village inn. Although American villages were superior to the German in most "merits, excellences, conveniences, and privileges," he believed that American hotels were inferior. One exception, apparently, was the Munich hotel, which he described so humorously to Mrs. Langdon in one of his early letters. Here the closets smelled, the tablecloths were dirty, the cuckoo clock woke them up at regular intervals, the window shades had to be put up and down with a ladder, and Clara Spaulding's bed collapsed twice during the night. There was also that hotel where their chandelier had nine burners, but they had to light eight of them in order to see the ninth.

These exceptions, it will be noted, make no criticism of the

personnel. The warmhearted friendliness of the German people
was among the traits which endeared them most to Mark Twain.
They were a "kindly people," he emphasized, whose chief characteristic seemed to be a goodwill to men. An unforgettable dem-
onstration of this characteristic was provided at the opera in
Hanover, where a once-famous tenor was giving a special performance. The renowned voice was now cracked and pathetic;
nevertheless, the audience gave the old man a storm of applause.
The people did not care that now, as Mark Twain's friend observed, " 'he only make like a cat which is unwell.' " This applause was a revelation to Mark Twain:

> Where and how did we get the idea that the Germans are a
> stolid, phlegmatic race? In truth, they are widely removed from
> that. They are warm-hearted, emotional, impulsive, enthusiastic,
> their tears come at the mildest touch, and it is not hard to move
> them to laughter. They are the very children of impulse. We are
> cold and self-contained compared to the Germans.[62]

Probably, Mark Twain would not have enjoyed this opera
even if the tenor had been in perfect voice. He was not an opera
lover. *Lohengrin,* he said in his notebook, was the kind of intense
but incoherent noise which reminded him of the time the orphan
asylum burned down. (His family had heard the opera in Mann-
heim.) "The racking and pitiless pain of it remains stored up in
my memory," he said, "alongside the memory of the time I had
my teeth fixed."[63] In the book he toned down his complaint
somewhat, although he made no effort to deny that the banging
and crashing of *Lohengrin* sounded to him like a shivaree.

At Baden-Baden the family went to the park one night to hear
the band play the "Fremersberg." A beautiful air ran through the
piece; then came the majestic chanting of the monks. Mark Twain
was convinced that the "Fremersberg" must be very low-grade
music, because it so stirred him and uplifted him: "I was full of
cry all the time, and mad with enthusiasm." He wished that classi-

cal music could move him like this but said that he had never heard enough to be able to enjoy it. "I dislike the opera," he confessed, "because I want to love it and can't."[64] He was sensitive to the fact, it seems, that he could not appreciate the favorite music of what he called the "higher and better people," the people among whom he had begun to move.

Mark Twain's sensitivity to the tastes of a more cultivated society had set him to reading Ruskin and making a study of art following his first trip to Europe. This study seems to have helped. No longer, for example, did Turner's painting of "The Slave Ship" remind him of a tortoiseshell cat having a fit in a platter of tomatoes. He become, in fact, a Turner enthusiast. As for his early preference for the bright new copies of the Old Masters: "That was a mistake of large dimensions. The Old Masters were still unpleasing to me, but they were truly divine contrasted with the copies." The credit for the mellow richness, however, belonged most likely to Old Time, not to the Old Master: "Perhaps the picture was a clanging bell, until Time muffled it and sweetened it." At any rate, he could now find some pleasure in contemplating certain of the Old Masters, "but still it was a calm pleasure; there was nothing overheated about it."[65]

This time Mark Twain did not denounce the early painters for toadying to the medieval princes, but he did inveigh against their female nudes. His Victorianism was stronger now than his republicanism. In warm and living detail, he complained, artists were allowed to portray that which an author would be burned for describing in cold type. It was not right. A "Venus" by Titian was, in his opinion, the vilest and most obscene picture the world possessed.

He also believed that the drawing of certain Old Masters was as faulty as their morals. He mentioned a figure with two right legs and horses that looked like "bladders on legs." In his notebook he was more outspoken than he was in *A Tramp Abroad,* attacking most sarcastically the unrealistic shapes and colors found in the old paintings. "In good art," he judged, "a correct complexion is the color of a lobster, or of a bleached tripe or of a chimney sweep—there are no intermediates or modifications."[66] He privately assured himself also that his own ignorance of the rules of art did not disqualify him as a critic, for a man might criticize a dinner without being a cook.

It is significant that for publication Mark Twain made concessions here, just as he did with regard to music. He conceded that to the skilled eye, the trained eye, there was something beautiful about the old paintings, just as certain women have an indefinable charm in their faces which makes them beautiful to their intimates. With concessions like this he was able to flaunt humorously his Western ignorance and at the same time defer to Eastern refinement. This was frequently his way.

So much for the fine arts, seldom among his enthusiasms. At concerts in Germany he was less interested in the music, as a rule, than in the sensible way the performances began on the dot and latecomers were not seated until the end of the first musical number. He also approved the fixed price of five cents in advance for checking coats and hats. America, he said, should learn these customs. One practice, however, he thought must be very uncomfortable and uninspiring to performers in the theater. Audiences would remain still and cold, saving up all their applause until the end of each act, and he disapproved.

The nature of his working habits seems to have caused Mark Twain, most of his life, to compose manuscripts about two to five thousand words in length. At times these pieces were published independently; at other times they were made parts of longer units. For this travel book he composed more of these short pieces than he knew what to do with. Six of them ended up as appendices, although they might better have been woven into the main text. Two others found their way into print elsewhere, while at least one more is still unpublished. "The Great Revolution in Pitcairn" and "The Stolen White Elephant," both somewhat longer, may have seemed too irrelevant. He might have made room, however, for his twenty-seven-page manuscript (unpublished) on the Schefflers (coopers) and their charming tradition of putting on elaborate street performances every seven years.

Appendix A, "The Portier," extols the Continental concierge as a "most admirable invention, and most valuable convenience." This man, said Mark Twain, is polite as a duke, speaks from four to ten languages, and seems to know everything. Mark Twain then explained how the various hotel employees were paid in Europe. He hoped that the "feeing system" would soon be imported into America.

Appendix B is about Heidelberg Castle, the romantic old relic on the hillside by the Schloss Hotel. Most of this sketch is straightforward description of the castle within and without, by night and by day. Mark Twain also indulged in some nonsense about the famed Heidelberg Tun, the wine cask as big as a cottage topped by a dance floor.

Appendix C, which might well have been used as a fifth chapter on Heidelberg University, is an amused account of how a student selects his own days for confinement to the College Prison and what his life is like while he lives there. Mark Twain knew an American student who promised the constable to report on his first free day. Visiting this young man in his cell, he was attracted by the inscriptions on the walls and the elaborate carvings with which prisoners had ornamented the tables.

Appendix D is the well-known "Awful German Language." This runs to some nine thousand words and, to anyone who has studied German, is one of the funniest things Mark Twain ever wrote. For many years he had great fun satirizing the German language, which contained words so long, he said, that they had perspective. Surely, he complained, there could not be another language so slipshod and systemless, so slippery to the grasp. He let off steam in his notebook: "godam language with 16 THE'S in it. & where a turnip has a sex & a young lady hasn't. (Die Rübe—Das Mädchen)."[67] Mark Twain says that he heard an American student, in one of his calmest moods, remark that he would rather decline two drinks than one German adjective.

Next comes the short, lively "Legend of the Castles," which could easily have been inserted in the body of the book, as were half a dozen other German legends of various types. This one is full of dialogue and builds to a tearfully happy climax.

The final sketch, Appendix F, is an informative and interesting study of "German Journals." Mark Twain was annoyed at finding so little to read in German newspapers. They seemed to be almost all advertisements. There were, he said, only 1654 words of reading matter in his Munich paper, not enough to fill a single column of the average daily newspaper in America. As a former newsman, he made a formidable list of all the things one *could not* find in the German daily, then listed the few things one *could* find:

> A child's handful of telegrams, mainly about European national and international political movements; letter correspondence about the same thing; market reports. There you have it. That is what a German daily is made of. A German daily is the slowest saddest and dreariest of the inventions of man.

He was disgusted. There was, however, a silver lining of sorts; at least this kind of paper did no harm. "That is a very large merit," he added, "and should not be lightly weighed nor lightly thought of."

These Appendices obviously have more to do with the foreign scene than do many of the stories and personal anecdotes with which he spiced the main text. To be sure, some of these stories are delightful, but who would think of looking in *A Tramp Abroad* for Jim Baker's Bluejay Yarn or the misadventures of Nicodemus Dodge? Mark Twain's fantastic search for a lost sock in a dark bedroom could have taken place in Carson City, and the average American ant is probably no smarter than the ants on whose stupidity he spent so many pages.

As for the legends, these may be padding, but they do enrich the Continental atmosphere of the volume. Some of them are sentimental or tragic; others are clever or romantic. Mark Twain did not make fun of them this time, as he sometimes did in *The Innocents Abroad*. He played them straight. His knowledge of German, moreover, was good enough to appreciate Heine's beautiful poem "Die Lorelei," and his ear was true enough to reject the only English translation he had at hand. Therefore, while he permitted a comic illustration of the Rhine maidens, he made his own serious translation of the poem. To the surprise of many readers, the translation is smooth, poetic, and readily singable.

Not all of the personal anecdotes in the book, of course, are irrelevant to the foreign scene. Several, indeed, give valuable insights into both the observer and the observed. In Baden-Baden one Sunday the family went to a fashionable church and sat behind a little old lady who was plainly and cheaply dressed. Mark Twain's heart went out to her, so embarrassed and out of place did she appear. At the end of the service, as he was about to offer the little lady a lift in his carriage, the entire congregation arose and stood still as she walked up the aisle. She was the Empress of Germany. "No,—she had not been so much embarrassed as I had supposed," he said. "My imagination had got started on the wrong scent, and that is always hopeless; one is sure then, to go straight on misinterpreting everything, clear through to the end."[68] Even allowing for the customary exaggeration, we get a picture here of a warmhearted American democrat who, nevertheless, has nothing but respect for royalty, especially when royalty is modest and unassuming.

This anecdote is introduced by a comparison of American and European ways of keeping the Sabbath. The Germans kept the

commandment to "rest" by abstaining from work, whereas the
foolish Americans abstained also from play, even though play,
argued Mark Twain, was generally the most effective form of
"rest." In the United States, as a result, Sunday was a day of
boredom. In Europe it was "the free day, the happy day," on
which a person could break the Sabbath in a hundred ways without committing any sin.

Mark Twain also liked the German custom of bowing, even to
strangers, on leaving a room. He liked the cigars which cost only
two cents apiece. He enjoyed the military music played by bands
in all the towns of Germany. On his frequent hikes he came to
appreciate the faggot-gatherers who kept the forests clean and
beautiful and free from underbrush. He was not quite sure what
to think of the German custom of allowing children to have
wine with dinner. Nor could he ever, either then or in later years,
make up his mind about the fat German "feather-beds" or the
eight-foot-high German stoves. With equal eloquence, depending on his mood, he sometimes praised and sometimes cursed
the heavy down-filled comforters and the enormous space-heat-
ing "monuments."

Restricted to his notebook was a surprised observation about
the robust parlance of the German dinner table: "German good-
society conversation, in which both sexes say Lord God, how good
it is! Jesus C! By God! Es ist verdammt gut! (the soup) D—d
good.—said by a lady."[69] Because it was his own practice to confine colorful language to the privacy of his home or to masculine
society, Mark Twain probably did not approve of such talk coming from women in public.

Germany, after all, was not perfect, and he was too honest to
pretend that it was. He complained of the high hack fares in
Heidelberg, of books which fell to pieces when opened, and of
the cleaners who ruined his family's clothes in Munich. That
German coffee and cream were poor was less surprising to him
than his discovery that Rhine wines were vinegary. It annoyed

him to see so many German men combing their hair in public. The church bells of the Continent often got on his nerves, and what he called the "church manners" of Munich were as bad, he said, as the theater manners were good. The reader wonders whether it was an art gallery, palace, or antique shop which caused him to explode in his notebook: "I wouldn't have such rubbish in the house. I do hate this antiquarian rot, sham, humbug; cannot keep my temper in such a place—& never voluntarily enter one."[70]

In Baden-Baden he found the baths so cheap, yet so luxurious and beneficial, that he went to them often. The shopkeepers were quite a different matter. After describing an experience with a boorish, contemptuous female, Mark Twain said that her manners were typical of many Baden-Baden shopkeepers. They would swindle you if possible, he said, and would insult you whether they succeeded in swindling you or not. They were said, however, to be polite to Russians, Germans, and people of rank. A friend advised him to pose as a Russian prince in order to see the abyss to which servility could descend.

The first third of *A Tramp Abroad* deals with Germany. This portion is drawing to a close before Harris is brought in. The remainder of the book is mostly about outdoor life in the Alps during the three happy weeks the two men wandered about together, between August 15 and September 7. This was a region of magnificent scenery but few other guidebook sights and very few people. For this reason Mark Twain was thrown more than ever upon his ingenuity in finding things to write about. More often than not he fell back upon his old poses of Simpleton and Tenderfoot. He devoted over forty pages, for example, to his farcical ascent of the Riffelberg, in the course of which he tried furiously at one time to spar a glacier off the rocks with his Alpine stick to make it move faster. He also worked in humorous tales from the Pacific slopes and anecdotes about a number of ridiculous tourists from the United States. And there was always that surefire device of making fun of himself—pretending to be acquainted with a certain young lady, climbing Mont Blanc by looking through a telescope, making a public display of himself in his nightshirt while mistaking a sunset for a sunrise.

In spite of this buffoonery, however, Mark Twain made clear his genuine love for the Alps. He was impressed by the skill and heroism of early Alpinists, from whose accounts he quoted more than thirty pages. And his descriptions of the great peaks and ranges became poetic in feeling. Particularly beautiful are his word-pictures of Mont Blanc, once in the sunshine and once by moonlight. The reader must be wary, however, because in the midst of his eloquence Mark Twain sometimes liked to play a joke. The imaginary view from the summit of Mont Blanc is couched in masterly prose, even as Popocatepetl is seen smoking far to the south and the stately range of the Himalayas appears in the purple glooms over to the southwest.

"Switzerland," said Mark Twain, "is simply a large, humpy, solid rock, with a thin skin of grass stretched over it."[71] Yet he fell in love with that humpy rock. He was wise, perhaps, to do no actual mountain climbing, but he and Twichell hiked to their hearts' content. At times the Alps may seem to have been little more than a spectacular playground for Mark Twain. More often they dazzled him with their awesome peaks and plunging valleys, their waterfalls and great lakes. He loved the picturesque chalets, the mountain trails, and particularly the fast-rushing streams beside which he frolicked like a boy, chasing sticks he tossed into the current. A hike from St. Nicholas to Zermatt, he said, was a wonder-filled experience, for nature in that region was built on a stupendous plan:

> There is nothing tame, or cheap, or trivial,—it is all magnificent. That short valley is a picture gallery of a notable kind, for it contains no mediocrities; from end to end the Creator has hung it with His masterpieces.[72]

Mark Twain sought to impart to his readers a sense of that

spell which people feel in the Alps, he believed, and in no other mountains. It is a deep, nameless influence, he said, which always leaves behind it a restless longing, a "longing which is like home-sickness, a grieving, haunting yearning, which will plead, im-plore, and persecute till it has its will."[73] Only these mountains, in all the world, he felt, took one by the heartstrings. Nearly five months after his vacation with Twichell he wrote to his old friend from Munich:

> O, Switzerland! the further it recedes into the enriching haze of time, the more intolerably delicious the charm of it and the cheer of it and the glory and majesty and solemnity and pathos of it grow. Those mountains had a soul; they thought, they spoke—one couldn't hear it with the ears of the body, but what a voice it was!—and how real! Deep down in my memory it is sounding yet.[74]

For a while Mark Twain tried to serve as guide and courier for his party, but he soon gave it up. It was not worth the money it saved. "Without a courier, travel hasn't a ray of pleasure in it, anywhere;" he said, "but with him it is continuous and un-ruffled delight."[75] He detailed the myriad ways a courier could be useful and closed by recommending "one who might fairly be called perfection." This was a young man named Joseph Very. Many years later in the 1890's Mark Twain would seek out Joseph Very and engage his services again.

Joseph Very was not Swiss. He was a Pole. Despite his love for the Alps, Mark Twain did not like the Swiss people. In the smaller shops, he said, they cheated the tourists when they could and frequently hounded them out onto the sidewalk and ran down the block bickering. Swiss men, moreover, practiced de-liberate rudeness on the sidewalks. One day in Geneva, said Mark Twain, he watched a young dandy on three occasions plot col-lision courses with other strollers. Once this man even forced a lady to stop dead in her tracks, while he lounged by in front of her. Mark Twain later saw this "curious game" played in Paris,

but there it seemed less for pleasure than simply from indifference
to other people's rights. American manners, he observed, were
the butt for jests in refined Europe and yet:

> Even the most degraded woman can walk our streets unmolested,
> her sex and her weakness being her sufficient protection. She
> will encounter less polish than she would in the old world, but
> she will run across enough humanity to make up for it.[76]

Mark Twain's inherent gallantry was also affronted by the
sight of so many women laboring in the fields of Europe. He saw
aged grandmothers doing the work of animals while groups of
men sat around smoking their pipes. There was at least one Swiss
woman, however, whom he would have enjoyed seeing at work
in the fields. This was the ponderous female who appropriated
his seat on the train, snuffling that she had lost the use of her legs
and had to keep them stretched out on the opposite seat. At the
border she hopped up and marched away, proud of her little
deceit.

Although Mark Twain made no secret of his dislike for the
Swiss people, he did cover up his extreme repulsion at certain
localities. He had made no effort to do this in his first travel book.
Readers of *A Tramp Abroad,* for instance, laugh at Harris when
he complains about the filth and squalor of the town of St. Nicholas. Harris, after all, is just a sort of gentle Mr. Brown. Furthermore, it is emphasized that he has been finding fault all morning
because they happen to be in a Catholic canton: " 'It ain't muddy
in a Protestant canton when it rains . . . They don't have those
lop-eared dogs in a Protestant canton.' "[77] There is no good
nature, however, in Mark Twain's private remarks about St.
Nicholas. He called it an "inhabited privy" where the streets ran
liquid dung. "This canton," he asserted in his notebook, "may be
called the fundament of Switzerland."[78]

Mark Twain also was less pleased with Italy than he ever let
his readers know. The only city which was new to him was Turin,

which he made sure to describe in glowing terms. He praised its "roominess," in particular, its vast paved squares and extravagantly wide streets. From the handsome houses and shops to the fine-looking military officers and laughing populace there was not a single aspect of Turin which failed to please him.

He also made it clear that not all Italians were as dishonest as they were reported to be. He described three episodes in which Italians could easily have cheated him but did not. Furthermore, instead of execrating St. Mark's Cathedral in Venice as the most hideous building in the world, this time he said that its ugliness charmed him. Too many buildings, he argued, mixed the beautiful and the ugly in ways which made the spectator uneasy, but one could be calm before St. Mark's. Its details were "masterfully ugly," with no misplaced beauties intruding anywhere. The result was a "grand harmonious whole of soothing, entrancing, tranquilizing, soul-satisfying ugliness." Then his memorable picture of the old church: "Propped on its long row of low thick-legged columns, its back knobbed with domes, it seemed like a vast warty bug taking a meditative walk."[79]

A Tramp Abroad, one must conclude, was designed to suggest that Mark Twain enjoyed Europe more than he actually did. His notebooks and letters always reveal his private reactions much more accurately. There he railed as usual against the beggars, the poor food, the wretched Continental lamps. Shopkeepers swindled him, he complained, and scoundrels kept passing him counterfeit money. He hated statues which had an "offensive & obscene fig leaf." The government lottery he considered to be a very bad thing for the poor, and almost all Italians were poor. Privately, too, his antipathy toward the Catholic Church was nearly as strong as in 1867. "Rome seems to be a great fair of shams, humbugs & frauds," he noted. "Religion is its commerce & its wealth, like dung in the Black Forest."[80] From this city he confessed, in a well-known letter to Howells:

I wish I *could* give those sharp satires on European life which
you mention, but of course a man can't write successful satire
except he be in a calm judicial good humor—whereas I *hate*
travel, and I *hate* hotels, & I *hate* the opera, & I *hate* the Old
Masters—in truth I don't ever seem to be in a good enough
humor with *any*thing to *satirize* it; no, I want to stand up before
it & *curse* it, & foam at the mouth,—or take a club & pound it
to rags & pulp.[81]

A Tramp Abroad does not really end; it just peters out. For
some reason, the months in Paris and the weeks in Belgium, Holland, and England are barely mentioned. On these countries there
are merely a dozen hasty lines. Mark Twain was immeasurably
glad to get home, he said, so glad that he thought nothing could
ever get him out of the country again. "Europe has many advantages which we have not," he concluded, "but they do not
compensate for a good many still more valuable ones which
exist nowhere but in our own country."[82]

There are indications that Mark Twain at one time intended to
include a chapter comparing life in Europe with life in America.
His notebook suggests this, as does an eleven-page manuscript
which he did not publish. Consistently, the one preeminence he
claimed for the United States, and almost the sole preeminence,
was the comfort, the convenience of her homes, hotels, and railroad trains. In regard to modern luxuries, in short, Europe was
disconcertingly backward. Her wealthy classes were obliged to
live in "stately sepulchres"; her poor had to herd together in
"morgues." On the other hand:

> *Outside* of the house,—well, that is another matter altogether.
> When we come to that, America must take a back seat. Not a
> moderately back seat, but a seat away to the rear. In Europe an
> invisible eye seems to order & govern & watch over everything
> & everybody like a tireless & unsleeping providence.[83]

He went on to give examples. Excellent law enforcement in

Europe, he said, prevented builders from cluttering up the sidewalks with material, prevented blackguards from howling about
the streets at night, and even prevented cabdrivers from over-
charging their passengers. The trouble with the United States, he
thought, was that officials were so concerned about reelection that
they did not attend to business. He also admired the country roads
of the Continent. He liked to walk the brightly lit city streets and
sit in the open-air restaurants. The thing which seems to have impressed him most favorably of all in Europe, however, was the
wonderful spirit of the people: "everybody is glad to do his
neighbor a kindness; nobody is insolent, not even the metropoli-
tan dry-goods clerk."

It is evident that much of this is contradicted by complaints
voiced in Munich, Baden-Baden, and elsewhere, and it is also
evident that when he wrote this, his anti-republican feelings were
still running high. By praising the people of Europe he was
probably trying to demean the society of the United States and its
government. In these years a particular grievance was the shabby
way the United States treated its foreign diplomats. His 1879
notebook is pockmarked with acid comments. Bayard Taylor,
the charming man-about-the-world, had come over on the boat
with Mark Twain to serve as Minister to Berlin. The two men
became warm friends. After only a few months in office Taylor
died. "Beggarly government," cried Mark Twain, "to pay but
$17,500 at Berlin, Paris—can't *board* for that. Bayard Taylor
could not get a decent house, had to *furnish* one—took all his
advance—then he died."[84]

From mid-November, 1878, until mid-February, 1879, the
Clemens family lived in Munich. They then made the unhappy
decision to go to Paris for the spring. The weather was cold and
damp when they arrived on the last day of February. Their cab-
man seemed brutally ill-mannered, and their first hotel room was
dingy, cold, and hideous. They changed quarters, but for months
the rain and chilly fog persisted. "France has neither winter nor

summer nor morals—" Mark Twain asserted, "apart from these drawbacks it is a fine country."[85]

This Paris sojourn was miserable. At the end of six weeks Mark Twain wrote to Frank Bliss that he had been sick, sick, and sick again with rheumatism and dysentery. Four-fifths of the time, he complained, he had been confined to bed, an awful setback. In polite understatement Paine observes that this visit to Paris gave Mark Twain a bad impression of France "from which he never entirely recovered" and that henceforth Mark Twain "had no great love for the French as a nation."[86] The truth is that from this time until the day of his death Mark Twain's dislike for the French amounted to a contempt, a loathing, a repugnance, which was unique in his international experience.

In later years, as we shall see, he brought his Francophobia out into the open, but in the 1870's he confined it to his notebooks and to manuscripts which he decided not to publish. There is evidence that he planned a full-scale assault upon the French, probably in *A Tramp Abroad,* but later considered it out of harmony with the prevailing lightheartedness of the book. He worked up over thirty pages of rough notes in which he compared French civilization with that of Dahomey. The barbarism of the latter was to be preferred, he said, because it was more frank and open. As for morality, there was no great Frenchman alive, he charged, without a mistress, and it was quite in fashion for French women, once they were married, to take lovers.[87]

From these notes may have come "The French and the Comanches" article, which seems to have been designed for the book but was never used. The article is savage in its sarcasm. The French, he argued, were not really more cruel than the Comanches, "only more ingenious in their methods." In one thing, though, the French stood almost alone: "The spirit of massacre seems to be theirs by divine right." So pious was the Frenchman, said Mark Twain, that he thought nothing of killing his neighbors to make them pious, too. And in spite of the "gigantic vanity" of the average Frenchman, he cringed with rabbit-like meekness under insult and abuse. Together with the Turks, Dahomians, and Comanches, concluded Mark Twain, the French were among the partly civilized peoples of the globe. Americans should pity the poor Frenchman and try to raise him up—"this disparaged and depreciated link between man and the simian."[88]

In addition to this article there exists a forty-six-page manuscript for which Mark Twain must have done considerable research. In a somewhat scholarly fashion, complete with footnotes, he compared French customs of courtship and marriage with those of such races as the Chinook Indians, Kaffirs, Abyssinians, and Zulus. His emphasis was upon the barbarism of the premarital and marital customs of the French. "Plainly," he decided, "there is much less sentiment than 'business' about a French marriage."[89]

Nothing less than the Grand Prix was able to interrupt Mark Twain's bleak mood in France. His colorful pages caught the festive, electric atmosphere of race-day and of the great race itself. In his enthusiasm he did not even appear unduly distressed by the fact that the occasion brought out the "French Goddesses of Liberty" (prostitutes) in large numbers. The annual event was too exciting for him. He was much more interested in observing the French plainclothesmen, whose duty it was to keep foreigners from being cheated *by the government* on ticket prices at the Grand Prix. Had Mark Twain wished to carry his travel account as far as France, what a charming chapter he might have made of all this![90]

During these months abroad Mark Twain filled his notebooks with anti-French comments, nearly all of which were left out by his editor. "In certain public indecencies," wrote Mark Twain, "the difference between a dog & a Frenchman is not perceptible."[91] "With French dressmakers always take a sample or they use cheaper materials."[92] He found fault even with French apartment houses, newspapers, and pipe tobacco. It was emblematic to him that Frenchmen lashed their horses, whereas Germans did not. And there was not a single Frenchman big enough, he said, to see any greatness in Germany or in a German citizen. He called France the "artificial nation," whose language and people were both "sophomoric and theatrical." The French, in short, were "Devotees of the trivial."[93]

These were among his gentler criticisms. His Victorian morality rebelled whenever he considered the sexual morals of the French. "The nation of the filthy-minded," he called them.[94] To be witty in France, he said, was very simple; one merely needed to be dirty. French literature seemed to him to confine itself to two specialties—science and adultery—and the nation seemed to interest itself mainly in "high art & seduction."[95] Contamination, he believed, started in the tender years, when young girls were reared in an atmosphere "suffocating with nastiness." In view of French history and literature, he said, a man must be a fool to believe in the cleanliness of the average French girl's mind. "Frenchman speaking admiringly of a little girl—'What! Seven years old & still virtuous? The little angel!'"[96]

"France," said Mark Twain, "has usually been governed by prostitutes."[97] This seemed appropriate. He set about to make up sayings, several of which he used in later writings. "'Tis a wise Frenchman that knows his own father."[98] "They have bestialities which are unknown in civilized lands . . . Scratch a F & you find a gorilla."[99] "A Frenchman's home is where another man's wife is."[100]

Curiously, in the midst of this censure Mark Twain paused to say a kind word about the exquisite artificial flowers made in France. This led him to believe that the French must have some redeeming qualities. He thought of one:

> This nation is not wholly savage—it has a surface humanity which crops out in hospitals, asylums, places for succor of wounded & drowned people. It is capable of being raised to a quite fair sort of civilization by the right sort of Am & Eng missionaries.[101]

Had these hospitals and asylums been found in any country but France, they would have suggested far more virtues to Mark Twain than a mere "surface humanity"—of this we can be sure.

Thoughts of France did nothing to sweeten Mark Twain's opinion of mankind in general during these months. It is not surprising, then, to discover in the midst of these notes the beginnings of a sardonic pessimism: "If hereafter the mightier the Empire the grander the ruler, the[n] the Devil & the Deity will contrast like the Czar of Russia & the Governor of Rhode Island."[102]

It is regrettable that we know so little about Mark Twain's ten days in Belgium and Holland en route to London. The Low Countries seem to have delighted him, but he scarcely mentioned them in his writings. He found the elaborate service in the Brussels Cathedral "highly impressive." For once he was in the proper mood, for he saw nothing at all ridiculous in the swinging censers, the old women selling candles, the many bells, and what he called the "remote bowing and mumming." It was there he heard the most majestic organ music and men's voices he had ever listened to. "Never heard anything," he stated "that rose to the sublimity of those sounds."[103]

In the Netherlands he was captivated equally by the people and by the countryside. "How very pretty & fresh & amiable & intelligent the middle-class Dutch girls are," he exclaimed. "Wish they would come over to us instead of Irish."[104] And after the many sordid spots he had visited elsewhere in Europe, it was a joy to see one of the great dairies in Haarlem, where everything was scoured clean and shining. As for the countryside, with its noble woods and idyllic atmosphere: "No wonder William III pined for Holland—the country is so green and lovely and quiet and pastoral and homelike. Boats sailing through the prairies and fat cows and quaint windmills everywhere."[105]

In June, 1878, Mark Twain began to jot down notes about the English people while he was still living in Heidelberg, more than a year before his family crossed the Channel. Perhaps he had been observing Englishmen at the hotel or English students at the university. At any rate, he made a memo that the best English characteristic was a plucky standing up for one's rights. No other people, he thought, agreeing with Emerson, approached the British in this manly trait. "It makes every man in the whole nation a policeman—" he said, "the administration of law can never go lax where every individual sees to it that it grows not lax in his own case, or in cases which fall under his eyes."[106]

At about this time Mark Twain heard a curious report concerning events on famed Pitcairn Island in the South Pacific. He dramatized the report for his travel book but ended by submitting the piece to the *Atlantic Monthly,* where it appeared in March, 1879. "The Great Revolution in Pitcairn" described a colony of English castaways who are leading a peaceful, carefree existence when an American reformer suddenly appears on the scene. This American manages to have himself declared king, whereon he turns the island into a tiny, pretentious empire with all the elegancies and extravagances of a great monarchy. Everyone is soon either at court or in the military service; no one is left to till the soil or manufacture necessities. After a while the people become disillusioned, revolt, and once more hoist the British flag. The nobles are reduced to commoners, the military is dispersed, the useful industries are revived, and Pitcairn reverts to its former happiness.

Mark Twain's anti-American sentiment kept cropping up as he roamed the European continent in the summer of 1878. His Bermuda visit of 1877, with its admiration for British ways, was still strong in his memory. As the months went by, however, he grew more and more critical of the British, perhaps from reading the London newspapers which found their way into his hands. He began to look askance at the pious conceit of the British. They should cease to patronize the Zulus and other blacks, he said, since they themselves had been equally benighted only a century ago.

"They are a very fine and pure and elevated people, now," he asserted, "but what they were between the Roman Invasion and the time within the memory of a centenarian was but a small improvement upon the Shoshone Indians."[107]

It may have been about this time that he decided to give his romantic old tale of the prince and the pauper a carping and critical tone. At any rate, during that winter of 1878–79 Mark Twain seems to have lost his veneration for England and to have begun to view it dispassionately. The family was in England from July 20 to August 23, 1879, but Mark Twain's record of these weeks is remarkably scant and objective. London provided the usual round of social affairs, even though it was not the season. Because he was trying to put together his new travel book about the Continent, however, the family did not travel very much; they did not even get up to Edinburgh to visit their old friends.

They did, however, accept an invitation of long standing to spend a week with Reginald Cholmondeley at Condover, and Moncure Conway recalls accompanying them on a visit to Stratford-on-Avon. Mark Twain even made a special trip to Lake Windemere to talk with Charles Darwin. Unfortunately, even on such promising material as this Mark Twain seems to have taken few notes, or else they have been lost. The inference is that he had now abandoned any notion of putting England into a travel book—ever. From habit he did take a few passing notes, but they are trivial stuff—comfortable railroads, trusting shopkeepers, hateful hotel rooms, boring picture galleries and theater (he could not understand the actors), and a most depressing church service where the congregation was wooden-faced and the music was "always the perfection of the ugly."[108] Nothing here to make a book or even a chapter.

Had Mark Twain written about England following that visit, the book probably would have been a great deal less enthusiastic than one he might have written after his three visits of 1872–74. His love for the English, which peaked in 1877, plummeted fast during the next two years. A reason is suggested in an observation made at the end of his 1879 notebook:

> All English individuals are kind and likable—the newspapers are snobbish, pretentious, and they scoff at America, or contemptuously ignore her. English preachers and statesmen try to draw the two nations together in friendship and mutual respect —the newspapers, with what seems a steady and calculated purpose, discourage this. The newspapers are going to win in this fight. The nations are at their friendliest now—the widening apart has begun—the separation will be complete in a generation. (1879) [M. T.'s date]
>
> For some years a custom has been growing up in our literature to praise everything English and do it affectionately. This is not met halfway, and so it will cease. English individuals like and respect American individuals, but the English nation despises America and Americans. But this does not sting us as it did when we were smaller. We shall presently be indifferent to be looked down upon by a nation no bigger and no better than our own.[109]

This is an interesting echo of Washington Irving's complaint sixty years earlier, even to the final sentence about America's growing indifference to British opinion. The gentle Irving had urged his countrymen to refrain from retaliation. Mark Twain, though, was not a man to make the soft answer. During the next decade, as we shall see, he retaliated in a pair of novels which still make the English shudder.

The above criticism of England was something which Mark Twain kept to himself at this time. There was no need to antagonize a large segment of his reading public just before issuing his new travel book. When he was asked if he was planning a book on England, he had his answers ready, and none of them hinted at his new acrimony. For one thing, he said, his conscience told him that England's shortcomings were also America's, by and large. For another thing, the *real* interest lay in domestic manners and customs, and it would be rude to abuse the confidence of his

English hosts. "Private matters are private matters," he said, "and it is not right to meddle with them."[110]

Lastly, England was too grave a country, he believed: "not a good text for hilarious literature." "I could have written a million books about England," he added, "but my publishers would have hired the common hangman to burn them. . . . No, I have looked the ground all over; there is nothing funny in England."[111]

There is an irony here. Mark Twain was implying that humor and satire were the only stocks-in-trade of his travel books, whereas, in point of fact, many of the best chapters of *A Tramp Abroad* are serious in tone. Too often the humor degenerates into monotonous horseplay that has nothing whatever to do with Europe. Much of it seems forced, as if the author were desperately trying to substitute for the gorgeous sequence of sights and adventures from which he had fashioned *The Innocents Abroad*.[112]

While he was working on his second travel book, Mark Twain complained to Howells that the book would contain "profitable reading" only "in spots": "there's not much material for a larger amount."[113] There was actually plenty of additional material, as we have seen, but he chose not to draw on it. He used the first months of his trip only, being anxious, no doubt, to have the book largely written by the time he got home. But the book just did not write itself as easily as he expected, and he had no newspaper letters to work from this time.

The novelty of the Old World, furthermore, had now vanished for Mark Twain, and with it was gone the excitement of foreign travel. It took a conscious effort now to assume his old comic pose as Simpleton, Sentimentalist, or Tenderfoot. Never again would Europe or the Near East appear so baffling and exotic to him as it had appeared in 1867. Since that time he had traveled widely, read a great deal, and become head of a respectable New England household.

In short, Mark Twain was a different person in 1879—not at heart, but in mind and prospects. Never again could he barnstorm in Europe as a sort of wild young American Adam from the Pacific slopes. From its inception *A Tramp Abroad* had no chance of approximating the bubbling spontaneity of its predecessor. Gone from Mark Twain's nature was the untutored Americanism, half-amused but bristling, of 1867. Twelve years of associating almost exclusively with people of culture in the East and abroad had cost him much of the charming innocence which had animated his first travel book. The chasm between Mark Twain and the Old World was contracting. On this latest excursion, for example, he even brought home foreign furnishings and bric-a-brac worth well over five thousand dollars.

III

Nationalist

T HE chasm between Mark Twain and the Old World might have continued to narrow had he done any traveling in the course of the next decade. However, those sixteen months of, as he put it, gadding around Europe with three women and two small girls gave him his fill of travel for years to come. He stayed at home during the eighties. Gradually, his love for republican institutions returned to him and, for a while, completely arrested any tendency to Europeanization. When next he went abroad, in 1891, it was because of necessity, both economic and social, not because the Old World held any remembered charms for him.

On his return from Europe in 1879, Mark Twain took up work again on *The Prince and the Pauper,* which he had pigeonholed just before he went abroad. This was to be a children's book, and he found the writing of it a relief from the task of padding out *A Tramp Abroad.* And the following summer he was again more interested in the adventures of his wandering prince than he was in those of his new picaresque hero, Huckleberry Finn, whose story he had also recommenced telling by this time.

The adventures of neither boy were described for their humor or thrills alone. The author's purpose frequently lay deeper. In the case of the prince, the adventures were sometimes a medium through which Mark Twain repaid England for her insults to

America. We know how these insults had lately begun to rankle in him. It was no trouble for him to digress now and then from his romantic plot, a plot which was derivative anyway, in order to introduce some rather mature and realistic criticism of supposedly Merrie Olde England.

The subject matter was close at hand. The Blue Laws of seventeenth-century Connecticut were just now being vilified in *Blackwood's Edinburgh Magazine*, so Mark Twain decided to show that the British were living in a glass house and should be careful about throwing stones. He would show that these Blue Laws were actually humane when compared with the barbarity of the British penal code of still more recent times. Certain Englishmen themselves were outspoken in their shame for British "justice." At a diplomatic dinner in London in 1880 John Bright, then a member of the Cabinet, strongly denounced the Bench:

> For two hundred years, the Judges of England sat on the Bench, condemning to the penalty of death every man, woman, and child who stole property to the value of five shillings; and, during all that time, not one Judge ever remonstrated against the law. We English are a nation of brutes, and ought to be exterminated to the last man.[1]

That the English were, or had been, a nation of brutes was an underlying theme of *The Prince and the Pauper* (1881). As for the old laws of Connecticut, they were greatly maligned, said Mark Twain. In reality, they were "about the first *sweeping departure from judicial atrocity* which the 'civilized' world had seen." He called them "humane and kindly."

> There never has been a time—under the Blue-Laws or any other —when above *fourteen* crimes were punishable by death in Connecticut. But in England, within the memory of men who are still hale in body and mind, *two hundred and twenty-three* crimes were punishable by death! These facts are worth knowing —and worth thinking about, too.[2]

Among the Mark Twain Papers are dozens of pages of notes made in preparation for this novel. There are lists of medieval terms, idioms, and expressions. There are references to books, such as Scott's, from which he could draw details about tournaments, banquets, court etiquette, coronations. Some of the notes describe atrocities which might be used in his story. Many suggest narrative episodes, and still others contain historical statistics: "60,000 in prison for debt & crime at one time. 72,000 executed in Henry's reign, for *theft & robbery*."[3]

History had long been Mark Twain's favorite reading, and he now saturated himself in the data and details of early England. He was determined to be accurate. He bought an old map of London and studied it minutely. Although he may never have achieved what Francis Hackett calls the *then*-mindedness of the antiquarian or the professional historian, at least Mark Twain knew his facts well enough to make very few mistakes unintentionally. It was not by accident that his picture of Europe in his foreign novels is a rather simple, elemental black-and-white. Stephen Leacock underestimated the sophistication of Mark Twain when he charged that he saw every king as a tyrant, every knight as a bigot, and old-time justice as mainly torture.[4]

As a matter of fact, in this first foreign novel Mark Twain was not particularly concerned with either kings or priests. Old-time justice was his target. The only king, Henry VIII, is relegated to the minor role of a sick old man and devoted father. And the royal court is painted with a merciful brush. Moreover, only two priests appear in the book, both in small roles. One priest is insane, the other is courageous and warmhearted. In this book, Mark Twain was no more interested in challenging the authority of Church or Crown than was little Tom Canty, the pauper in the story. In certain ways Tom Canty was a sort of "Missouri democrat," as De Voto calls him, but it is significant that, when he had the opportunity, he made no effort to reform the royal court along democratic lines. He happily forgot the royal debt, in fact, and he tripled the number of servants.

Mark Twain's leniency with the cherished British institutions of monarchy and the established church enabled *The Prince and the Pauper* to make a brisk sale in England and to elicit reviews which were quite complimentary. Only the *Saturday Review* and the *Athenaeum* cried down the book. Neither of these journals, said Mark Twain, would compliment the Holy Scriptures if an American had written them.

Reviewers in America were almost unanimous in lauding the novel as the first book in which Mark Twain had displayed notable talents as a serious writer and as a true literary artist. Few objected to the discord created by the injecting of sharp satire into a tale for children. Most critics acclaimed particularly those aspects of the novel which differed most widely from Mark Twain's earlier work and which conformed most carefully to the standards of the genteel tradition.[5]

To illustrate the barbarity of the old penal code of Great Britain, Mark Twain selected the close of the reign of Henry VIII. The plan was to oblige Henry's son, Edward, to live for a while among the starving and oppressed people of the realm and thereby to understand the causes of their suffering and crime. This schooling would account for certain mildnesses which distinguished the short reign of Edward VI. To work this plan, Mark Twain hurled the young prince among the burly rogues and vagabonds who were ravaging the countryside. They thought he was just a crazy boy. Even though these outlaws suffered cruelly because of the king's law, they harbored no ill will toward the king himself. They had, instead, a genuine affection for him. Cried their leader:

> ". . . we be bad men, in some few trifling ways, but none among us is so base as to be traitor to his king; we be loving and loyal hearts in that regard. Note if I speak the truth. Now—all together: 'Long live Edward, king of England!' "[6]

The hearty thundergust of cheering warmed the heart of the prince whose father had just died. What a thrill and comfort it was to witness the loyalty of these homeless vagrants! Inherently a kind and fair-minded boy, he had resolved long ago, on his very first day in rags, that he would do something for them as soon as he came into power:

> "When I am king, they shall not have bread and shelter only, but also teachings out of books; for a full belly is little worth where the mind is starved, and the heart. I will keep this diligently in my remembrance, that this day's lesson be not lost upon me, and my people suffer thereby; for learning softeneth the heart and breedeth gentleness and charity."[7]

As the weeks went on, Edward saw living proof of the fact that it was a crime to be hungry in England. The branded and mutilated body of a man named Yokel was a constant reminder. Yokel had had one ear cropped off by the law and bore a slave's "S" burned on his cheek. Now, if caught, he would hang. Yokel's one consolation was that already his wife and children had died of starvation and his mother been burned as a witch. They might be in heaven or in hell, he cried, " 'but the kindly God be thanked, they bide no more in England.' "[8]

The penalty of death was prescribed for crimes ranging in character from witchcraft to larceny above the value of twelve pence. Legal punishments specifically condemned in the novel were boiling to death, roasting to death at a slow fire, hanging, mutilation, and torture on the rack. " 'Would God I had been blind!' " the prince cried after watching two harmless women burned to death for being Baptists. And on witnessing a gruesome example of political vengeance, he exclaimed, " 'The world is made wrong; kings should go to school to their own laws at times, and so learn mercy.' "[9]

Tom Canty, the pauper, meanwhile, was living the soft life of prince, then uncrowned king. Both humor and amiable satire were employed in describing his embarrassing experiences at court. Many of Edward's adventures, too, were comic, because this book was essentially a romance for children. To portray sixteenth-century England as a truly horrifying place to live seems to have been an afterthought, a way to answer England's insolent criticisms of the United States. Both British monarchists and American democrats, however, could be gratified by the way Tom Canty and King Edward eventually worked together to humanize the judicial system of old England.

In a way, of course, the censure in *The Prince and the Pauper* was merely the whipping of a dead horse. The barbarous old laws had been modified long before. Had Mark Twain attacked a currently popular institution such as hereditary monarchy or aristocracy, that would have been another matter and he would not have got off so easily in Great Britain. As yet, however, he was at peace with the entire caste system. In fact, there was much of Tom Canty's romanticism in his own soul—a romanticism which bred deference and even awe in the presence of the nobility. Several times within the next few years, for example, he went into Canada—Ottawa, Montreal, and Toronto—to secure British copyrights for his books. On one occasion he was handsomely entertained by the Marquis of Lorne and his wife, a daughter of Queen Victoria. Unsure of protocol, he was afraid to send even a small remembrance to them directly, so he mailed it instead in care of Colonel De Winton, "you who know all about the proper observances will protect me from indiscretion . . ."[10]

The Prince and the Pauper, nevertheless, was Mark Twain's first tentative step away from the unqualified praise of England which had marked his writings of the 1870's. Perhaps it was his research for this novel which spurred him to hours and hours of labor in designing and patenting an educational game based on the history of England. This was a major project from 1883 to 1885. For a time his notebook was filled almost entirely with this subject. He began with England but planned to branch out later. He called it "4000 Historical Facts & Memory-Improver," worked out rules and a scoring system, drew sample illustrations of his own, managed to adapt the game to several joined cribbage boards, and, on August 18, 1885, secured a patent.[11]

In his zeal Mark Twain had visions of this game's sweeping the world and bringing in millions of dollars. Chess, whist, and other useless games would be forgotten. Had not his own daughters enjoyed playing—and learned a great deal, too—a simplified version of the history game with stakes driven along the driveway and up the hillside? The patented game, unfortunately, was extremely complex. It was so large and intricate that almost no one could play it. For several years, however, perfecting it gave Mark Twain a great deal of pleasure and kept active his interest in European history.

A new interest also began to attract Mark Twain about this same time. He delved into books written about the United States by English tourists. It might be expected that he took exception to their unflattering remarks about America, but not so. In *Life on the Mississippi* (1883) he quoted from the early accounts of Mrs. Trollope and Captain Marryat. To our tender-skinned citizens, he said, these accounts had seemed prejudiced and condescending, but in reality they were generally "calm, truthful, reasonable, kind."[12] He also defended certain disparaging judgments by Charles Dickens.

So interested did Mark Twain become in this subject that he wrote an entire "Tourist Chapter" for his river book. At the written request of his publisher, however, he consented to leave it out. This chapter is a staunch defense of Mrs. Trollope's 1827 volume on the customs and manners of the United States. Although she was cursed and reviled over here, said Mark Twain, her alleged prejudices were simply the reactions of a humane spirit against inhumanities and of an honest nature against humbug. Above all, he insisted, Mrs. Trollope told the truth and Americans knew it:

> Indeed, all those tourists aimed at the truth; did their honest best to tell it . . . And with hardly an exception they told their harsh truths in the kindliest language, and still with reluctance; and siezed [sic] eagerly upon every pleasant truth that offered, and made as much as they possibly could out of it.[13]

In this deleted chapter Mark Twain also denounced those timid British tourists who tried to temper their criticism of America by means of false flattery or else by criticizing England as well. These creatures, he said, give you a slap, then turn and kick a member of their own family, stupidly imagining that the kick heals the slap. They succeed only in offending both parties. One hopes that Mark Twain was judging unfairly the intentions of such tourists, because this very practice was one which he himself, perhaps unconsciously, followed quite often.

The inclusion of this chapter in *Life on the Mississippi* would have offset Mark Twain's well-known strictures on the romanticism of Sir Walter Scott. The South, he thought, had not yet recovered from the "debilitating influence" of Scott's novels. These novels, with their false sentimentalism, upset man's moral judgments, he said, and made him unfit to play a part in real life. The influence of medieval England, he maintained, was evident everywhere in the South, even in the basic structure of society itself. Scott's enchantments had turned back the wave of progress by setting the Southern world in love with sham European grandeurs and with degraded forms of both religion and government. Scott had created such a love for rank and caste and had shaped Southern character so banefully that, but for him, there might have been no Civil War. "He did measureless harm," said Mark Twain, "more real and lasting harm, perhaps, than any other individual that ever wrote."[14]

In railing against Scott, and later against Fenimore Cooper, Mark Twain may have been hoping to deromanticize himself, as it were. Sometimes, as a foreign critic points out, "the grown-up man is inclined to let the heroes of his youth pay for the absorbing idolatry they evoked from the child."[15] Scott, moreover, may have glorified the decayed forms of Old Europe, but so did Mark Twain idealize the bygone days of the great river. Blissfully he overlooked its pimps and harlots, its murders, robberies, and gambling, its skin-games and thriving sucker-trade. Never did he succeed in completely deromanticizing himself—fortunately.

During 1884 Mark Twain wrote in his notebook, "Anything from foreign travel pleases best."[16] Histories, diaries, confessions, and autobiographies headed his reading list, but he was also interested in special books about Greece and India at this time. Being an impatient man, however, he would toss aside books that bored or angered him. "When this fellow isn't praying he is always lying," he scribbled in the margin of a travel book he began to read in 1884. "Oh give us a rest," says another note. And, "Whose gush is this."[17] It appears that the first twenty and the last ten are the only pages he was able to read. Not everything from foreign travel pleased him best.

Why did Mark Twain not go abroad during this decade, if travel books still interested him so much? His recent tour may still have galled his memory. Besides, he had three daughters now, two of whom were well along in school and best not disturbed until summer vacation, the very months when he got most of his writing done at the Elmira farm. During the rest of the year he was extraordinarily busy with his newly established publishing house, his writing, his numerous investments, and his demanding social and platform commitments. The family did plan to go over in the summer of 1884 but changed plans on the excuse that too many of his investments had turned out badly. Mark Twain explained to friends abroad that he felt obliged to "settle down to work & restore things to the old condition; & one can work better at home than in Europe."[18] As to just where he could work best, Mark Twain seems to have been uncertain.

In addition to *The Prince and the Pauper, Life on the Mississippi,* and *Huckleberry Finn,* he planned a book on Hawaii at this time. Chapter I opens with a description of the Islands as the "peacefulest, sunniest, balmiest, dreamiest haven of refuge for a worn & weary spirit the surface of the earth can offer."[19] The three fragments total seventeen pages. The second fragment is dramatic and sentimental, while the third is a farce about the King's purloined spittoon. The idea of setting a novel in a romantic spot which he loved so well was a good idea, but he seems to have dropped it after one short sitting.

Mark Twain's notebooks during the 1880's prove his continued interest in the foreign scene. For some reason, Paine omitted nearly all of these foreign allusions from the published volume. Apropos of nothing, in 1885 a note appears about having seen Russian ladies strip themselves naked and walk down the beach into the Black Sea to swim. In the same year Mark Twain deplored the beating of twenty Chinese by a mob of white brutes in San Francisco. His affection was still warm for the industrious, peace-loving Orientals. In 1883 and 1884 he went out of his way to help General Grant to befriend both them and their government.[20]

These were the days in America of "No Irish Need Apply," and Mark Twain was not immune to the prejudice. He considered the Irish to be roughnecks, not quite civilized. Their Catholicism made them even less lovable to him. He had no patience with their independence movement:

> The Irish rage yet over what they call the tyrannical siezure [sic] of their country 700 years ago by Henry II—forgetting that Ireland was *given* to that King in 1156 by their beloved god the Pope—& that Henry went over in 1171 & claimed & took his own with but little opposition from the pope's Irish slaves.[21]

One day Mark Twain tried to find an adjective or two to classify the different nations of the world. The men of Ireland stumped him—or was he being coy? Paine did not reproduce Mark Twain's cancellations, and he skipped the sentences about the Parisians and Roman Catholics:

The English. The arrogant nation. The ~~French~~ Parisians, the
adulterous nation. The Americans, the material nation. The Germans the patient nation. The several Roman Catholic countries,
the ignorant nations. The French, the ~~thrifty~~ volatile nation. The
Scotch the thrifty nation. The Italians, the hot-blooded, kindhearted nation. The Irish, the nation of chaste women . . .[22]

Incidentally, among the Mark Twain Papers there is preserved
an engraved document announcing that on August 24, 1886,
Mark Twain was elected Corresponding Member for Life of the
Scottish Society of Literature and Art. Mark Twain, who still
had a soft spot in his heart for the Scots, had this mark of honor
mounted and framed in New York City. It was among his possessions when he died a quarter-century later.

During this decade Mark Twain's interest in the German language continued to show itself both in his notebooks and in his
private correspondence. Dozens of times he lapsed into German
in his notes. He copied lines of German poetry and made lists of
German words and expressions. Eight entire pages he wrote in
German, tossing in an occasional word in English when his vocabulary spluttered. The subject matter made no difference—
Grant's autobiography, the Paige typesetter, stray ideas, individuals, anything at all. Never in French or Italian, only in German.

When he was away from home, he also liked to break into
affectionate German in his letters to Livy. From St. Louis on
January 11, 1885, he even sent her a six-page English translation
he had just made of Chapter Six of the German prose version of
The Pied Piper of Hamelin. It was hard work, he said, but he
meant to translate the rest of the story later. (He never did.) On
December 14, 1884, he wrote a two-page letter to Susy entirely
in German and another to little Jean, age four. To amuse his
daughters he also translated nursery rhymes into German verse
and made up his own light verse with abundant seasonings of the
German tongue. Again, it was always German.

Unfortunately, the eighties showed no indication that Mark

Mark Twain's notebook entry, August 15, 1885.

Twain was losing his contempt for the French people. In 1881
he became morbidly fascinated by *The Memoirs of the Duke of
Saint-Simon on the Reign of Louis XIV and the Regency*. The
three thick volumes reinforced his low opinion of the French.
Over the years he read and reread Saint-Simon, making snappish
comments in the margins:[23]

> The Court is a family of cats & dogs, who are always quarreling
> over scraps of offal.[24] Persistence in making French people is
> but little creditable to God.[25] From the year AD 300 to the year
> 1800 may be described as the age of pious W—S.[26] . . . these
> low scoundrels, these shams, these play-acting, sentimental
> pukes! How French it all is![27]

This aversion carried over into Mark Twain's notebooks, less
frequently now than in the 1870's, but still with the smell of
sulfur. "An isolated & helpless young girl is perfectly safe from
insult by a Frenchman," wrote Mark Twain, "if he is dead. A
dead Frenchman has many good qualities."[28] On the very next
page, however, he admitted that some Frenchwomen were perfectly decent, an admission which is startling in its uniqueness.
Before long he was back on the offensive: "Write a 'French' novel
—37 cases of adultery, & they all live happy to the end."[29] And
finally, "Who could endure a French Christ?"[30]

It is likely that Mark Twain did not really despise modern
France as much as it sounds or even as much as he convinced himself that he did. To seek a tangible villain and to flay him or it
without mercy was ever his way. At times he seems to have been
doing little more than exercising his imagination and his flair for
invective. These outbursts gave him both pleasure and relief. They
helped to keep his vocabulary flexible, his sense of outrage astir.
Even Mark Twain himself may not have been consciously aware
of these psychological needs. Surely, his wife was not. "How I
wish that you were less ready to fight," she exclaimed, "and more
ready to see other peoples [sic] side of things."[31]

During the latter part of the eighties a new animus preoccupied Mark Twain, causing him almost to forget the French. In
1879, as we have seen, he had begun to lose his admiration for the
British; nearly ten years later, long separated from their shores,
he began to express his disenchantment with the entire undemocratic Establishment of Great Britain. Charitably, he had stood
up for those old English travelers who had criticized America's
semibarbarous Frontier, but he was not a man to permit the English of his own day to deride both the modern culture which he
loved and some of his close friends. It was time to loose his sense
of outrage upon the British.

Charles Dudley Warner, his good friend and next-door neighbor, was under attack in British journals for his recent observations about England. The abuse so angered Mark Twain that he
began to draft a hot reply. He attacked the Anglican Church,
hereditary class privilege, and the British crown itself. The United
States, he said, had not had three presidents to be ashamed of,
whereas most of England's rulers were merely "animated rubbish," not even fit (a major insult!) to sit in the United States
Congress. As for the British actress Lily Langtry, the only reason
she was drawing crowds in the United States, he said, was because Americans were so surprised to discover *one* Englishwoman
of beauty. He did not publish this sixteen-page manuscript.[32]

In 1886 Mark Twain published a short but cogent article which
broadened the assault he had made upon Sir Walter Scott. This
time he was advocating international copyright. It would help to
keep out of America such noxious matter as the "semiannual
inundation from Zola's sewer." In language reminiscent of
Whitman's *Democratic Vistas* he castigated foreign novels:

> They fill the imagination with an unhealthy fascination for
> foreign life, with its dukes and earls and kings, its fuss and
> feathers, its graceful immoralities, its sugar-coated injustices and
> oppressions; and this fascination breeds a more or less pro-
> nounced dissatisfaction with our country and form of govern-

ment, and contempt for our republican commonplaces and sim-
plicities; it also breeds longings for something "better," which
presently crop out in diseased shams and imitations of that ideal
foreign life.[33]

Then there was Matthew Arnold, the apostle of culture, who
was drawn across the Atlantic in 1883 and again in 1886 by the
lure of the dollar on the lecture circuit. To Arnold the New
World signified a failure in whatever things were elevated or
beautiful. He was certain he knew what America was, says Lionel
Trilling. It was "raw and conceited and vulgar and grasping and
commercial and Philistine and prostrate before bunkum."

Although Arnold seems to have comported himself with poise
and even friendliness, the newspapers made him out to be a
difficult, arrogant guest. Americans began to boil and seethe, and
by then Mark Twain's boiling point was as low as anyone's.
America, he urged, should retaliate by criticizing England according to New World standards. He told Howells that Napoleon
would have conferred an incalculable blessing on the entire world
if he had invaded England and destroyed the feudal aristocracy.
Mark Twain was particularly distressed by the crushing defeat
of the British Liberal party by the Conservatives in 1886.

So Mark Twain begain to fill quires of paper with caustic, but
unpublished, replies to Arnold. Many of the replies were personal, until Arnold died in April, 1888. At that time Mark Twain
noted simply, "Matthew Arnold's civilization is *superficial
polish.*"[34] Thereafter, he transferred his wrath to England in
general and to her most revered institutions. The nobility and
hereditary government were his primary targets. From the summer of 1888 until the summer of 1891, when he went abroad
again, Mark Twain wrote about England in his notebooks with
what he called a "pen warmed-up in hell." Here are samples
from the summer of 1888 alone:

How superbly brave is the Englishman in the presence of the

awfulest forms of danger and death; and how abject in the presence of any and all forms of hereditary rank.

The kingly office is entitled to no respect. It was originally procured by the highwayman's methods; it remains a perpetuated crime, can never be anything but the symbol of crime. It is no more to be respected than the flag of a pirate. . . . if you cross a king with a prostitute the resulting mongrel perfectly satisfies the English idea of nobility. The ducal houses of Great Britain are mainly derived from this gaudy combination.

The system has for its end the degradation of the many to exalt the few, the misery of the many for the happiness of the few, the cold and hunger and overworking of the useful that the useless may live in luxury and idleness.

In a constitutional—figurehead—monarchy, a royal family of chimpanzees would answer every purpose, be worshiped as abjectly by the nation, and be cheaper.

The man who believes there is a man in the world who is better than himself merely because he was born royal or noble, is a dog with the soul of a dog—and at bottom is a liar.[35]

Although Mark Twain continued these charges for the next three years, the charges began to diminish both in frequency and intensity. He admitted that Americans worshiped the Dollar, but maintained that this was a worthier god than Hereditary Privilege. The dollar represented a contribution to the world's wealth, not a robbery from it. He also accused England of pensioning "the rich whore with millions, the poor private with a shilling a month, she was always shabby and a humbug." And his patriotic fervor made him denounce "These wretched American women who buy titles (and noble tramps) with their money—mongrel breeders; should have a bench show of their children."[36]

Mark Twain's Anglophobia diminished between 1889 and 1891, partly because business troubles were starting to preoccupy him, but mainly because he had discovered a most satisfactory outlet for his wrath. In 1884 he had been introduced to the Arthurian legends of Sir Thomas Malory. He was enthralled by Malory's characters, as well as by the quaint old culture of Camelot. What fun it would be, he thought, to drop a nineteenth-century American into King Arthur's Court and to see what would happen!

Two years went by before he did anything about it. Then, just for fun, he began to write *A Connecticut Yankee in King Arthur's Court*. He had no intention, he told Mrs. Fairbanks, of belittling the "great & beautiful *characters* drawn by the master hand of old Malory." Nor was satire his purpose. He simply wished to contrast life in the sixth century with that of his own day. The book would not even be published, he assured her. He intended to write three chapters each summer for thirty years simply as holiday amusement.[37]

Mark Twain's intentions, however, underwent a drastic change the moment it occurred to him that this very book might be the perfect weapon with which to strike back at England. From that moment the "beautiful characters" of Malory commenced to take on the garish hues of satire. Nor did Mark Twain write only three chapters each summer. Under the spur of Matthew Arnold's indictments, he completed the long novel for publication in 1889, drawing upon his notebooks for occasional inspiration. One modern critic conjectures that if it had not been for Matthew Arnold, "the Boss never would have entered the lists."[38] This may be a simplification, but enter the lists the Boss did, and with him went most of Mark Twain's thirst for revenge on England. Now the whole thing was out in the open for the world to see. There was something more courageous and cathartic about this than about all his little tablets crammed with secret fulminations.

Before we turn to *A Connecticut Yankee,* however, it will complete the picture to look briefly at these private papers, which still have never been published. Several notebook entries which Paine politely overlooked might be added to the half-dozen quoted above. "Yours is the civilization of slave-making ants," he told the British. "What a curious admixture of cur & lion is

the English character."[39] Soon thereafter he spoke contemptu-
ously of that worm-eaten social structure which Matthew Arnold
regarded as civilization. People bred in the shadow of royalty and
nobility, he said, could not see the humor of it all. One had to
get a perspective. "It's as funny as seeing quacks & prostitutes
gravely doing the rôles in a miracle-play."[40]

Then comes a note which Mark Twain himself canceled and
changed to one we have seen above: "Better the Almighty Dollar
than a tub of rancid guts."[41] It was Paine, however, who killed the
sweeping admonition that "Assassination of a crowned head
whenever & wherever opportunity offers, should be the first
article of all subjects' religion."[42] By 1891, as we have seen, Mark
Twain's republican ire was largely spent. Now he could only
mutter that the chief occupations of the nobility were adultery
and cheating at baccarat.

Among the sorties which helped to spend this ire were a paper
underlining the arrogant and boorish manners of English visitors
to the United States[43] and a paper scoring the behavior he observed in a fashionable English country house. He made fun of
the ladies who argued bitterly over who had precedence at the
dinner table. Their behavior, he said, was inferior to that of a
Pawnee squaw.[44]

Mark Twain also began to write an article blaming England
for the modern revival of the slave trade. The first regular English
slaver, John Hawkins, he charged, not only was knighted by
Elizabeth for his success in capturing and selling Africans, but
even selected a slave in chains for his knightly device.[45] In another paper, Mark Twain began to develop the idea that the word
"subject," as distinct from "citizen," was merely another name
for "slave."[46] At somewhat greater length, he sought to demonstrate that kings and nobles were nothing but "non-producing
idlers, cumberers of the soil," whose culture was like that of the
slave-making ant. "This isn't all there is of English and Euro-

pean civilization, of course," he added, "but it's perhaps as much as you can stand. . . . Now as to French civilization—but there are ladies present."[47]

Mark Twain also addressed a special reply to a "visiting critic." For ten pages he explicitly applied to England the standards of the New World. Judged by these standards, he concluded, the English people of all classes were coarse in nature, indifferent to the rights of others, brutal in their speech, and pitiful in craving the notice of royalty.[48]

Outstanding among these private papers is "The American Press." Mark Twain addressed this to Arnold's criticism of the "irreverence" of the newspapers in the United States. The newspapers of monarchical Europe, said Mark Twain, were obliged to maintain a "graveyard gravity of countenance: to laugh would expose the whole humbug." The devil's aversion to holy water, he said, was a light matter compared with the despot's dread of a newspaper that laughs. As far as the American press was concerned:

> Its frank & cheerful irreverence is by all odds the most valuable quality it possesses. For its mission—overlooked by Mr. Arnold —is to stand guard over a nation's liberties, not its humbugs & shams. And so it must be armed with ridicule, not reverence. . . . to my mind a discriminating irreverence is the creator & protector of human liberty—even as that other thing is the creator, nurse, & steadfast protector of all forms of human slavery, bodily & mental.[49]

It pleased Mark Twain at this time to think that monarchy as a form of government was on its way out in the world. His 1889 speech "On Foreign Critics" said that monarchy had already been on trial for thousands of years in Europe when the United States "invented" human liberty in its Constitution. In every case monarchy had been a convicted failure. It had never produced anything but a vast, a nearly universal, savagery, with a thin skin of civilization on top, and the main part of that was nickel plate and tinsel.[50]

Mark Twain was temperate enough to admit, in another paper, that the British monarchy was making steadier progress toward liberty than were the other monarchies of Europe. This progress, he believed, would continue. Always this progress would be at the expense of kings, priests, and nobles. Always it would be to the advantage of commoners, because "in my scheme of a best & worthiest civilization there isn't anybody *but* commoners. Therefore, when you move the commoner onward, you move the whole nation."[51]

Russia, unlike England, was making no progress. Alexander III struck him as quite a different character from his father, the polite gentleman who had entertained the Innocents in 1867. "The cannibal who infests the Russian throne," said Mark Twain, must laugh in scorn at his miserable and abject slaves. Who could choose between the "twin civilizations of hell & Russia"? Thus Mark Twain began to warm up for his elaborate "Czar's Soliloquy" of 1905.

It will be noted that Mark Twain's nationalistic fervor was causing him to contradict many of his anti-democratic pronouncements of the late 1870's. In those days, enamored of the British, he had frankly admired their aristocracy and envied their government by the enlightened minority. He had decried the ignorance of the masses and therefore distrusted the republican form of government. No longer. Now he proclaimed, "The few here are always wrong—the body of the people is usually right."[52]

In his newfound enthusiasm Mark Twain attacked the aristocracy of money and social class which was being created in the United States. He saw in it the danger of a titled caste, an hereditary nobility. In particular he hated to see the reverence which ordinary citizens were beginning to show for these rich upstarts.[53] As criticism and warning he wished to get out a cheap paperback

edition of the anti-aristocratic compilations of George C. Standring, a freethinking English printer.

Offsetting the aristocratic trend was the rise of the labor
movement in America. Mark Twain viewed with boundless enthusiasm the growing political power of the productive masses.
His long article on "The New Dynasty" extolled these masses
as one king we need not fear. They were, he claimed, the "right-
ful sovereign of this world . . . our permanent shield & defense
against the Socialist, the Communist, the Anarchist . . . and
against all like forms of political disease, pollution, & death."[54]

These frequent and abortive attempts by Mark Twain to say
what he wanted to say on many subjects close to his heart must
have been very unsatisfying. Of all these unpublished manuscripts
we have been surveying, only a few run to more than ten pages.
Most of them were inspired by strong emotion, but by little else.
What he needed was a new vantage point, a new perspective,
from which he could view mankind, and especially England, in
the light of his new theories. In years to come he would experiment with viewpoints as divergent as those of an angel, a devil,
and a microbe, but now he tried writing "Letters from a Dog to
Another Dog, Explaining & Accounting for Man." After listing
faults such as cruelty, malice, envy, ambition, immodesty, and
servility, which exist only in man, the dog explains that man has
long been recognized by the other animals as the "base original"
from which they have all ascended.[55]

We can see the germ of *The Mysterious Stranger* in this, but
Mark Twain was not getting much further with these dog letters
in unburdening himself of his new political and social theories.
Furthermore, as he must have known, he was being rather dull.
He could never peddle this stuff, except on his reputation alone,
and no one would have much pleasure reading it. His whole approach had been wrong; fiction was the proper approach.

To his surprise, perhaps, he discovered that fiction was already
to be found in his yarn about the Yankee in Camelot. He had

designed it in 1886 as a humorous diversion; he would retain the humor but lace it liberally with the serious thoughts and passions which burned within him. Experience had taught him, as Walter Blair has pointed out, that the best way to make an idea tasty to most Americans was to serve it up with a sauce of native-grown humor and horse sense.[56]

In writing *A Connecticut Yankee,* Mark Twain had more in mind than striking back at the British. Revenge was a strong motive for a while, but fortunately it was ennobled by a belief that he was laboring as a sort of modern-day Cervantes. He was convinced that *Don Quixote* had swept the world's admiration for "medieval chivalry-silliness" out of existence, and that novels such as *Ivanhoe* had restored it. Therefore, he in turn would endeavor to undermine the "pernicious" work of Sir Walter Scott. It has been suggested that he may even have used *Don Quixote* as a model.[57] At any rate, he was determined to attack the entire sentimental myth about life in the Middle Ages. He would be the modern American realist scrutinizing the romantic medieval world of Scott's novels and poetry, of Tennyson's *Idyils of the King,* of William Morris' *Early Paradise,* and of the Pre-Raphaelites. "No church, no nobility, no royalty or other fraud," he maintained, "can face ridicule in a fair field and live."[58]

That *A Connecticut Yankee* had a further aim was recognized by E. C. Stedman, in a letter he wrote to Mark Twain on July 7, 1889:

> *Some* blasted fool will surely jump up and say that Cervantes polished off chivalry centuries ago, etc. After a time he'll discover, perhaps, that you are going at the *still existing* radical principles or fallacies which made "chivalry" possible once, and servility and flunkeyism and tyranny possible now.[59]

Many readers, especially abroad, objected that Mark Twain did not provide a "fair field." An extreme view was that the novel was a masterpiece of vulgarity which distorted history and took malign joy in debasing everything honored by time. Andrew Lang, a friend and brilliant champion of Mark Twain in England, refused to read this particular book. In high places there was a feeling that the novel was little more than an assertion of smug nationalism.

Most readers, though, delighted in the fusion of comic adventure, burlesque, and fierce satire. The American labor press, in particular, acclaimed *A Connecticut Yankee*. Dan Beard himself was an active Socialist and many of his illustrations for the book were more explicit than the text. Mark Twain was delighted with them. The Slave Driver had Jay Gould's face, Merlin had the features of Tennyson, and both the Prince of Wales (later Edward VII) and Wilhelm II were portrayed as Chuckleheads. (Several years later Mark Twain met both monarchs in friendly circumstances; as far as we know, neither made mention of these likenesses.)

The most perceptive critics denied that the amazing novel was aimed solely at England or even solely at medieval times. They also denied that Mark Twain had smugly deserted the problems of modern America. William Dean Howells in his review for *Harper's* emphasized that *A Connecticut Yankee* was not primarily an attack either upon England or upon chivalry but rather an assault upon thirteen centuries of reputed Christian civilization which, under the pretense of serving God, had enslaved the children of God.[60]

In his notebook Mark Twain jotted down a reminder to himself for this novel:

NOTE FOR YANKEE

The first thing I want to teach is *disloyalty,* till they get used to disusing that word *loyalty* as representing a virtue. This will beget independence—which is loyalty to one's best self and principles, and this is often disloyalty to the general idols and fetishes.[61]

Himself a Mugwump, Mark Twain had plenty to say elsewhere about unthinking loyalty to one's political party. Here, however, he was concerned with England, where he believed the situation to be even worse. Loyalty to fetishes made the common man in England content with his enslaved position, he noted, and caused him to revere with affection a creature such as Nell Gwyn. Herein lay the real tragedy. Spirit and manhood must have been drained out of the people. The fault was the government's. "That government is not best which secures mere life and property—" he stated, "there is a more valuable thing—manhood."[62]

Harboring these thoughts and feelings, Mark Twain began to shape the career of Hank Morgan, the Hartford factory foreman, whom he had already dropped into Camelot. With luck and Yankee ingenuity Hank Morgan soon made himself Boss of the realm, the power behind King Arthur's throne. Then his problems as a ruler began. His goal was to transform England into a republic which would flourish under a kind of laissez-faire capitalism. First of all he must teach the masses to be disloyal to the ancient institutions, for these were the mere "clothes" of the nation, and they were worn out and ragged. He must teach the masses that the only just political power was inherent in the people, not in the few unproductive aristocrats. He sized up the situation:

> So to speak, I was become a stockholder in a corporation where nine hundred and ninety-four of the members furnished all the money and did all the work, and the other six elected themselves a permanent board of direction and took all the dividends. It seemed to me that what the nine hundred and ninety-four dupes needed was a new deal.[63]

The Boss hoped to achieve the New Deal by means of education and peaceful persuasion. He established schools, began a newspaper, and introduced the technology of the nineteenth century. Top priority among his projects was a Man-Factory for selected individuals who showed any glimmer of having spirit or independent thought. After several years, however, it became apparent that a peaceful revolution would not be possible among these human animals. They had been reduced to a dead level of resignation, of dumb, uncomplaining acceptance of whatever might befall them. "Their very imagination was dead," lamented the Boss. "When you can say that of a man, he has struck bottom, I reckon; there is no lower deep for him."[64]

Disenchanted, the Boss was almost sorry he had ever set out to remodel old England. He was now forced to admit the historical fact that "goody-goody talk and moral suasion" had never won any people their freedom. With reluctance he bowed to the immutable law that "all revolutions that will succeed must *begin* in blood."[65] He thought of the blood of the French Revolution and of the blessing it finally brought. What England needed, he acknowledged, was a Reign of Terror and a guillotine, but he thought he was the wrong man for the job.

Time and again the Boss had the feeling that he was living in France before the Revolution. In a way he was. During 1887 and 1888 Mark Twain was reading with great interest Taine's *Ancien Régime* and Carlyle's *French Revolution*. We have observed his interest also in the *Memoirs* of Saint-Simon. He was thinking of publishing all three of these massive works. In 1888 he was also perusing Lea's *History of the Inquisition,* an excellent source of information about ecclesiastical trials, tortures, and executions. As well as any of his critics, Mark Twain realized that his novel did not portray accurately the laws and customs of England in the sixth century. His current reading colored all his thoughts. He did maintain in his Preface, however, that his book was no libel on Arthurian England, because all these laws and customs did exist in England and elsewhere at later times, and conditions had been steadily improving down through the centuries.

They had been improving, that is, everywhere except in Russia. In a discarded Preface for *A Connecticut Yankee,* Mark Twain had much to say about the wretched empire of Alexander III. Exile to Siberia, he said, concentrated all the bitter inventions of the black ages for the infliction of suffering. This Preface also had much to say about the barbarism of old English laws, though he had said it all before, in *The Prince and the Pauper.* The opening paragraph is straightforward: "My object has been to group together some of the most odious laws which have had vogue in the Christian countries within the past eight or ten centuries, and illustrate them by the incidents of a story."[66]

A Connecticut Yankee often misfires, because it was seldom written in that calm, judicious good humor which Mark Twain considered essential to effective satire. Often it repels rather than persuades. Hank Morgan's reading had led him to expect Camelot to be instinct with lofty ideals and refinements; instead he found ignorance, filth, crime, tyranny, superstition, and a pervading brutishness. Except to observe briefly the coarseness of the knights and ladies, Hank loitered little in the great hall. When he became Boss, his concern for the poor led him into the unlovely secret places far beneath the veneer of feudal splendor. In these places he became very angry indeed.

As Howells remarked about Mark Twain, "No one can read *The Connecticut Yankee* and not be aware of the length and breadth of his sympathies with poverty."[67] Nor can a sensitive reader long remain unaware that many of Mark Twain's assaults on the past strongly hint at evils surviving in Victorian England and elsewhere. (The very failure of the Boss in the end suggests the author's disillusionment with the whole materialistic society of America in general and perhaps with the Paige typesetter, that invention in which he was losing a fortune, in particular.) And always the measuring-stick was the same one used in his early books: the spiritual and physical well-being of the masses.

Although King Arthur himself was as fine a man as the monarchical system could produce, he was wholly indifferent to the welfare of his subjects. The system itself must therefore be at fault. Regardless of his kindly nature and good intentions, Arthur was a victim of his training, of his ingrained sympathy for his own class. "He was as unfitted for a judgeship," said the Boss, "as would be the average mother for the position of milk-distributor to starving children in famine-time."[68] Justice, as a result, was a term of no meaning, and people who were not slaves in name were slaves in fact. The Boss concluded:

> The truth was, the nation as a body was in the world for one object, and one only: to grovel before king and Church and noble; to slave for them, sweat blood for them, starve that they might be fed, work that they might play . . . And for all this, the thanks they got were cuffs and contempt; and so poor-spirited were they that they took even this sort of attention as an honor.[69]

By coincidence, the Brazilian throne crumbled shortly before *A Connecticut Yankee* came from the press. Mark Twain swam in "oceans of satisfaction." He was convinced that within fifty years the thrones of Europe would be selling at auction for old iron:

> It is enough to make a graven image laugh, to see apparently rational people, away down here in this wholesome and merci-less slaughter-day for shams, still mouthing empty reverence for those moss-backed frauds and scoundrelisms, hereditary king-ship and so-called nobility.[70]

The democratic Boss was willing to admit that unlimited power was the "ideal thing," when it was in safe hands. The despotism of heaven, he said, was the one absolutely perfect government. On earth, however, power inevitably fell into wicked or corrupt hands, making despotism the worst possible form of government for man.

At Camelot power fell into the Boss's own hands. He did not

handle it wisely. He was skilled enough to make a revolver and run a telegraph line, but in more important matters, as Mark Twain told his illustrator, Hank Morgan was a perfect ignoramus. His philosophy could not withstand the temptations of power. As an early advocate of freedom and progress, he spoke for the author. But as an ordinary man corrupted by power, he was marked for satire and ultimate destruction. He became a victim of ruthless ambition in what he confessed was a "base hankering" to be the first president. He was finally transformed into just the right man to lead a bloody revolution, a massacre which annihilated the entire knighthood of England: "we fifty-four were the masters of England! Twenty-five thousand men lay dead around us."[71]

The dichotomy in the Boss's character reflected the conflict in Mark Twain between an optimistic view of historical progress and a growing pessimism. The Boss embodied both the hopes and the fears of his creator. The conflicts between elements within his own character should not be overlooked in the drama of the more obvious conflicts between two types of society. Early reviewers, especially, made this mistake, just as they had with *Huckleberry Finn*. It is too easy to oversimplify the nationalistic bias of the novel by overstressing the innocent Americanism of its hero.[72]

An early illustration portrays a checked-suited Yankee with a straw in his hand, tickling the nose of a stately British lion. It was also Mark Twain's purpose to have his Yankee ride this lion with cruel spurs and a sharp bit. At times, therefore, the great knights of England were set to playing baseball in full armor and to wearing advertising slogans for soap and stove-polish. At other times the Boss inspected their pitiless dungeons and condemned the entire nobility of England as "tyrannical, murderous, rapacious, and morally rotten."[73]

In attacking the system of hereditary caste, Mark Twain made use of his wide reading. He described in detail the slavery of serfs to aristocratic landowners. He explained how the treasury was drained by royal grants, how high positions, especially in the army, were allotted on the basis of blood alone. Most disillusioning of all, he showed how class snobbery filtered down even to the impoverished coal-burners, who haughtily spurned the paupers below them.

Outside the royal court Mark Twain showed the common people chained to existences of perpetual misery and humiliation. To the physical bondage of lord and prelate were added the invisible bonds of ignorance, custom, terror, and superstition. The only "justice" they knew was at the cruel whim of some nobleman or wealthy priest. By law they were required to inform on their friends, even members of their own families. Confessions, whether true or not, were extracted by torture. A man might be hanged for pilfering a bit of cloth, whereupon his whole estate would be confiscated, beggaring his widow and children. "Men write many fine and plausible arguments in support of monarchy," observed the Boss, "but the fact remains that where every man in a State has a vote, brutal laws are impossible."[74]

Mark Twain developed a theory that each nation loathed a particular class of crimes above all others. England hated crimes against property. This put the poacher at the very bottom of the scale; there was no one below him. He was the "English Satan." Mark Twain even began an article on this subject. Unfortunately, he said, English judges, unlike American, were men of inherited wealth and so not qualified to understand crimes which were the natural outgrowth of desolation and hunger.[75]

The desolation in *A Connecticut Yankee* is similar to that in *The Prince and the Pauper,* and so are the inhuman laws. There is an important difference, however. This difference reflects the change in Mark Twain's attitude toward England in general and monarchy in particular. The paupers and vagabonds in the earlier novel felt a proud affection for their king. The paupers and serfs in Arthur's realm felt nothing but fear and hatred for all men of rank.

Too late, however, the Boss discovered that his most formidable enemy was not Aristocracy but the Church. Its theology did not concern him as much as did its political and economic power and the sway it held over the superstitions of the masses. He saw the Church as a machine created as a prop for the monarchical system and as the chief transgressor against human dignity and freedom. By inventing "divine right" and by perverting the Beatitudes, the Church made a virtue out of spineless humility and meanness of soul. "In two or three little centuries," said the Boss in disgust, "it had converted a nation of men to a nation of worms."[76]

The Boss, like his creator, made no mention of the Church's role in fostering scholarship or the arts. To him, any Established Church was an established crime, an "established slave-pen." It grew rich, he said, even in Victorian England, on property taken by force from the poor. And it achieved dominance of simple minds through fear, oppression, and chicanery. It paralyzed human thought.

In spite of all this, it is going too far to assert that either the Boss or Mark Twain believed that the world would never be free until "men had hanged the last king in the guts of the last priest."[77] The high ecclesiastics in Arthur's court were grossly immoral, but, said the Boss, the "great majority of these that were down on the ground among the common people, were sincere and right-hearted, and devoted to the alleviation of human troubles and sufferings."[78] Indeed, the only priests who actually participated in the narrative were men of excellent character, devout, unselfish, and fearless. One of them even dared to speak out strongly against the rulers and laws of England.

Mark Twain was more charitable toward the priests than he was toward the ladies of the court. These high-born females looked with amusement upon bloodshed and upon the torturing of prisoners. As for their conversation, it would have made an Elizabethan whore blush, reported the Boss. And in their morals they were nothing but modified savages: "The fact is, it is just a sort of polished up court of Comanches, and there isn't a squaw in it who doesn't stand ready at the dropping of a hat to desert to the buck with the biggest string of scalps at his belt."[79] And, the Boss added (from what experience?), the highest ladies and gentlemen of Victorian England were no or little cleaner in their talk and moral conduct than were the members of King Arthur's court. A bold accusation, not for the Boss, but for Mark Twain, who already had many personal friends among the upper classes in England! He was attacking not only the hereditary power of the anachronistic House of Lords but also the morality of the class it represented.

More good-natured was Mark Twain's approach to the great extra-moral pastime of the nobility, that "most chuckle-headed trade" of knight-errantry. The Boss considered it ridiculous to be obliged to joust with every strange knight encountered on the road. These knights, moreover, seldom bothered to observe "those chivalrous magnanimities" which he had read so much about. And his first day in a suit of armor presented a dozen practical discomforts never mentioned by the romancers.

The lovely young Demoiselle Alisande la Carteloise is the author's most delightful exhibit in his case against romantic sentimentalism. The Boss was led by Sandy, as he called her, on a mission to rescue forty-five beautiful maidens who had supposedly been abducted by an evil sorcerer. After extensive searchings they came upon a drove of hogs. Breaking into tears, Sandy called them by aristocratic names and fondled them affectionately. They were, she insisted, her friends, now transformed into swine by enchantments. "My land," cried the Yankee, "the power of training! of influence! of education! It can bring a body to believe anything."[80] Poor Sandy, ignorant and superstitious, had simply lived so long amid the fictions of the medieval world that she could not distinguish them from the facts of the real life around her. In this way she resembled Don Quixote himself, or the boy in Mark Twain's story "A Curious Experience," or, indeed, so the author would imply, many readers who breathed too freely of the enchanted air of such romancers as Scott and Tennyson.

The Boss, like his creator, came to the conclusion that "training" was all important, was, in fact, all there was to a person. What we call "nature," said the Boss, is really just heredity and training. "We have no thoughts of our own, no opinions of our own; they are all transmitted to us, trained into us."[81] Being a practical man, he tried to counteract the training of the Dark Ages by an intensive training program of his own. He scoffed at the notion that certain people were not capable of self-government. He opened his Man-Factory, established a newspaper, schools, and many types of Protestant churches. History had taught him that the masterminds of all nations invariably sprang from the masses, not from the privileged classes. It was a self-proven fact, he maintained, "That even the best governed and most free and enlightened monarchy is still behind the best condition attainable by its people."[82] A wave of democratic optimism swept away his fears that the people had been dehumanized beyond redemption:

> A man *is* a man, at bottom. Whole ages of abuse and oppression cannot crush the manhood clear out of him. Whoever thinks it is a mistake is himself mistaken. Yes, there is plenty good enough material for a republic in the most degraded people that ever existed—even the Russians; plenty of manhood in them—even in the Germans [sic!]—if one could but force it out of its timid and suspicious privacy, to overthrow and trample in the mud any throne that ever was set up and any nobility that supported it.[83]

And so the Yankee pursued his dream of setting up a republic in England as soon as the aging King Arthur should die. First he must break the back of chivalry. This he did, in his opinion, by riding on his pony into the lists and killing a dozen armored knights with well-aimed bullets. Symbolically, the feudal system died in that arena, and England seemed ready for its New Deal.

The Boss had been in power for ten years already. He had trained thousands of men.

Sure enough, the people tossed their hats with joy when the new republic was proclaimed. Then came the unexpected, the fearful Interdict of the Catholic Church. Only a handful of boys remained true to the Boss, while the masses cowered before the fury of the Church. Superstition had not been educated out of the masses, for it was in their blood and bones. This was the ultimate, crushing disenchantment for the Boss. Reluctantly he went forward with battle plans against the entire knighthood of England in the despairing hope that he might possibly cure the political disease, even though the patient might die. The hope proved vain. Although the knighthood of England was destroyed, the Boss himself was finally outsmarted by his vengeful old enemy, Merlin.

The climax of *A Connecticut Yankee* reflects the growing pessimism of Mark Twain. Like the Boss, he was an aggressive modernist who was enthralled by the scientific progress of the nineteenth century. He was convinced that his own age was the greatest in world history and that his own nation was the greatest of the age. At the same time, he was having grave misgivings. Perhaps technology was proceeding too fast. Perhaps scientific growth was outstripping spiritual growth. Perhaps, as Emerson feared, the machine might soon be in the saddle, riding man. The frightful carnage to which his modern Yankee resorted suggests these misgivings. Science, the prodigy that was counted on to save humanity, might prove to be, instead, the very force that would annihilate it.

Humanity as a whole will always see itself mirrored in this novel, but the fact has not vindicated the novel in the eyes of the British. Nor has the considerable criticism which the Boss directed at such alleged evils in the United States as the income tax, "poor whites," corporation practices, slavery, and the protective tariff.[84] To the British, the book has seemed unpardonably abusive, although, as we have seen, it barely suggests the full fury of Mark Twain's Anglophobia. The author was afraid, in fact, that he had pruned it until it had lost its power. If he could write it over again, he told Howells, he would not leave out so many things, for they burned within him. It angered him, therefore, when his London publishers suggested drastic revisions. He explained to them all the trouble he had already taken to "soften" the book:

> Now, mind you, I have taken all this pains because I wanted to say a Yankee mechanic's say against monarchy and its several natural props, and yet make a book which you would be willing to print exactly as it comes to you, without altering a word.[85]

His charitable intent, he added, was to "pry up the English nation to a little higher standard of manhood." He refused to revise the book again, although he did work hard to compose a Preface which would not hurt his sales on either side of the Atlantic.

This letter seems more honest than the one he later wrote to his friend Andrew Lang in London, begging him to use his vast influence to explain to Europe that *A Connecticut Yankee* was designed with the sole purpose of entertaining the masses. The British, he complained, kept criticizing the novel by the "culture standard." The book was not written to instruct, he told Lang, but merely to amuse.[86] But, as we have seen, Andrew Lang would not even read the book.

In later life Mark Twain almost certainly had regrets for having dealt so harshly with the British. His fires of patriotic vengeance soon burned out. Only a few weeks before his death, however, he read the Yankee's story for the first time in twenty years and wrote his daughter that he was "prodigiously pleased with it— a most gratifying surprise."[87]

Ranging as it does from tears of hysterical laughter to a compassionate fury too deep for tears, *A Connecticut Yankee* has few counterparts in American letters. No one knew better than Mark

Twain that his Arthurian England never had an objective reality. But he knew his history, and he had the power to recreate its lesser-known phases. By exposing some of the forgotten aspects of medieval life, he hoped to tickle the nose of the arrogant British lion and to twist its tail. Further than this, he wanted to confront old-fashioned privilege with modern-day humanity and thereby to dramatize the merits of democratic society. If he did not make a complete success of it, his failure at least has fascination.

It would be many years before Mark Twain was able to look again on monarchical government with tranquillity. His attitude toward the aristocracy, however, underwent some interesting changes shortly after his invasion of Camelot. These changes began in the winter and spring of 1891, while he was working on his next novel, *The American Claimant,* which ran in American newspapers and the *Idler Magazine* in England later that same year.

The American Claimant is a curious book. In it Mark Twain sought to interweave several social theories of the day with parts of his old Colonel Sellers play and selections from his anti-Arnold tracts. At least one revelation must have been soothing to British tempers: Mark Twain did not hate aristocrats indiscriminately. What he hated was the system in which great titles were automatically handed down to men of the most ignorant and corrupt kind. In a private note he said that he had no objection to making eminent men dukes, on condition that their titles would not pass on to their sons.[88] He appears to have wondered whether he had not been somewhat unfair in his condemnation of the aristocracy, or even of the monarchy. This thoughtful paragraph looks as if it were intended as the opening of *The American Claimant:*

CHAP. I

Perhaps the most warping & narrowing habit a man can acquire is that of encouraging his inborn disposition to look at only one side of a thing. If persisted in, a time will come when the thing *has* only one side for him. If he approves it, it is wholly beautiful & flawless; if he disapproves it, it is utterly ugly, & thick-spotted with faults. Yet in truth, few things are entirely bad or perfectly good. As regards to one matter, this injurious habit seems to have become almost universal in America. By habit our people have come at last to imagine that a democracy is the only perfect form of government, & that the monarchical form is thoroughly bad—so completely bad that it would be vain to try to find any rational excuse for its existence. And when they speak of monarchy it is always with heat, always with bitterness.[89]

Mark Twain must have realized that he himself had been speaking of monarchy with as much heat and bitterness as almost anyone else. And it had long been his habit to look emotionally on only one side of many things. He fought against this habit, but frequently he lost the fight. At this particular time, it looks as if he wanted to mitigate some of the strictures of *A Connecticut Yankee* by demonstrating that not all aristocrats were monsters; nor, for that matter, were all so-called democrats much to be proud of.

At any rate, it is hard to imagine a finer young man than the aristocratic hero of *The American Claimant*. The only son and heir of the Earl of Rossmore, young Berkeley comes to the United States to make his way in the world by personal merit. His claim to the title, he has learned, is spurious. Therefore, he will study at first hand the democratic way of life he has been admiring from afar.

At first the Englishman is carried away by enthusiasm for the wholesome principles he hears expressed, particularly by a newspaper editor who extols the freedom and irreverence of the American press. He is disillusioned, however, to discover that principles and practices are quite different matters. The American branch of his own family, for example, revels in the very idea of hereditary caste. Colonel Mulberry Sellers, head of the branch, even writes to the aged Earl, laying claim to the title.

Colonel Sellers is obviously under the baneful influence of Sir

Walter Scott's romances. He calls members of his family by such titles as "Lady Gwendolen." He sends his daughter to "Rowena-Ivanhoe College," where everything is "redolent of royalty." He makes a seal of the Rossmore crest and calls his humble place in Virginia "Rossmore Towers." The silly old Colonel, however, is different only in degree from his compatriots. Berkeley is told that any American would jump at the chance to gain a title. The truth, he finds, is that Americans do not really despise aristocrats; they admire and envy them.

> "I believe I understand—yes, I think I get the idea. You have no blame for the lucky few who naturally decline to vacate the pleasant nest they were born into; you only despise the all-powerful and stupid mass of the nation for allowing the nest to exist."[90]

His republican friend is glad that Berkeley has finally been able to get that simple thing into his head.

In this manner Mark Twain turned his criticism away from the peerage itself and upon the common people, in America as well as in Europe. In spite of their democratic pretensions, Americans, he said, loved lords and yearned to bask in their society. The United States, moreover, was developing a social hierarchy as rigid and nearly as self-perpetuating as that of England. One evening young Berkeley wrote in his diary: " 'It does rather look as if in a republic where all are free and equal, prosperity and position constitute *rank*.' "[91]

After his outburst in *A Connecticut Yankee*, Mark Twain was trying to see the other side of this nobility business. He had shown how England looked to a democratic Yankee; he would show also, as did Henry James, how the United States looked to an aristocratic Englishman. Berkeley was as disillusioned in America as Hank Morgan was in Camelot. And, it must be confessed, Berkeley was a more estimable product of hereditary privilege than Hank Morgan was of republicanism, and incomparably more estimable than foolish old Colonel Sellers.

The truth is that Mark Twain was quickly discarding England as his political *bête noire* and was settling now upon Russia. We have noted the comments on Siberian exile which he made in his original Preface for *A Connecticut Yankee*. In his new book even Colonel Sellers was concerned about Siberia. His grandiose scheme was to purchase it, convert it into a republic, and thereby attract all the Russian "slaves" away from the Czar.

A number of unpublished writings also attest to the extent of Mark Twain's new animosity. By editorial request, in 1890 he wrote a long letter to "Free Russia" condemning the atrocities of the Czar. He described the Czar as a "granite-hearted, bloody-jawed maniac," who did not deserve to live in this world. The proper way to demolish the Russian throne, he said, was by revolution. Because revolution was not feasible yet in Russia (as in Camelot?), there was only one thing left to do: "keep the throne vacant by dynamite until a day when candidates shall decline with thanks. Then organize a republic."[92]

As might be expected, Mark Twain did not mail this letter. Nor did he publish its still more strongly-worded sequel, "The Answer," which was purportedly Alexander III's reply to the United States. The Czar addresses "Impertinent Republican Scum." He frankly boasts of his cruelties and of the fact that he is the worst usurper on a throne today. He calls his government a "ferocious travesty" and admits that his throne is "built upon broken hearts." The American people he calls "shams & humbugs," because they know all these things yet contrive to treat him with respect. "Oh, incredible, unspeakable, unimaginable hypocrisy!" he cries. Never will he respect any petitioners, he adds, until they have the honesty and the courage to call him what he is, "a bloody-lipped beast, a ghoul, a hyena."[93]

"The Answer" is obviously the prototype for the elaborate "Czar's Soliloquy" which Mark Twain published in 1905. In the early nineties, however, he cautiously kept these fulminations to himself. He wrote more on the Czar, too. Sometimes he got started

on the Hell-Russia kinship,[94] and sometimes he advocated a sensible crusade, which would "make a bonfire of the Russian throne
& fry the Czar in it."[95] Less fiery was the cablegram supposedly
sent—collect—by the Czar to Col. Mark Twain in Washington.
At this time, 1890, Mark Twain was in the vanguard of those
battling for strong copyright protection. The cablegram objected
to an international copyright law on the ground that it would prevent the Czar from continuing to "doctor" American literature
in such a way as to keep the Russian people pleased with Siberia
as a summer resort. "We should be obliged to let you say your
say in your own way," complained the Czar. "Voila! my empire
would be a republic in five years and I should be in Siberia myself."[96] A similar message allegedly came from the Sultan. He
complained that such a copyright law would undermine the
social structure of his empire and make Turkey a republic within
ten years.

With *An American Claimant* and these anti-Czarist papers of
1890–91 another phase of Mark Twain's career came to a close.
He would go abroad again now, and things would change. But
during the eighties, at least, he had returned with ardor to the
brash American point of view which had animated his writings in
the sixties, but which he had largely abandoned during his anti-
republican phase in the seventies. Antagonized by British criticism
of the United States like many an author before him, Mark Twain
looked on himself in the eighties as spokesman for his nation. He
became the latest apostle of an aggressive and militant democracy.
At the end of the decade his nationalism grew so unashamed that
he wrote as if America were the center of the world. *A Connecticut Yankee,* indeed, has been termed the era's most powerful expression of the "democratic humanitarianism which underlies so
much of our middle-class economic critique."[97]

"Humanitarianism" is the key word here. Mark Twain did not
always write fairly or even consistently, but never—never in his
life—did he waver from his search for those things which were

best for the ordinary man. This was the ruling passion of his life. In the words of Stuart Sherman:

> He did not and could not give a "square deal" to the South or to Scott or to Europe or to the Arthurian realm. He refused all recognition to aristocratic virtues which retarded the complete establishment of the brotherhood of man. He was not, like some exquisite men of letters, a democrat in his study and a snob in his drawing-room; he was of the people and for the people at all times.[97]

IV

Ambassador-at-Large

URING a lecture tour in 1869, a year
before his marriage, Mark Twain sent a revealing and prophetic
letter to his prospective mother-in-law. He informed Mrs. Langdon that he had quit swearing and drinking and had become a
well-mannered Christian. This was revealing, but not true—or at
least not for long. He also assured her that he was not marrying
Livy for her money. He had been paddling his own canoe since
he was thirteen, he said. "If we get into trouble we will sell our
point lace & eat our shucks in a foreign land, & *fight it out* . . . "[1]
Not only biblical, this was also prophetic.

Twenty-two years later, in 1891, this bold promise was put to
the test. He and Livy got into deep trouble. Both as an investor
and as a businessman Mark Twain had proved to be an unlucky
tyro. Money was coming in fast from his royalties, but it was
going out even faster in day-to-day living and entertaining expenses, in backing inventions, and in trying to run his own business. In particular, the Paige typesetting machine had already
swallowed over two hundred thousand dollars of his own money,
and his publishing house, begun so bravely with *Huckleberry Finn*
and the *Memoirs* of General Grant, was now on the brink of
failure.

By 1891, Mark Twain said, he had seen all of the foreign
lands he wished to see except heaven and hell. Nonetheless, he

determined to do what he had done in 1878 and 1879; namely, take his family to Europe once more and write another travel book. So it was that on June 6, 1891, the Clemens family again embarked for Europe. Susy and Clara were in their late teens now; Jean was eleven. This time Livy's companion was her sister by adoption, Susan Crane, recently widowed. The seventh member of the party was Katie Leary, who had long been, and would remain, a faithful servant in the Clemens household.

To Frank Finlay in Ireland, Mark Twain wrote that they planned to wander awhile on the Continent, then return home by way of England after two or three years. The plan went awry, however. Little did they guess that they had already bid farewell to their only real home and would not return to live in the States for nine long years.

Apparently, they did not wish to visit England just yet. The obstreperous Hank Morgan was still spreading his unpopular brand of Yankeeism there. Besides, Mark Twain's anger at the British was not quite dead. That autumn on the Continent he was stirred to note, "As long as time shall last, history will spit in England's face for her treachery to Napoleon's trust in her."[2] He also scouted the hypocrisy of the British people in shouting or singing "God Save the King" with the mouth only, neither higher nor lower. And he continued to assert that the first and only gospel of all monarchies should be rebellion against Church and State.

So they bypassed England and went first to France and Switzerland. Before sailing, Mark Twain had contracted to write six travel letters for the McClure Syndicate and the *New York Sun*. He would be paid a thousand dollars for each letter. But he refused to allow the letters to be published in Europe, despite the fact that he was reported to be "more valuable on the continent than any writer, English or American."[3] The letters, he feared, might be mutilated by the foreign press: "If my letters are syndicated in Europe they will be robbed of freedom—better not do that. I want to speak of certain things in a [vocabulary] which *they* would not print."[4]

Mark Twain apparently expected his reports to be more critical than they actually turned out to be. He wrote the first five letters during the summer of 1891 as the family moved about from one health resort to another. Susy and Livy were both in poor health. His own rheumatism was so painful that he had even tried to dictate part of *The American Claimant* into cylinders of his phonograph. And so the family spent only a short time in Paris and Geneva before taking the water treatment at Aix-les-Bains.

"Aix, the Paradise of the Rheumatics,"[5] was a serious and highly flattering description of the entire resort area and its inhabitants. (The baths, by the way, took nearly all the pain from his arm.) Aix-les-Bains he found to be an "enchanting place" where the nineteenth century rubbed elbows with the Middle Ages. The climate, the town, the hack-drivers, the baths, the gambling hall, the theaters, the countryside—everything was pleasing to Mark Twain. Not even an Irving or a Longfellow could have expressed greater delight.

From Aix the Clemens party went to Bayreuth for the Wagner Festival. "At the Shrine of St. Wagner" is the good-humored report of an untrained listener in a community gone music-mad. Sometimes, said Mark Twain, he felt like the one blind man where all other men could see, "the one groping savage in the college of the learned and always during service I feel like a heretic in heaven."[6] One such "service" was *Tristan und Isolde*. But he enjoyed the Festival as a whole and did it high justice in this descriptive letter. He was not really still as insensitive to great music as he sometimes liked to pretend. He was intoxicated with joy, he said, in the music of *Tannhäuser* and *Parsifal*.

In Bayreuth the Clemenses encountered a lovely German princess with whom they all fell in love. Her heart was said to be as kind as her face. Obviously this put a strain on Mark Twain's anti-aristocratic principles. All he could say, as he gave in to her charms, was that royal personages of her character set back the clock of progress by reconciling people to monarchy.

The third of Mark Twain's letters came from a spa in Bohemia: "Marienbad—A Health Factory." Paine reported that this letter was "of the same general character as those preceding,"[7] but it was not. It was written in a mood both bitter and contemptuous. Save for the scenery and the modern architecture, nothing in Marienbad made a favorable impression on Mark Twain. Nor was his disposition improved by the constant rains and cold which kept him indoors much of the time. On these cold days he found the towering white German stove to be no better company than a corpse: "Of all the creations of human insanity this thing is the most forbidding."[8]

He did not even enjoy the baths in Marienbad. Being forced to abide by the severe regimen seemed as disagreeable to him as having the gout. He also got so tired of hearing people discuss their ailments that he wrote a "love" poem with the refrain, "Oh, Darling, how's your liver?"[9]

His temper was abraded, too, by observing the identical "strange barbarism" he had noted many years earlier in Geneva. Consciously and intentionally, he reported, the best-dressed men and women, not the others, would swerve from their paths on the sidewalk in order to crowd one into the gutter. This infuriated Mark Twain, especially when practiced on young ladies. "It is a mistake," he said, "that there is no bath that will cure people's manners. But drowning would help." Then he added:

> However, perhaps one can't look for any real showy amount of delicacy of feeling in a country where a person is brought up to contemplate without a shudder the spectacle of a woman harnessed up with dogs and hauling carts. The woman is on one side of the pole, the dog on the other, and they bend to the work and tug and pant and strain—and the man tramps leisurely alongside and smokes his pipe. Often the woman is old and gray, and the man is her grandson. The Austrian national ornithological device ought to be replaced by a grandmother harnessed to a slush cart with a dog.[10]

Small wonder that Mark Twain disapproved of having his daughters become too friendly with the men of Marienbad. Susy was nineteen now and Clara seventeen. The latter recalled that it was at this time that her father gave unmistakable evidence of what she called an "ingrained objection to foreign suitors."*[11]

Letter Number Four to the *New York Sun* was entitled "Playing Courier." It described the comic adventures of the Clemens party when Mark Twain decided to act as courier on the trip from Aix to Bayreuth.[12] Most of the letter was dialogue, not very enlightening to his readers, but at least lighthearted.

At the end of August, 1891, the family passed through Nuremberg on the way to their beloved Heidelberg. For almost a week they lived in their old apartment at the Schloss Hotel, then tore themselves away to move south into Switzerland. From Lucerne they traveled to Brienz, then to Interlaken, from which city Mark Twain mailed his fifth letter, "Switzerland, the Cradle of Liberty." As the title suggests, he found the atmosphere of Switzerland extremely wholesome, morally as well as physically, after that of the neighboring monarchies. It was refreshing, he wrote, to breathe air that had known no taint of slavery for six hundred years.[13] The bulk of the letter, however, was given over to an old legend, a comic anecdote, and a description of the magnificent Jungfrau. The anecdote was about the King of Greece, who was traveling incognito on the train and being abused by a bumptious American tourist. The satire on the American suggests that Mark Twain's hatred of kings was dying out.

While relaxing at Ouchy, on Lake Geneva, shortly after leaving Interlaken, Mark Twain decided to take a short trip on his own. First he looked up Joseph Very, his favorite guide from the seventies. Then at Lake Bourget they hired a boat and boatman to take them on a peaceful float down the Rhône River to Arles.

* *Although the objection, as a rule, remained strong, in 1909 he was proud to give Clara's hand in marriage to Ossip Gabrilowitsch, a brilliant young pianist and conductor—and a Russian.*

Mark Twain in London, 1872

Mark Twain in Berlin, 1892

Mark Twain in London, 1899

Mark Twain's notes for a London lecture

A suggestion to writers from
Mark Twain

**"Innocence Abroad
(in search of a copyright)"**

Thomas Nast caricature of
Mark Twain in Canada

Joseph Keppler (Spy) caricature
of Mark Twain, 1885

Mark Twain sitting for Miss Theresa Feodorowna Ries, 1898

Mark Twain chatting with King Edward VII and Queen Alexandra

"Be good and you will be lonesome"
Following the Equator, 1895

Mark Twain and his lecture
agent, Carlyle Smythe, 1895

NOTICE
ALL STOWAWAYS WILL
BE PROSECUTED AT HONOLULU
AND RETURNED TO THIS PORT.
BY ORDER.

Mark Twain, Clara, and Livy, departing for Australia, 1895

"More Tramps Abroad"

Arrival in England, 1907

Mark Twain at Oxford, receiving
his degree, 1907

Mark Twain with British Members of Parliament, 1907

William Dean Howells

H. H. Rogers, with Mark
Twain, 1908

Cecil J. Rhodes, 1889

King Leopold II

Mark Twain with Helen Allen,
Bermuda, 1908

Mark Twain being carried ashore
after his last trip to Bermuda, 1910

Mark Twain at Clara's wedding, October, 1909 (*left to right:*
Mark Twain, Jervis Langdon, Jean Clemens, Ossip Gabrilowitsch,
Clara, Joe Twitchell)

Not only would this be a vacation from his strenuous travels, but also it might provide adventures for another book. It was by then mid-September.

Unfortunately, as he confessed to Clara, their only adventures were drifting into rough waters now and then. The trip was serene and restful, but nothing of special interest happened. Every day or two he wrote Livy about the gorgeous sunrises, about breakfasting and dining ashore with the hearty peasants. The crumbling ruins which studded the hillsides made history flood over him once again—the history this time of the successive conquests by Gauls, Romans, Visigoths, Saracens, and Christian Crusaders. "These are pathetic shores," he told Livy.

For ten days the three men drifted with the current, gazing across at towns which appeared horribly ugly, noted Mark Twain, unless seen from a distance in just the right light. He practically ignored his notebooks. He did, however, make the mistake of trying to create an entire travel book out of this uneventful journey. Thinking no doubt of 1878, he wrote to Joe Twichell that he should have been along. Joe's presence might have helped.

Mark Twain put Joe (Harris) into the account anyway, together with several other imaginary, fun-loving characters. He wrote 174 manuscript pages for this book, which was to be entitled *The Innocents Adrift*. Having so few real facts to inspire him, however, he was frustrated in his effort to recapture the freewheeling charm of *The Innocents Abroad*. Dated notes prove that he at least read over the manuscript in 1894 and again in 1904. Evidence also suggests that the second half may have been written later and at several different times. But Mark Twain finally gave it all up as a bad job and never published it. Years later his biographer completely retailored the loose, rollicking book-fragment and printed it as a mild descriptive sketch for the sewing-circle.[14]

The Innocents Adrift discussed the Old Masters once again. This time, as if the author were apologizing for his youthful indiscretions, he treated them with kindness. Most of the traveling companions frankly envied those people whose eyes were trained to detect genuine beauties in the old paintings.

The vulgarity of French fiction was also discussed, and again Mark Twain modified one of his early opinions. He did not deny that Zola's *La Terre* was more coarse and vulgar than American novels. But now he admitted that this did not prove that French life was any more repulsive or brutish than American life. The "untranslatable incidents" of *La Terre,* he said, had counterparts all through American society. The distinction, therefore, was not between national moralities, but simply between literary customs. In a short paper probably written at about this time Mark Twain deplored the sustained "filth" of *La Terre* but insisted that the book was true—true also of towns in every state of America. That, he said, is the real reason for our hatred of Zola.[15]

It is interesting to see Mark Twain deliberately ignore this opportunity to blast the French. He leaned over backward to be kind. Perhaps the Rhône trip left only memories too pleasant to mar. Perhaps, too, he was at last trying to combat his penchant for generalizing about French manners and morals. In *The Innocents Adrift* he made his most perceptive explanation of this failing:

> Well, I will say this; that a man's impressions of a people is a thing which in the course of years generalizes *itself* out of a multitude of experiences whose details pass from his memory, but the sum of whose meaning remains as a verdict. That verdict might fall one way with you, & the opposite way with me. And I won't say but that a half a dozen very striking instances, all on one side, may not carry your verdict against a hundred testifying for the other side—because by chance the hundred might happen to be less striking & impressive, all put together, than the half dozen.[16]

How true! Sometimes, of course, generalizations lead one to verdicts that are favorable. Mark Twain proceeded to give a good example of this by relating a story about three Englishmen whose coolness and raw courage prevented a panic among the passengers on a ship during an emergency at sea. He told this story in support of Harris' encomium of the British for their probity, their persistence, and their rational calmness in the crises of life. These words, it will be noted, were the most charitable Mark Twain had written about the English in more than ten years.[17]

This Huck Finn river idyll completed, Mark Twain gave away the boat in Arles and made his way back by rail to Ouchy and his family. The plan was to winter in Berlin, a gay capital where they had a number of friends and relatives. Mark Twain wrote an amusing sketch about their first apartment at Körnerstrasse.[18] The family, however, were embarrassed to discover what a shabby address theirs actually was, so they soon moved to a handsome apartment at the Hotel Royal on Unter den Linden.

In Berlin that winter Mark Twain was surrounded by a brilliant company of people eager to do him honor. The American Minister was William Walter Phelps, whom Mark Twain had known in the States. And at the Emperor's court was a Clemens cousin, now married to a German general. Mark Twain's books were on display everywhere. He himself was recognized joyously whenever he appeared on the streets. As in London nearly two decades before, he was a social lion in a foreign capital which he loved. It was especially gratifying to him, moreover, to find that in German academic circles his writings were already being treated seriously and with respect.[19]

Mark Twain's facility with the German language, which had just replaced Robert Browning as his current passion, increased rapidly that winter. He plowed through the slovenly newspapers and on occasion would practice his uncertain grammar in an exchange with some amiable tradesman. For fun he translated nursery rhymes both from German to English and from English to German. And during the nineties he sprinkled even his business correspondence with German words and phrases. Most of all, perhaps, he enjoyed giving prepared speeches in a humorous mélange of English and German. The students loved these speeches. He had done this sort of thing in his play *Meisterschaft,* which he wrote for the German class meeting in his home in 1887 and 1888. In 1897 he even translated one of his stories, "A Singular Episode," into German, but Livy would not allow him to publish it.[20] John T. Krumpelmann, who has examined the matter with care, reports:

> When Mark Twain left German territory (May, 1899) he could read even journalistic German with facility. He could understand the spoken word with little difficulty. He could, if in a mood to try and if given time to shape his phrase, speak simple German haltingly, and probably ungrammatically. He could even write German prose, which, although not flawless, was good and commendable.[21]

Mark Twain made up his mind to be enthusiastic about Berlin. The result was predictable. Even his private notebooks contain almost no criticism of Berlin or its society. Only one matter really angered him. He thought it infamous that the government recognized only two Churches (Catholic and Lutheran) and subsidized these two at the expense of other Churches and of nonchurch people. That one of the state-supported sects was Catholic did not particularly annoy him, as it would have done a few years before; he was swiftly making his peace with Catholicism. He was flattered to be invited to contribute to the Catholic periodical *Christ's Poor.* And in 1894 he even put Jean in a convent school, hoping that it might make a "good strong unshakable Catholic of her."[22]

Among the German characteristics which Mark Twain admired was the sensible attitude of the people toward the nobility. In contrast to French newspapers, the Court Gazette of the German papers, he said, could be covered with a playing card. The German newspapers respected titles, he said, the British papers revered them, the French papers adored them. In France, said Mark Twain, if a duke's dog caught cold, they would stop the presses to cry about it.

In February, 1892, Kaiser Wilhelm II commanded a dinner to honor Mark Twain, whom he placed at his right hand. A modest, factual note on the occasion is all that appears in Mark Twain's notebook. Howells informs us that Mark Twain valued the distinction but was never very proud of this particular dinner, since Wilhelm II was still a "rather cockahoop sovereign."[23] Mark Twain was impressed, however, by the courage displayed several days later by the royal family in riding openly among revolutionary mobs which had risen against the government. But it was only for his autobiography fourteen years later that Mark Twain recalled the details of the dinner. It still troubled him that he seemed to have committed some *faux pas* which offended the Kaiser, and, surprisingly, he blamed himself, not any false pride on the part of Wilhelm II.

From one source only do we have testimony that Mark Twain was dissatisfied at this time with the ruling classes of Germany. An American journalist who knew him in Berlin during the nineties reported that Mark Twain despised the "monarchical atavism" of the Prussians, whom he considered to be stupid, malicious, and arrogant, in contrast to the Austrian aristocrats. Mark Twain was also alleged to have denounced the warlords and to have viewed a royal reception with "amazement and disgust."[24] This report, significantly, was not made until shortly after World War I, when it was hard for Americans to be objective about Germans. Mark Twain himself, after witnessing a reception given the King and Queen of Württemberg, wrote in his notebook, "I would like to be Emperor myself for awhile."[25]

As a matter of record, Mark Twain never expressed anything but pleasure in his associations with the royalty or aristocracy of any nation. Invariably he reported them to be people of cultivation and charm. On one occasion when the wife of one of his friends was cruelly snubbed by a German prince, who pointedly ignored her proffered hand, Mark Twain's democratic ire was not aroused in the least. He simply pitied the social naïveté of the woman. By 1892 his association with court personages had more or less reconciled him to aristocracy, as being in the natural order of things. That summer in Nauheim he was delighted to accept an invitation from the Prince of Wales, later Edward VII, to meet and talk. The men liked each other immediately.

It was from Berlin in the spring of 1892, soon after his dinner with the Emperor, that Mark Twain sent off the last of the six letters he had promised to the *New York Sun.* This letter, entitled "The German Chicago," was more carefully planned than the others. Except for the haphazard naming of streets and numbering of houses, Berlin was uniformly delightful to Mark Twain. Most of the city, he said, looked as if it had been built just last week. He praised its strict building code, its spaciousness, its great central park, its brilliantly lighted streets. All about the city were a prevailing cleanliness, beauty, blooming health.

Still more impressive was the magnificent government of the German capital. It stopped at no expense, marveled Mark Twain, where the public health, comfort, and convenience were concerned. Taxes were not only levied, they were also collected. The police, courteous but persistent, kept coming until the taxes were paid in full. Berlin was the best-governed city in the world, he thought, with method and system in all details, however great or small:

> And it is not method and system on paper, and there an end—it is method and system in practice. It has a rule for everything, and puts the rule in force; puts it in force against the poor and powerful alike, without favor or prejudice.[26]

In America, said Mark Twain, he did not know if we could venture to ask our most illustrious citizens to serve on a board of aldermen. He was not even sure we could elect them. In Berlin, however, the very best men in the city considered it an honor to serve gratis as aldermen, and the people had the good sense to elect them year after year. As a result, Berlin was a thoroughly well-governed city.

The Berlin post office department was such a miracle of efficiency that Mark Twain had heard it extolled in France and England. Now he wrote a twenty-page (unpublished) article about it.[27] The post office department was responsible also for the telephone, telegraph, *rohrpost* (pneumatic), and the best railway guide in the world. It permitted no ugly poles or wires in all of Berlin. And its services were so cheap, so prompt, and so excellent, said Mark Twain, that he could hardly believe they were related to America's "Western Union gravel trains" and "so-called telephones." "There seems to be no red tape, no standing on quibbles, anywhere," he said. "To get the work done, & done promptly & in the best possible manner is apparently the broad law of the Department." What was the secret? Simple. The department was run on the merit system by university graduates who were not under political patronage. Unmolested by official caprice, he said, these men served the country, not a party.

Later in 1892 Mark Twain worked on an article which frankly compared many things in Europe and America. This may have been designed as a chapter for his travel book, for he never published it, either. "Some National Stupidities" was generally critical of Europe for not advancing scientifically in the past twenty-five years and for not importing valuable ideas from overseas, for example, American arctics, gumshoes, typewriters, fountain pens, and modern elevators. The article was Philistine in tone, taking only occasional sideswipes at such things as the detestable cabmen and dishonest shopkeepers of Paris. Oddly, almost a third of the article was devoted to praise of the German stove, the very "monument" he had cursed in Marienbad only the year before. This was one thing America should import and work on. "I think that as a rule we develop a borrowed European idea forward," he said, "and that Europe develops a borrowed American idea backward."[28]

As if to offset his changed opinion of the German stove, Mark Twain now turned violently against the railroads of the Continent. He apologized for having once praised them. Further experience, he admitted, had taught him that they were slow, dirty, inefficient, uncomfortable, and "ingeniously inconvenient." The so-called European system, he said, was devised either by a maniac or by a person whose idea was to exasperate the traveler in all conceivable ways.

"Some National Stupidities" opened in an objective fashion, but as soon as it began to list the shortcomings of Europe, the needle got stuck in the groove. Mark Twain had persuaded himself to find almost no faults in his Berlin essay; now he was persuaded to find almost no merits. He seems to have sensed this and to have become a bit embarrassed by his severity—hence his tongue-in-cheek brag at the end:

> We are a great people. We have always been a great people, from the start: always alive, alert, up early in the morning, and ready to teach. But Europe has been a slow and discouraging pupil from the start; always, from the very start. It seems to me that something ought to be done about this.[29]

One half expects him to add, "Well, I wasn't planning to do much of anything next week, anyhow."

Mark Twain or another member of his family pasted in a scrapbook several items about him that appeared in German newspapers during 1891 and 1892. One item mentioned the huge fees he was paid for his writings and, ironically, estimated his fortune at two million dollars. Another quoted him to the effect that all foreigners were really guests in the countries they visited and should behave accordingly. They should not speak harshly or sarcastically of these countries: "Especially he who goes to a foreign country to express ideas on his observations must do so only with such intention and conviction that one can feel how well the writer means and how he respects the legitimate characteristics of each country."[30]

The longer Mark Twain lived in Europe, the harder it became

for him to write about it. Mature and experienced, he found the Old World growing so familiar to him that it may have seemed inadvisable to try to slip back into his early poses. Roles suitable to a bumptious young nobody were hardly fitting for an international figure whose hair had grown white with the years. This narrowed down his perspectives and made travel writing more difficult. Also going poorly were his other writings, although he continued to pile up a great deal of copy, despite his rheumatism. In search of health and inspiration he finally took his family out of Berlin in March, 1892, and settled in a warm, quiet haven in Menton, on the south coast of France. After a three-week rest they crossed into Italy, where they visited Pisa, then moved south to Rome for a month's stay.

From Rome the party went to Florence. As usual they went directly to the best hotel, but found it to be a "huge congerie of rats' nests, furnished with rubbish, probably bought at prayer auctions."[31] In spite of the odious accommodations, they all fell in love with Florence, its climate, and the surrounding countryside. On the hills to the east they finally located a charming villa, which they promptly leased for the following winter. Immediately Mark Twain began to copy Italian words and phrases into his notebook, as well as to drop them into his personal letters. Italy, he seemed to know, had a place in his future.

Two weeks in Florence, another two in Venice, and then it was June—time to head back to Germany out of the heat. They took what Mark Twain called a "tangled route" by way of Lake Como and Lucerne. After establishing his family in Bad Nauheim for the summer, he set sail in mid-June, 1892, for the United States on a business trip to check up on his publishing house and the Paige typesetter. This was the first of the six rather cheerless missions he made alone before he took his family back with him briefly in May, 1895.

After only a couple of weeks in the States, Mark Twain returned to his family in Nauheim, where he worked on a number of different stories and sketches for the rest of the summer. In a short piece called "The Cholera Epidemic in Hamburg" he censured the German press for its "eternal lethargy" in reporting information about the disease's toll in that city. To the rest of the world, said Mark Twain, the epidemic was like a tragedy being enacted behind a heavy curtain. He then indicted the German newspapers in general once more: "an Irish stew made of unrelated odds and ends, a mere chaotic confusion and worthless."[32]

He worked also on *Tom Sawyer Abroad,* a novelette which ran serially in 1893 and 1894. The story, unfortunately, does not take his young hero through adventures in Europe; it simply drops him in a balloon onto the Sahara Desert. There are sandstorms, mirages, lions, caravans, and robbers, but much of the story is made up of Tom's debates with his two old companions, Huck and Jim. Few of the debates have anything to do with matters outside the United States. On one occasion, however, Jim seems to voice the author's opinion about the Crusades. Jim never did see any use for them. To him they were just like burning down the house of a complete stranger, murdering his family, and stealing his land. The romantic Tom, on the other hand, wished to organize another Crusade and to sweep into Jerusalem. "Now Tom," commented Huck in disgust, "he got all that notion out of Walter Scott's book, which he was always reading."[33]

On another occasion it was Tom who, with his superior education, spoke for the author. Huck had just made some foolish statement about the importance of the vast Sahara when Tom quickly withered him for judging things merely by their size. England, he pointed out, was the most important country in the world, yet you could put it in China's vest-pocket: "'And look at Russia. It spreads all around and everywhere, and yet ain't no more important in this world than Rhode Island is, and hasn't got half as much in it that's worth saving.' "[34] It may be no mere coincidence that this was the summer that Mark Twain met the

Prince of Wales and spent a cheerful afternoon and two evenings
in his company. At any rate, his Anglophobia was obviously dead
at last.

The happy mood of Nauheim carried over to the Villa Viviani
in Florence, to which the family moved at the end of September,
1892. There were times that winter, however, when they missed
their Berlin friends and the gay social life. They wished it were
easier to get from Italy to Germany. As Mark Twain explained
it to the American Minister in Berlin, it was obvious that God
had never intended to travel Himself and had, therefore, been
careless in making the world:

> It would have been better to take more time & do it right, it
> seems to me, than to rush it through, helter-skelter, in 6 days,
> just for reputation. There's a heap more rocks than there is any
> use for, & instead of being set off to one side out of the way,
> they are piled right up everywhere that a person has to go.[35]

The Clemens family fell in love with the ancient, fortress-like
Villa Viviani, where they lived quietly until the middle of the
following June. Mark Twain even wrote to Washington for some
seed-corn to plant in the garden, and later he asked for some
choice Southern watermelon seeds. His enthusiasm bubbled over
in a letter to Mrs. Fairbanks:

> To me this serene and noiseless life out here, with the unimagin-
> able beauty of the view—which is never twice the same . . . —
> is heaven, & I want to stay in this one when I die. . . . I can
> work here every day in the month; there is no feeling of dulness
> [sic] or laziness or lack of interest.[36]

Little did he guess that he would be staying in Florence, at
another villa, with Livy when she died many years later. They
never forgot those happy months in Florence.

As for his working every day, it was here that he now began and
largely completed the longest novel of his later life, *Personal*

Recollections of Joan of Arc (1896). This was truly a labor of love, started in a perfect setting. To him, Napoleon I and Joan were the greatest glories of France, "that wonderful man and that sublime girl who dwarf all the rest of the human race."[37] By reason of her youth and sex, Joan seemed incomparably the more splendid. A modern critic has perfectly grasped Mark Twain's fascination with the Maid of Orleans: "She was the incarnation of youth and purity and power. She was the unique instance in history of the young girl whose innocence not merely *existed* but *acted* in the gross world of adult affairs."[38]

Whereas the advantages of Hank Morgan in Camelot had called up Mark Twain's bitterness and pessimism, Joan of Arc's evoked his most profound tenderness, a kind of "secular Mariolatry," as Carl Van Doren has termed it. Most of the book was easy to write, said Mark Twain. For the climactic trial scene and the execution, however, he constantly referred to at least ten sources, English and French, so that no historical nugget might escape him. These last scenes, he insisted, were "history pure and simple,—history stripped naked of flowers, embroideries, colorings, exaggerations, inventions." Never before, confessed Mark Twain, had any book cost him "so much cautious and painstaking execution."[39]

Some readers praised *Joan of Arc* as the author's supreme literary achievement, whereas others denounced it, for various reasons—excessive reverence, broad Western humor, or sheer miracle-mongering and mystic claptrap. George Bernard Shaw argued the interesting point that Joan was burned for neither heresy nor politics but "essentially for what we call unwomanly and insufferable presumption."[40] To all readers, however, it became apparent that the iconoclastic author of *A Connecticut Yankee* could also command the accents of adoration and create a Scott-like mood of medieval romance. "No Bayard," it has been said, "ever did his devoir more knightly to his lady than Mark Twain to Joan."[41]

In private Mark Twain continued to rain criticism on France, but he managed to keep his rooted dislike for the French out of this romantic novel. Although it would have been an easy thing to do, he did not arraign the Catholic Church, Monarchy, or Aristocracy as institutions. Nor did he pause to inspect the squalor of the French peasants or slum-dwellers. His predominant interest was Joan.

The Dauphin was accurately portrayed as a weakling, controlled by unscrupulous favorites. His chief crime, as Mark Twain saw it, was his ingratitude to the Maid, his refusal to ransom her, and his later reluctance even to try to clear her name. This struck Mark Twain as being still more abominable than Scotland's permitting the last moments of Robert Burns to be darkened by the fear of being imprisoned for a paltry debt.

The chief villain of the novel was the servile and conscienceless Pierre Cauchon, Bishop of Beauvais, who was serving as president of the ecclesiastic court at Rouen. He was a puppet of the British, and he dominated a "kennel of mastiffs and bloodhounds harassing a kitten."[42] But Mark Twain made it clear that Cauchon was not typical of the clerics, most of whom balked at his treachery. By playing down the political and ecclesiastical subtleties of the situation, Mark Twain was lenient with State and Church, much more lenient than Shaw, and made the trial fundamentally a clash of good and evil.

The soldiers of England, it is interesting to note, were depicted as forthright and brave, whereas those of France were mired in a slough of despond and cowardice. " 'By God,' " cried a British soldier at Joan's trial, " 'if she were but English, she were not in this place another half second!' "[43] The French people under British rule, moreover, were shown to be quite content, for this rule was "fair and kindly." The reader understands Mark Twain's regret that the sublime Maid had not been born across the Channel.

Mark Twain did not attempt here to paint a broad canvas of

fifteenth-century France. On one occasion only did he suggest
that the peasants were generally treated like animals, and only
on rare occasions did he dramatize the brutality of the Middle
Ages. Satire was not his purpose here. In general, he tried to
enter into the credulous spirit of the century, with its ignorance,
mysticism, and superstition. He was not debunking, not censur-
ing; he was romanticizing a glorious life and death.

Europe rejoiced in this third and last of Mark Twain's European novels. Andrew Lang, who would not even read the Yankee
yarn, was so delighted that in 1900 he asked Mark Twain's permission to dedicate his own new book, *The Maid of France,* to
him. Unfortunately, Mark Twain mislaid the letter and forgot
to reply.

Joan of Arc, begun so blithely in Florence, was brought to its
conclusion amid months of despair and heartbreaking interrup-
tions. The panic of 1893 accelerated the collapse of Mark Twain's
publishing house early the following year. Within only months
the Paige typesetter also failed. In March, 1893, Mark Twain had
to be in the States for six weeks; then in August he went back
again. This time he stayed all winter. No sooner did he rejoin
his family in Europe, in March, 1894, than he had to sail off once
more the following month. His stay in the States this time was
too short, and he was obliged to sail yet again in July.[44] Then
late in February, 1895, only two months before completing *Joan
of Arc,* Mark Twain made his fifth business trip to America
within less than two years.

The net result of this feverish shuttling across the Atlantic was
failure. At the age of sixty Mark Twain found himself completely
wiped out and some one hundred thousand dollars in debt, since
he had honorably undertaken to pay off the obligations of his
firm. His personal fortune was gone, and so was Livy's. On their
silver wedding anniversary, February 2, 1895, he presented Livy
with a five-franc piece as a symbol of their reduced circumstances.

There is something both touching and amusing about the efforts of the Clemens family to economize in Europe. Livy and the girls were not brought up to it, and Mark Twain had long since grown out of the habit. In Europe they did escape the expenses of entertaining almost continually, but still they lived in the best hotels and leased very fine houses, as befitted an international personage. Most of the time they lived in hotels, the most expensive way to live. On August 7, 1894, when things looked black indeed, Mark Twain wrote impatiently to his older brother, Orion, that he could not stand writing for low pay: "And by George I can't afford it, either, with family expenses of $1,700 a month, scrimp & economize as we may."[45]

Just three months later Mark Twain explained proudly to his new financial adviser that the family was moving from their Paris hotel (The Brighton) and renting a four-bedroom house. This was the lovely, rambling house of the artist Pomroy. The studio, which they used for everything, was forty feet long, forty feet high, and thirty feet wide. It had a vast fireplace on each side and a musicians' gallery at one end. It may have been the best substitute they could find for their Hartford home, but it could hardly have been cheap. His letter to Henry H. Rogers went on, "Mrs. Clemens is digging for servants now. She has dug up a cook, & is close after a manservant & a chambermaid. . . . We expect to save $200 a month, housekeeping, *but*—we'll wait & see."[46]

All this time it was costing them two hundred dollars a month, plus taxes, to maintain their Hartford home untenanted, in the vain hope that they would live there again. A nostalgic visit to their home in 1895 again impressed on Mark Twain how tasteless and ugly were the interiors of European houses compared with their main floor in Hartford, and dinner in a beautiful New York apartment increased his contempt for the "hideous and spirit-depressing" homes of Europe: "How poor and shabby and gawky

and lubberly and shammy and stupid Europe is, when it comes
to living! Those people are half cultured in those things and not
quite that."[47]

There is some evidence that, after completing *Joan of Arc,*
Mark Twain undertook research for a book based on the theory
that Queen Elizabeth was actually a man. Allegedly, he talked
about the project, which, like *The Prince and the Pauper* and *Joan
of Arc,* was to be a serious one. " 'I will then have three serious
books to my credit,' " he is quoted as saying, " 'and after that I
will be damned—"thrice damned," Elizabeth would have said
—if I allow anybody to take me for a mere funmaker.' "[48]

The older Clemens girls were sometimes separated from the
family by their studies during 1893 and 1894. Susy, now in her
early twenties, was allowed to go to Paris one summer to train
her voice for opera. Clara, two years younger, was sent to Miss
Willard's School for American girls in Berlin and had a marvelous time. During the summer of 1894 Clara was even permitted
to go off by herself to Fleulen in Switzerland. This is most surprising, in view of her parents' Victorian sense of propriety.
They had hoped she would live in a respectable peasant home
and did not like at all the idea of her staying in a public hotel.
Perhaps she was amused at her father's admonition not to sit out
on her balcony unless it was perfectly private—"not under fire
of curious eyes." Above all, he warned her, she must "keep on
the safe side & out of range of foreign criticism & remark."[49]
We can guess that he was actually more concerned for Clara's
safety than for her reputation, but that he did not wish to embar-
rass or alarm her. She was barely twenty.

During the summers the Clemens party, perhaps minus a
daughter or two, moved freely around Bavaria, Switzerland, and
finally France. Rouen attracted them, as did the French resorts
of Étretat, in the north, and Bourboule-les-Bains, in the south.
Then, most curiously, in view of their unhappy experiences of
1879, they decided to spend the winter of 1894–95 in Paris.

But no place interested Mark Twain enough to stir him to write about it. Europe was fast becoming too much of a familiar second home to him.

He was not, however, becoming reconciled to France. The French critic Paul Bourget helped see to that. Bourget impressed Mark Twain as a nasty sort of Gallic Matthew Arnold, sniping at American society in general and at American women in particular. Mark Twain took special exception to Bourget's assertion that the United States had adopted "pell-mell all the best & worst" of French civilization. In characteristic rage Mark Twain composed a forty-seven-page rebuttal entitled "Have We Appropriated France's Civilization?" Item by item he showed that it was a matter of historical fact that France had learned her most valuable lessons from the United States—religious and political freedom, equality before the law, mercy for the petty transgressor, and almost everything related to science and to the welfare of the common man. Even the English, he said, had contributed more to civilization than had the French. He listed thirty-three English contributions and only twelve French, including the guillotine. Then he got sidetracked into making lists for Italy, Spain, Germany, Russia, China, and Turkey. In the midst of these lists his excitement dissipated. He never published the paper.[50]

A portion of this material Mark Twain did use in a paper which he published in the *North American Review,* January, 1895. "What Paul Bourget Thinks of Us" scoffed at the Frenchman's effort to manufacture hard and fast principles for explaining *the* American girl, *the* American woman, *the American* lust for sudden wealth. In the first place, said Mark Twain, there must have been a conspiracy in the United States to fill Bourget up with all kinds of extravagant misinformation and "airy inaccuracies." Secondly, Americans were such a mixture of peoples that there was not a single characteristic which could safely be called "American." The yearning to get rich quick, for instance, was equally strong the world over. The Old World simply lacked opportunities for satisfying it. "And if I could furnish an American opportunity to staid Germany," he added, "I think I could wake her up like a house afire."[51]

The Frenchman, said Mark Twain, made the mistake of thinking that it was possible for him to do more than simply photograph the "exteriors" of the United States. No foreigner was qualified to report the "interior" of any nation, its life, its thought, its soul. Knowledge of these things could be acquired only by years and years of unconscious absorption.

> Observation? Of what real value is it? One learns peoples through the heart, not the eyes or the intellect.
> There is only one expert who is qualified to examine the souls and the life of a people and make a valuable report—the native novelist.[52]

The essay then branched out into Mark Twain's customary indictment of French marriages and morals. Bourget, criticizing Americans as upstarts yearning for roots, had remarked that whenever an American got bored, he could always try to find out who his grandfather was. Mark Twain replied with the barb that whenever a Frenchman got bored, he could always set out to discover who his father was.

A second French critic replied to Mark Twain in the same periodical, but the reply was another red flag to a bull. Mark Twain wrote a sarcastic "Little Note to Paul Bourget," pretending to believe that Bourget was responsible for the reply, too. The periodical did not print Mark Twain's second paper, perhaps because he was not doing well in the exchange. Certain it is that the Frenchmen were showing more reasonableness than Mark Twain. They were even employing the very same argument which Mark Twain himself had featured in his first travel book and many times since then. France, said this argument, could teach America some of the "higher pursuits of life":

She can teach her, not perhaps how to work, but how to rest, how to live, how to be happy. She can teach her that the aim of life is not money-making, but that money-making is only a means to obtain an end.[53]

Mark Twain found it impossible to answer this argument. All he could say was that these lessons referred to intangible things not subject to measurement and therefore not provable. Philistine though he still was in many ways, he could hardly contend that these lessons were not important. He just knew from experience that America was the place for him and that France was not. On his final business trip to the States he wrote to Livy, "I can't describe to you how poor & empty & offensive France is, compared to America—in my eyes. The minute I strike America I seem to wake out of an odious dream."[54]

Two months later he brought the entire family back to the States, in the latter part of May, 1895. It was not the end of the odious dream, however; it was only an interruption. At the farm in Elmira, Mark Twain spent the next two months preparing lectures and readings to be given clear across the continent and on around the world. He dreaded the prospect. He was almost sixty now, carbuncles were torturing him, and he was sick to death of travel. Pride and honor, however—plus the strong urging by Livy—demanded that he pay off those company debts. So he resolved to talk himself hoarse throughout the British Empire and—this time, for sure—to write that third travel book.

After lecturing his way west on a zigzag route which took him sometimes into Canada, Mark Twain sailed from Vancouver on August 23, 1895. Livy and Clara accompanied him, for he could not bear the prospect of being separated from his whole family for more than a year, and he needed Livy's nursing. In Australia they would later be met by Carlyle Smythe, a tour agent who would travel with them and make all the arrangements. Mark Twain would welcome Smythe's company after four years of traveling with a bevy of females.

Livy, who had been plagued with poor health in Europe, actually thrived in the course of the long journey. Near the end of it she told her husband how glad she was to have traveled so much and seen so many beautiful places: "How many beautiful, beautiful pictures I have in my mind," she said. ". . . they are a great comfort to me."[55]

Mark Twain was not so lucky. In Australia and New Zealand he was twice bedded with carbuncles, and he missed a great deal of sight-seeing in Ceylon and India because of coughs and colds. Whenever possible he got up and lectured. He did manage to get the material needed for his travel book, but it was not much fun for him, except when he was actually on the platform. This he never ceased to love.

The book, *Following the Equator* (1897), was written in blood and tears. Mark Twain's eldest daughter Susy died unexpectedly before any of them could get back to America. Although the outside aspect of the book had to be cheerful, he confessed, its secret substance was made all of bitterness and rebellion. Furthermore, this was the first time he had written a book without the relief now and then of shifting to other work. He would rather go hang himself than have to do the same thing again. As he put it to Howells:

> I wrote my last travel book—in hell; but I let on, the best I could, that it was an excursion through heaven. Some day I will read it, and if its lying cheerfulness fools me, then I shall believe it fooled the reader. How I did loathe that journey around the world!—except the sea-part and India.[56]

In spite of his best effort, *Following the Equator* is graver and gentler than his first two travel books. It is also less personal. There is almost nothing about the lectures, about the constant round of teas, dinners, receptions, and balls, or about day-to-day activities. In place of the personal anecdote, he now provided an unusual amount of historical background, description, and gen-

eral information. Never had he had such long stretches of leisure
at sea—leisure in which to read up on where he was going. He
marked passages and whole sections of books from which he
wanted to quote. He wrote reminders to himself to cite so-and-so's
books about island life and to draw from so-and-so for information about the Trappists. More than ever he was becoming
a researcher, depending less and less on his unaided observations.
He wanted, it seems, to furnish the reader with something more
solid and valuable this time. Also something the reader could
count on. "Quote all sorts of authors," he told himself, "to back
up any doubtful statement about India."[57]

He took this advice. Entire chapters of *Following the Equator*
are little more than long sections lifted from a book of history
or from someone's study of strange customs. This was a time-
saver, too. Later he discovered that much of this secondary material would not be needed at all. With the aid of Chatto, his
London publisher, therefore, he "ripped out a raft of reprint
matter . . . It improves the book to leave it out."[58] The resulting
volume, as Paine has well described it, is the "thoughtful, con-
templative observation and philosophizing of the soul-weary,
world-weary pilgrim who has by no means lost interest, but only
his eager first enthusiasm."[59]

Mark Twain's introduction to the East began in Victoria, B.C.,
where their hotel was staffed with porters and elevator boys from
Japan. In their politeness and intelligence he found them quite
similar to the Chinese, whom he had admired years before in
California.

Seven days after sailing, Mark Twain felt his heart pound to
see Diamond Head in the sunset. For twenty-nine years, he said,
Hawaii had represented to him a paradise he had longed to
visit once more, particularly now that its "little monarchy sarcasm" had given way to a flourishing republic. The Islands looked
so reposeful and unworldly in the sunset that he yearned to go
ashore and never leave. What a heartbreaking irony that no one

was permitted to land! Cholera had broken out on the Islands. Mark Twain could only gaze with sadness from the deck of the "Warrimoo," while hundreds of Islanders gazed back at the man they had bought tickets to hear.

Although he never got to observe this island republic, Mark Twain was puzzled to know what had caused the downfall of the monarchy, which, in his day, had been so liberal and democratic. He decided that King Liholiho's mistake was in trying to be a reformer:

> This is mixing fire and gunpowder together. A king has no business with reforming. His best policy is to keep things as they are; and if he can't do that, he ought to try to make them worse than they are. . . . Will it be believed that the first thing he did was to destroy his Established Church, root and branch? He did indeed do that. To state the case figuratively, he was a prosperous sailor who burnt his ship and took to a raft. This Church was a horrid thing . . . It was the best friend a king could have, and the most dependable.[60]

The "Warrimoo" next put in at the Fiji Islands, where Mark Twain was immediately charmed by the handsome, clean-limbed natives. He also felt a special compassion for them. In spite of their obvious intelligence and their desire to rule themselves, they had been swallowed up by the British Empire. The British Commissioner had tried to pass off the conquest as just a sort of hermit-crab formality, but King Thakombau wisely observed, " 'Yes, but with this difference—the crab moves into an unoccupied shell, but mine isn't.' "[61] From this moment on, for many years, Mark Twain was to give a great deal of serious thought to the entire question of Christian colonization and imperialism.

On September 16, 1895, the Clemenses reached Australia. Spring was just beginning, and Mark Twain's welcome was even warmer than the weather. The colonials, he discovered, seemed more democratic and vivacious than the English, with little of their stiffness or reserve. From the very start they took to him, and he took to them. In Sydney for nine days, Mark Twain gave four lectures to houses which set his mind at rest regarding the success of the tour. The welcome which an American lecturer gets from a British colonial audience, he reported, "is a thing which will move him to his deepest deeps, and veil his sight and break his voice."[62]

This was the start of what turned into almost a royal progress through the British Empire. Packed houses and ovations, gorgeous entertainments for his family, honors both public and private—these were the custom from the day they landed in Sydney until the day, ten months later, they sailed from Cape Town, South Africa. And after four years on the continent of Europe, it was a treat for them to travel among people who spoke their native language—almost. The tour convinced Mark Twain of a fact which dominated his international thought for the rest of his life: "that the names England, America, India, Canada, Australasia, are but geographical expressions; that they but indicate the several homesteads of one great family—the great English-speaking family."[63]

Mark Twain thought Sydney to be every bit as fine as its citizens. Blessed with a magnificent situation, it was one of those rare cities which actually enhanced—not marred—its natural setting. What he called the "go-ahead spirit" of the place—skyscrapers, fast elevators—also impressed him. And the buildings, in their use of harmonious materials, were far more beautiful to him than the massive, coarse buildings of Europe.

He also praised the liberality with which Australians spent money on such public works as legislative buildings, town halls, hospitals, museums, libraries, art galleries, asylums, gardens, parks, and "pleasure grounds." This liberality, he said, was truly wonderful. It had no equal in America and would be hard to match in any country.

Carbuncle Number Two made it advisable for Mark Twain to avoid the heat of Queensland and to proceed, instead, directly to

Melbourne. The old connoisseur of railroads now got his first
taste of Australian trains. He had a fine new sleeping car, but
everything else he found to be "continental" and troublesome.
"Any detail of railroading that is not troublesome cannot honorably be described as continental."[64] When he was routed out of
bed at the border to change trains by lantern-light, he wondered
what paralysis of intellect was responsible for using tracks of different gauges in New South Wales and Victoria. He was not
amused. The trouble might lie, he thought, in the fact that the
railroad was a government monopoly. At any rate, he noted in his
journal: "The railroad is the only thoroughly European thing
here . . . slow trains, no drinking-water, no sanitary arrangements,
every conceivable inconvenience; an utterly insane system—the
jackass system."[65]

As usual, these notebook observations were more critical than
those he wrote for publication, and they were probably more
honest. Privately, Mark Twain spoke with feeling about the rats
and cockroaches and Ballarat flies of Australasia, but his book is
notable for their absence. Most remarkable of all, perhaps, is the
sanitary picture of an India without its extraordinary vermin,
filth, and squalor, its diseased beggars and swarms of mangy
beasts. His wife, who edited the manuscript, had much to do with
this, asking him, for example, to delete the cockroaches and other
things, which she labeled "*too* vulgar."[66] More important than
Livy's editing, however, was Mark Twain's realization that in
this particular book he was writing both *of* and *for* many of the
same people. And, as in England in the seventies, he was more of
a guest than a tourist. It would be tactful to ignore mentioning
the snake his daughter stepped on in her room and the large cock-
roach which walked across his face in bed. Clara's report of the
trip is much harsher than her father's.[67]

The broad-gauge and narrow-gauge railroads finally got Mark
Twain to Melbourne on September 26. He presented five readings here, even though his carbuncle kept him in bed most of the

two weeks he spent in the city. It also prevented his getting out into rural Victoria, as he wished to do. Melbourne was a stately, modern city, he said, but did not furnish him with anything to write about:

> The things which interest us when we travel are, first, the people; next, the novelties; and finally the history of the places and countries visited. Novelties are rare in cities which represent the most advanced civilization of the modern day. When one is familiar with such cities in the other parts of the world he is in effect familiar with the cities of Australasia.[68]

As it was, the only real "speciality" he could discover in the Victoria capital was horse racing. Melbourne was the Mecca of the cult, and the Melbourne Cup was the one, supreme Australasian National Day. The reader shares Mark Twain's regret that his visit did not include this great holiday. It would have made marvelous copy for his book, especially since he was resolved, he told the newspapers, to write only about his outward impressions of the countries he visited. In this he was true to the principle stated in his Bourget articles. He had no patience, he said, with globe-trotters who rattled through a country on a three-weeks' tour, then wrote a whole book about it "'out of their colossal incapacity for the job.'"[69]

On October 11 the party traveled on to Adelaide, where Mark Twain gave four readings in five days. The last two weeks of October were spent in working their way back to Melbourne, with lecture stops for several nights in Horsham, Stawell, Ballarat, Maryborough, Bendigo, and Geelong. These weeks are scarcely mentioned either in his book or in his journals, save for comments on the strange flora and fauna. The countryside he found to be singularly "unpretty."

Rather bored with his travels, Mark Twain then decided to make use of the history of Australia. This led him directly to the early function of Australia as a penal colony and thence to the subject of modern imperialistic methods. On these subjects it was impossible for him to keep his temper. Temporarily his old anger against England flared up again. Most of the convicts who had been exiled to Australia and brutally mistreated there, he said, were probably not noticeably worse than the average person left at home. Again he denounced England's old penal code. A nation which could look on unmoved, he said, while a freezing, starving woman was hanged for stealing some bacon or rags could not be called civilized. The same was true of a nation which snatched men and boys from their families for trifling offenses and sent them to the other side of the globe for many long years.

Equally cruel was England's extermination of the natives who occupied this subcontinent jail, which later became a colony. Few things in history made Mark Twain as heartsick as the account of the British plantation owner who wiped out a whole tribe of peaceful natives by inviting them to a banquet of Christmas pudding sweetened with sugar and arsenic. By means of robbery, murder, whiskey, humiliation, and grinding poverty, said Mark Twain, the British and French were taking over the Pacific Islands. "There are many humorous things in the world," he added wryly, "among them the white man's notion that he is less savage than the other savages."[70]

On November 1, while en route to New Zealand, where they would spend six weeks, the Clemens party paused briefly in Tasmania. Resting on low hills that sloped to the harbor, the town of Hobart seemed remarkably attractive to Mark Twain. In some detail he described the opulence and freshness of the entire region, giving special attention to the tidiness of Hobart, the "neatest town that the sun shines on." It was more like a "Junior England," he said, than any place he had ever seen.

But Mark Twain could not forget that this Junior England had been created only at the cost of killing or exiling all the Tasmanian natives. Many had been sent under guard to neighboring islands, where they pined away and died, "homesick on their alien crags."

> The Whites always mean well when they take human fish out of the ocean and try to make them dry and warm and happy and comfortable in a chicken-coop; but the kindest-hearted white man can always be depended on to prove himself inadequate when he deals with savages.[71]

In Mark Twain's opinion the Tasmanian blacks were a wonderful people who ought not to have been wasted. They should have been crossed with the whites, he believed: "It would have improved the Whites and done the Natives no harm."[72] The British looked on the natives as mere fanatics, and this enraged Mark Twain. "Patriotism is Patriotism," he cried. "Calling it Fanaticism cannot degrade it; nothing can degrade it . . ."[73]

Among the colonials, however, there was springing up a new kind of patriotism of which Mark Twain did not approve. This was represented by a political party which wanted Australasia to break loose from the British Empire. To Mark Twain this made no sense, because England never used her veto power anyway and could not even appoint a governor to whom the colonies objected. "Can't see," he noted, "that the British Gov't has any more authority here than she has over the constellations."[74]

Not only was Australasia already free in fact, but also it seemed to him to be the "modern heaven—it is bossed absolutely by workingmen."[75] As for the desire to break from the British Empire: "Australasia governs herself wholly—there is no interference; and her commerce and manufactures are not oppressed in any way. If our case had been the same, we should not have gone out when we did."[76]

It might be noted that diplomatic relations between England and the United States were seriously strained in 1895 and 1896. The Monroe Doctrine was challenged by England's activity in

Venezuela and British Guiana. Time and again in his book Mark
Twain referred to the "war-talk" and "war-flurry" of politicians.
The newspapers and the public, however, said Mark Twain, had
the good sense to realize that the English-speaking peoples might
dominate the earth in a hundred years, if they did not start fighting one another.

His six weeks in New Zealand did not interest Mark Twain
to any degree. His schedule took the family up the east coast of
South Island to the main cities of Dunedin, Oamaru, Christ-
church, and Nelson, then across to North Island to Auckland,
Gisborne, Napier, Hawera, New Plymouth, and Wellington. At
Gisborne extremely rough seas kept the family on board. Speaking engagements and ill health—Carbuncle Number Three—prevented him from sight-seeing among the mighty glaciers of New
Zealand and among the beautiful lakes, fiords, waterfalls, and
snowy grandeurs. This he regretted, but business came first. He
could not even get up into Rotorua to see the hot lakes and geysers, and he had to cancel his Napier reading on doctor's orders.
As a result, his few pages on New Zealand are drier and more
diary-like than any of his other travel writings. This does not
mean that he disliked New Zealand. On the contrary, he found
it to be a highly progressive country filled with friendly people.
Much of it had the beauty of a Junior England, he said, but he
wished the inhabitants might have been less provincially vain
of everything colonial and less jealous both of neighboring towns
and of Australia.

Several things in New Zealand impressed him particularly,
including the comfortable, efficient trains, though not the dirty,
overcrowded boats. He was awed by the large amount of public
money expended to acquire fine works of art for the local museums and galleries. But most of all was he pleased with the
enlightened attitude toward women. New Zealand law, he said,
specified that the word "person" invariably included women. To
Mark Twain this was a giant step forward, because, he was con-

vinced, "no civilization can be perfect until exact equality between man and woman is included."[77]

When he finally sailed from New Zealand on December 13, Mark Twain was ready for a rest. "Summer seas and a good ship—" he wrote, "life has nothing better."[78] Refreshed by "three days of paradise," he filled several more engagements around Sydney before embarking on the "Oceana" on December 23. On its voyage west the ship put in at Melbourne and Adelaide, where he lectured again. Then, finally, came the long, soul-refreshing voyage across the Indian Ocean. While on shipboard only one bit of news saddened him. He noted:

> Within this week Siam has acknowledged herself to be, in effect, a French province. A pity. It is plain that all savage & semi-civilized countries are going to be grabbed—I wish England might be the grabber, not France. India is better off for being grabbed by England.[79]

It seems that his mind was already made up about the British *raj* in India. He had read a great deal about India, of course, and had talked about it eagerly with Rudyard Kipling. It was the country he was looking forward to most excitedly. He had warned Kipling:

> I shall arrive next January, and you must be ready. I shall come riding my Ayah, with his tusks adorned with silver bells and ribbons, and escorted by a troop of native Howdahs, richly clad and mounted upon a herd of wild bungalows, and you must be on hand with a few bottles of ghee, for I shall be thirsty.[80]

India did not disappoint him. His profits were cut, because the halls were generally too small for the crowds who wished to hear him, but this did not trouble him greatly. He was too enthralled by the exotic sights and sounds and smells—authentic novelties at last! "INDIA THE MARVELOUS," he printed in large letters in his notebook. From the moment he went ashore in Ceylon, on January 13, 1896, until he sailed from Calcutta, on March 28, his

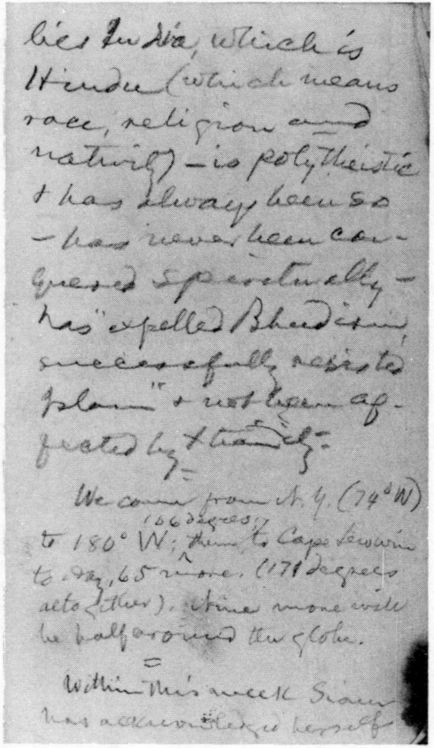
lies India, which is Hindu (which means race, religion and nativity) — is polytheistic & has always been so — has never been conquered spiritually — has "expelled Buddhism, successfully resisted Islam" & not been affected by Christianity.

=

We came from N.Y. (74° W) to 180° W; then to Cape Comorin to day, 65 more. (166 degrees; 171 degrees altogether). Nine more will be half around the globe.

=

Within this week Siam has acknowledged herself

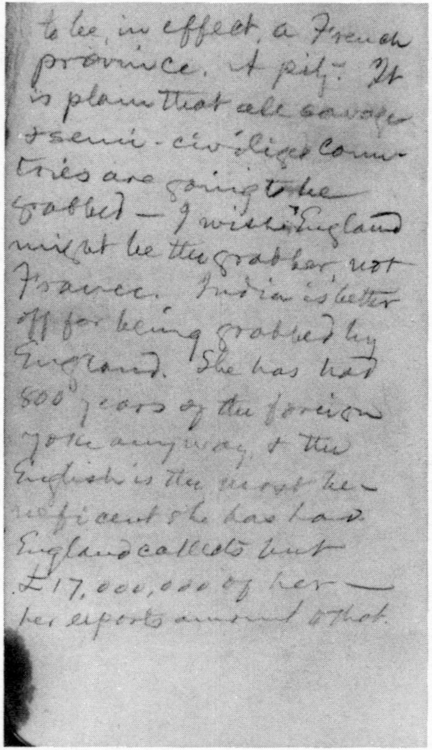
to be, in effect, a French province. A pity. It is plain that all savage & semi-civilized countries are going to be grabbed — I wish England might be the grabber, not France. India is better off for being grabbed by England. She has had 800 years of the foreign yoke anyway, & the English is the most beneficent she has had. England collects but £17,000,000 of her — her exports amount to that.

Mark Twain's notebook entry, January 4, 1896.

emotions reeled under the impact of this land of marvels. Although he spent a month longer in Australasia than in Ceylon and India, his book spent less time on it. As for South Africa, where he stayed just as long as in India—seventy-two days—he could work up only seventy-eight pages on that. India? Two hundred and ninety-four pages, and he could have written about it forever.

Even though Mark Twain spent only a day and a night in Colombo, it was long enough for him to taste the Oriental flavor of the city. Years before he had sampled what he called a "tempered Orient" in the Near East, but "Ceylon was Oriental in the last measure of completeness—utterly Oriental; also utterly tropical . . . "[81] Nothing was missing. The costumes were right, he said, the juggler was there with his basket of snakes and his mongoose, the flowers were ones found only in books at home, and out in the jungle were the proper beasts of prey and the wild elephant and the monkey. His imagination was catching fire.

Mark Twain's first ride in a jinrikisha, however, was not pleasing. After half an hour his small coolie grew visibly tired. This ended the fun for Mark Twain. Months later in South Africa his reaction was quite different. There he saw black Zulus so overflowing with strength that they laughed as they ran. It was a pleasure, not a pain, he said, to see these Zulus snatch a ricksha along.

On the day the Clemens party left Ceylon, word reached them of Dr. Jameson's defeat by the Boers in South Africa. Apparently there would be more excitement on that last leg of the journey than they had bargained for.

Six days on a "poor old ship" brought them finally to the mainland of India: *"January 20. Bombay!* A bewitching place— a bewildering place, an enchanting place—the Arabian Nights come again!"[82] Clara recalled that her father was like a young boy in his enthusiasm; he kept repeating, " 'This wonderful land, this marvelous land! There can be no other like it.' "[83] Writing a year later, Mark Twain said that the delirium of those

days in Bombay had still not left him and he hoped it never
would:

> When I think of Bombay now, at this distance of time, I seem
> to have a kaleidoscope at my eye; and I hear the clash of the
> glass bits as the splendid figures change, and fall apart, and
> flash into new forms, figure after figure, and with each new form
> I feel my skin crinkle and my nerve-web tingle with a new thrill
> of wonder and delight.[84]

They were ten days in Bombay. Because of bronchitis, Mark
Twain was confined to his room for the first five or six of them.
Livy and Clara did his sight-seeing for him—that is, such sight-
seeing as he could not do from his window and from his large
balcony over the street. The leading British and Indian inhabitants rivaled one another in their hospitality. Prince Kumar of
Politana permitted the visitors a rare sample of domestic life and
Oriental generosity, showering them with beautiful gifts. And
Lord Sandhurst, Governor of Bombay, entertained them at Government House on Malabar Point. Mark Twain wrote to his best
friend, "All over India the English—well, you will never know
how good and fine they are till you see them."[85]

It is significant that Mark Twain's India notebooks do not comment about England's role in that great subcontinent. Not until
he was forced to face colonial conquest in South Africa did he
speak of the Indian political situation. He had praised the laissez-
faire policy of Great Britain in Australasia, but there the relatively few natives had been killed or driven off. In India the case
was different. Here the millions of natives were actually living
among, and taking orders from, a few thousand conquerors. The
Indians had no legal powers of their own.

The drama of the situation appealed to Mark Twain. He seems
to have envisioned Warren Hastings, back in the previous century,
as a sort of modern Messiah bringing enlightened government
to a benighted people. Hastings had done many unprincipled
things, as Mark Twain well knew. But were they not justified by

the final result? Hastings had attached India firmly to the British Empire, "and that was the best service that was ever done to the Indians themselves, those wretched heirs of a hundred centuries of pitiless oppression and abuse."[86]

The *Calcutta Englishman* (unbiased?) of February 8, 1896, quoted Mark Twain as saying that the educational and industrial activity set in motion all over India and the security and prosperity visible everywhere convinced him that British rule was the best for India, whether the Hindus and Muslims liked it or not. Mark Twain, the report continued, regarded the English as the strongest race in the world physically and intellectually. Above all, they were a merciful people, the best kind for colonizing the globe.

As he moved across this wonder-filled land for two and a half months, Mark Twain became more and more impressed with the character of the men who were governing it. These were the men among whom he lived during this period. Nothing he heard or saw seems to have touched his anti-imperialistic nerve, which would become unbearably sensitive within the next five years:

> Indeed, if monuments were always given in India for high achievements, duty strictly performed, and smirchless records, the landscape would be monotonous with them. The handful of English in India govern the Indian myriads with apparent ease, and without noticeable friction, through tact, training, and distinguished administrative ability, reinforced by just and liberal laws—and by keeping their word to the native whenever they give it.[87]

This whole subject of colonialism, however, did not interest Mark Twain at that time one-tenth as much as did the Indian people, with their singular appearance, customs, and traditions. Even the land itself, although most of it was a monotony of dust-colored flats and scattered mud villages, had for him much the same enchantment he had once found in the barren hills of Palestine. The enchantment came from the haunting sense of the millions and millions of people who had flourished and died there, age after age: "it is this sense that gives to this forlorn, uncomely land power to speak to the spirit and make friends with it; to speak to it with a voice bitter with satire, but eloquent with melancholy."[88]

Even the horrifying old institutions of Thuggee and Suttee, already outlawed, helped spiritualize the ugliness of India for Mark Twain and to veil it with a macabre charm. With fascination he perused official reports of Thuggee, the cult of professional assassins, and copied many of their accounts and statistics into his twenty-five-page report. He explained the religious nature of Thuggee: how the Thugs robbed their victims but offered the dead bodies to their gods. He described the methods of strangulation, the assembling of the gangs, the limited season for their activities. He came to the conclusion that the main attractions of Thuggee were three: partly, piety; in larger part, gain; and perhaps chiefly, sport. This notion of hunting human quarry for sport was so novel to Mark Twain that he pursued it into a second chapter on Thuggee and its psychological bases.

It was more difficult for him to appreciate the motivation behind Suttee, the religious practice which involved widows' throwing themselves upon their husbands' funeral pyres in order to cremate themselves alive. Although he could not stomach the grisly act, Mark Twain could envision it better than Thuggee, because the Hindus' burning ghats were still operating in Benares. From an awning-shaded boat on the sacred Ganges River he watched the grim ritual of cremation, as stokers moved about poking the fires and adding fuel. He watched them hoist skulls and bones into the air, then slam them down and batter them to make them burn better. The sight, he said, was hard to bear.

The surrounding activity was equally revolting. Pilgrims bathed in the river and drank the holy water, he said, while charred bits of bodies floated by and while great sewers spewed their foul gush into the river, making it turbid and murky. He

was compelled, however, to admire the extraordinary piety of the
pilgrims and their faith in the purifying magic of the Ganges.
Indeed, the intense spirituality of all classes and ages of people
amazed him. He frankly envied both the Hindus and the Muslims
their religious faith. It must be largely responsible, he thought,
for the gentleness and basic goodness of Indian character. The
Indians spent hours kneeling in prayer, he said, while Americans
were robbing and murdering. He made the notation:

> These nations are religious countries, Xian countries are not. In
> these countries the *whole* people are religious;—profoundly, sin-
> cerely, heartily religious in Xian ones it is 1 in the 10 in
> Germany, 1 in 15 in Eng; 1 in 20 Amer.; 1 in 90 in France, &
> *that* a woman.[89]

The Holy City of Benares interested Mark Twain more than
any other place in India. He described it at length—its history,
fame, topography, temples, suburbs, and the masses which
thronged its streets. Everything was strange, utterly unlike the
whole of his previous experience. In this "religious Vesuvius,"
he said, he felt very much as an Oriental must feel when he is
dropped into the middle of London. Benares may have reminded
him of Jerusalem, but he did not say so. The whole region, he
said, seemed to ache with age and penury. The city itself was a
mass of buildings cloven with cracks which stood for streets; this
he could observe from atop the ancient 147-foot minaret, which
he climbed for the view.

> Yes, the city of Benares is in effect just a big church, a religious
> hive, whose every cell is a temple, a shrine, or a mosque, and
> whose every conceivable earthly and heavenly good is procurable
> under one roof, so to speak—a sort of Army and Navy Stores,—
> theologically stocked.[90]

His high regard for the religious atmosphere of India and for
the goodness of Indian character did nothing to improve his outlook on Christian missions overseas. His chief objection to the

"missionary trade," as he called it, was that its theological efforts were devoted to making people, especially children, traitors to the religion of their parents. Some natives, he learned, pretended to be Christian converts in order to gain material benefits from the white man. These "rice-Christians" were lazy and incompetent, no credit to the missionary effort. "Traitors to religion are of the same stuff as other traitors," he noted, "the poorest material in camp."[91]

If Mark Twain had no use for those missionaries whose goal it was "to make religious deserters"—and he thought they would have a pretty thin time of it among the hundreds of millions in the Orient—he still admired those who applied themselves to what he considered practical matters. Such were the New Guinea missionaries, who had weaned a whole tribe from its appetite for murder, pillage, piracy, and cannibalism. And such were the Trappist monks, who were training the South African natives in the monastery fields, shops, and schoolrooms. "That is a tangible piece of work," he explained, "one can see it with his eyes, feel it with his hands, so to speak. It is a distinct addition to the world's betterment."[92]

Mark Twain was especially pleased to find branches of the Salvation Army all over South Africa when he got there. "They are the missionaries for me," he exclaimed. "They feed the poor, they employ the idle, & ex prisoner, they reform the drunkard & the wanton."[93] All things considered, the missionary who appealed most favorably to Mark Twain was a sort of down-to-earth Peace Corpsman who ministered to social and material needs and left the soul alone.

In regard to India specifically, he was more amused than disturbed by the strict caste system of the Hindus. For some reason, he viewed it not as an instrument of hereditary power and privilege but rather as an appendage of a unique religion. Castes, he explained, were different in essence from mere social classes and titled distinctions. They bore an ingrained spiritual significance.

He told a reporter that this whole subject was a great mystery to him, a fascinating mystery. Anything more uncongenial to the Western mind, he said, could not be imagined. It is puzzling that Mark Twain did not write at least a full chapter on the caste system, especially since such a chapter would have led naturally to one of his favorite topics: theology. He could hardly help being intrigued, one would imagine, by the Hindu belief in the transmigration of souls and its ramifications, such as the sacredness of all animal life, especially cows and monkeys. It is also surprising that he did not describe one or two of the fantastic Hindu temples, so different from the cathedrals he enjoyed describing in Europe.

Something, of course, had to be left out of his book. In the Indian chapters he resorted less often than usual to anecdotes and irrelevancies. There was no need for padding. Still, he included about twenty-five pages concerning stories about Augustin Daly and P. T. Barnum, plus a chapter on comic misuses of the English language. The Australasia chapters made room for some forty pages of nontravel matter. To deprive Mark Twain of his freedom to ramble would be to rob him of one of his charms. In this particular case, however, he might have been wise to replace the airy charm of his digressions with the more substantial charms of India.

One thing in India it was impossible for any traveler to ignore: the Taj Mahal. Here, in a curious performance, Mark Twain fell back upon the descriptions and impressions written by others. In this way he worked in facts and figures and also provided his readers with the glowing words they expected. He acknowledged that these words were all true, and yet, in his own case, the famed mausoleum did not come up to expectations: "The Taj is a disappointment though people are ashamed to confess it. God will be a disappointment to most of us . . . St. Peter's, Vesuvius, Heaven, Hell, everything that is much described is bound to be a disappointment at first experience."[94]

He admitted that he was an "impressionist" reader and that his imagination had become overheated by drinking too much "pestilential literary hot Scotch" about the Taj Mahal. He would have to visit it fifteen times, he thought, to let his mind get rid of the imagined tomb and substitute for it the Taj of fact. His reason convinced him that the Taj was truly man's supreme achievement in the domain of the superb and the beautiful, but his other faculties were unable to appreciate the actual structure. "My Taj had been built by excitable literary people," he said; "it was solidly lodged in my head, and I could not blast it out."[95]

Of all the peoples of India, the Parsees impressed Mark Twain as being the most intelligent and up-to-date. These were the descendants of Zoroastrian tribes which settled around Bombay centuries ago, after being driven out of Persia. Although there were only about ninety thousand of them, they made up in importance what they lacked in numbers. They were highly educated, enterprising, progressive, well-to-do, and they kept an open purse, said Mark Twain, "for all great and good objects." "They are a political force, and a valued support to the government. They have a pure and lofty religion, and they preserve it in its integrity and order their lives by it."[96]

As might be expected, Mark Twain enjoyed many privileges denied to the ordinary traveler. In addition to the whirl of entertainments, he was often invited to attend special Indian ceremonies. These he enjoyed tremendously, for they were unique and picturesque. The Parsee burial at the Towers of Silence struck him as the perfection of reverence and sanitation, especially when compared with the Hindu burning ghats on the Ganges. After a month, when the bodies had been picked clean by vultures and the skeletons dried in the flaming sun, the bones were dropped with tongs into great wells with underground drains and charcoal filters. In the book of the Panchayet, the Parsee council, he wrote:

> One marvels to see here a perfect system for the protection of the living from the contagion derivable from the dead—I mean one marvels to see this proof that modern science is behind the ancients in this so important matter. S. L. Clemens.[97]

Mark Twain was guest also at a native bungalow to witness a ceremony in which Thakur Saheb Mansinghji, one of the Jain princes, was honored for having been knighted by Queen Victoria. The color and radiance of the native costumes made him more disgusted than ever with the drabness of Western clothes. At the ceremony he was also struck by the loveliness of the native complexions. Nearly all black and brown skins were beautiful, Mark Twain said, whereas a beautiful white skin was rare. He felt sorry for his own race, whose skin had no sort of chance against "that rich and perfect tint" of the Indian.[98]

He was also privileged to attend a Hindu betrothal ceremony one night in Bombay. The streets, a tumult of people and animals by day, were silent at midnight, but not vacant. Everywhere hundreds and hundreds of natives, tightly wrapped in blankets, lay asleep on the ground. There was scarcely room for the procession to drive between them in the dim narrow lanes of the native quarter. And every now and then a swarm of rats would scuttle across in front of the horses, carrying the plague which was soon to break out. Arriving at the bride's house—the groom entertained for a week at his own house—the procession was met with singing and dancing by high-priced nautch-girls, and there was also a band of strange instruments. Mark Twain withdrew at two o'clock in the morning. "Both of the children were a little elderly," he observed, "as brides and grooms go, in India— twelve; they ought to have been married a year or two sooner; still to a stranger twelve seems quite young enough."[99]

As Mark Twain was leaving these festivities, a giant Hindu brought him an invitation from the Gaikwar of Baroda to visit him and to give a lecture in his state. Mark Twain was happy to accept. The 250-mile trip was made in a luxurious railroad compartment, which he called the finest in the world for comfort and privacy. This put him in a proper mood to enjoy a delightful day in Baroda, an ancient princedom which was long celebrated for its wealth and its barbaric pomp.

His family was met at the station at 7:00 A.M. by swarms of

officials and servants, who took them to breakfast and escorted
them around for the rest of the day. From the comfort and safety
of a state carriage he looked down upon scenes which he often
found less than agreeable on those occasions when he was on foot.
In the narrow lanes near-naked natives squatted at their work,
"and then the swarm of ragged and noisy humanity under the
horses' feet and everywhere, and the pervading reek and fume
and smell! It was all wonderful and delightful."[100]

Baroda itself, crumbly and moldering, he thought "inde-
scribably quaint." His eyes were drawn to the intricately carved
house-fronts. Some of these massive structures were so battered
and worn and seemingly so burdened with the weight of age that
he got the feeling that they must have been a part of the original
Creation.

It was a mistake, however, to make him lecture that afternoon
in one of these antiques, the vast old hall where the durbars were
held. (The Maharani and two court ladies listened from behind
a screen.) The echoes were bad. As a sight the Durbar Palace was
fine, but it was hardly functional. Mark Twain liked his sights
to convey the dusky, romantic aura of antiquity, but he liked
functional things to be modern, comfortable, and efficient. It was
as a sight that he denounced the newly constructed palace of the
Gaikwar, because it was an unhappy mixture of modern American and European: "It is wholly foreign to India, and impudent
and out of place. The architect has escaped. This comes of over-
doing the suppression of the Thugs; they had their merits."[101]

It will be noticed that Mark Twain applied to India standards
which were quite different from those he applied to the rest of
the world, or to most of it. The reason is not hard to find. Europe,
for example, seemed to him a residence, a place to live. India, on
the other hand, was an immense and extraordinary museum to be
marveled at as one passed through. A Morris chair was a fine
thing for the home, but among the antiques of a museum it was
nothing but a crude monstrosity.

Before leaving the museum of Baroda, Mark Twain had the pleasure of watching the caravans of stately camels plod by and also the more dubious pleasure of taking a ride on one of the Gaikwar's elephants. Despite his trepidation, he was able to admire the costly howdahs of silver, gold, and ivory and the rich trappings of the elephants. He also wondered at the patience of the enormous beasts in obeying the prods of the little mahouts high on their necks. To his surprise, the owner of all these marvels, Sayaji Rao III, was an educated gentleman who had been to Europe five times and whose culture was European.

The Clemens party returned to Bombay before taking the long train trip more than eight hundred miles inland to Allahabad. For a full day Mark Twain watched mud villages drift by. Most of his printed observations upon rural life in India, however, seem to derive from Major Sleeman's India Service Report of 1839. This fat report, old as it was, served him as a basic source-book, but apparently the good Major had not prepared him for the experience of sleeping in the Indian night-costume, pajamas. Mark Twain had never heard of pajamas before. He hated them. They gave him the suffocating sense, he said, of being in bed with his clothes on. Several hours in them were all he could stand; then he put on his old nightgown and got to sleep.

Mark Twain's description of Allahabad confined itself to the British sector of the city, which was comely and alluring, he said, full of suggestions of comfort, leisure, and serenity. It was typical of areas in which English colonists lived all over the world. The cost of living in the colonies, he pointed out, was absurdly low for the average Englishman. People who had struggled for a livelihood in London or Liverpool could reside comfortably in Bombay, Allahabad, or Calcutta, with a private compound, a coach, and a family of servants. Many Englishmen, understandably, resolved to spend their last years in India or some other colony, where they would be regarded by the natives as people of consequence.

English friends took Mark Twain to the famous fort outside of town, but he showed less interest in the fort than in the throngs of pilgrims along the road. Thousands of them had been plodding along patiently for months from distant parts of India. They were going to a great religious fair just beyond the fort. The crowds were a thrilling, awesome sight to Mark Twain. In India they always were, especially at the railroad stations: "Thought this would all become commonplace in a week; three weeks of it have only enhanced its fascinations. I think I should always like to wait an hour for my train in India."[102]

The trip from Allahabad to Benares took only a few hours. We have noted his excitement in this holiest city of Hinduism. For the Christian tourist no other city in India holds the morbid fascination of this sprawling museum of idols, fakirs, burning ghats, beggars, temples, dusty pilgrims, and swarming sacred animals. Amid the overwhelming sights and sounds and smells, Mark Twain puzzled about the state of mind which reveled in such apparent insanity.

He seized the opportunity, therefore, to meet a genuine, living Hindu god. (In Bombay he had been called upon by a young Muslim deity, supposedly a direct descendant of Muhammad, but seems to have been little impressed by their half-hour chat.) Swami Saraswati proved to be a tall, emaciated man of sixty. By being born again and again into this world through one reincarnation after another, he had changed substance and arrived at a state of perfection. He was no longer part of this world. Several million Hindus worshiped him unquestioningly as a god; this to Mark Twain was the intoxicating thing about touching and talking with the Swami. The thrill came secondhand from millions of believers, just as the thrill of the Taj Mahal came from a thousand fervid writers. "By and by you sober down," mused Mark Twain, "and then you perceive that you have been drunk on the smell of somebody else's cork."[103] But he liked the Swami, and the two men—or rather the man and the god—got along well together. All in all, said Mark Twain, this was a most friendly and pleasant deity. The Swami suggested that they exchange autographs, which they did. Mark Twain gave him a copy of *Huckleberry Finn* in the hope that "it might rest him up a little to mix it in along with his meditations on Brahma, for he looked tired."[104]

The Swami had a pupil who interested Mark Twain intensely, because of the material sacrifices he had made for his faith. This pupil was a man of distinguished capacities and attainments. He was an educated man, a thinker, and a man of former wealth. With a splendid career ahead of him, he had given away his possessions and renounced the world in favor of religion. Mark Twain was unable to revere this man's gods, but the man himself won his reverence, a reverence not lightly given.

After Benares the Clemens party continued to the east coast, where Mark Twain read to packed houses in Calcutta. They dined with the Lieutenant-Governor of Bengal, visited Clive's fort and the museum, watched a review of the garrison, and dutifully did the expected sight-seeing. But the fine, large city seemed prosaic after Benares. Almost any city would have. A brief chapter was all that Mark Twain gave to his week in Calcutta.

The gruesome story of the Black Hole of Calcutta stirred him more than anything the modern city had to offer. No other city in India seemed to be so rich in historical memories, so rich in the evidences of British achievement. Nowhere else in India, said Mark Twain, did he get a more reassuring sense of the splendid administrative abilities of the English. But with its modernity and its colonial social life Calcutta did not seem to be the real India.

On February 14 they departed from Calcutta in an official railroad car, crossed the Ganges by boat, and the next day found themselves leaving behind the steamy Bay of Bengal. "Vegetable geysers" of bamboo lined the horizon as their train slowly climbed through fields of banana trees and past myriad villages. There

was no end to the villages. Dozens were in sight at one time, said
Mark Twain, making an immense city hundreds of miles long.
And always naked men and boys plowing the fields—what a re-
flection on Bavaria, France, and Austria, he exclaimed, where
women did all the hard and dirty jobs! Yet the brutish men of
central Europe, he said, piously chanted the famous hymn about
"India's coral strand" where

> Every prospect pleases,
> And only man is vile.

The last forty miles of the trip to Darjeeling took eight hours
but were continually exciting to Mark Twain. They were now in a
special mountain train. The little canvas-sheltered cars were
luxuriously comfortable yet gave them the sense of being out-
doors. Elephants crossed the tracks as the train climbed higher
and higher through ever thickening jungles. Mark Twain wished
that this leg of the trip could last a week, it was so wild and enchanting.

In Darjeeling he lectured, enjoyed the conviviality of the
Planters' Club (English), and visited the local bazaar. His cold,
it appears, kept him from joining the rest of his party when they
rode off on horseback to Tiger Hill at dawn for a view of Mt.
Everest. Livy went by ricksha. Instead, he contented himself with
gazing at the twenty-eight-thousand-foot peak of Kanchenjunga
from his windows and with watching the swarthy tribes of Ti-
betans who flocked by the hotel. The bazaar itself, he said, was
worth coming up from Calcutta to see, even if there had been no
mountains. And all over the British Empire he was grateful for
the hospitality of the English clubs, because the hotels were not
always as clean and comfortable as they might have been.

The climax of this side trip to Darjeeling was the descent back
to the valley in a little canopied handcar, which had no engine,
a powerful brake, and only six seats. For safety, a police inspector
and two guards preceded them down in another car. Whenever

they felt like it, they all stopped to admire the varied scenery. Halfway down they paused an hour for refreshments at the chief engineer's home. Again they stopped to watch a Tibetan dramatic performance out on the hillside. And all the time they were deep in the midst of trees, flowers, animals, and birds of the most exotic character. Mark Twain was in ecstasies:

> That was the most enjoyable day I have spent in the earth. For rousing, tingling, rapturous pleasure there is no holiday trip that approaches the bird-flight down the Himalayas in a hand-car. It has no fault, no blemish, no lack, except that there are only thirty-five miles of it instead of five hundred.[105]

From this day on, the remainder of India was anti-climactic to Mark Twain. On February 21 his party left Calcutta for a grand swing up through central and northern India, almost to the Afghan frontier and back again. They visited many places renowned for their beauty or their history. During these last five weeks, however, nothing was able to arouse his emotions as they had been aroused by Bombay, Baroda, Benares, and the trip into the Himalayas. Even his notebook entries became relatively meager. India, too, was growing more familiar to him. The thrill of discovery was past.

Following the Equator, as a result, became less personal after this. After composing a rather statistical chapter about the number of natives killed each year by tigers, wolves, leopards, snakes, etc., and the number of these wild creatures slain by the government, Mark Twain got out his books and pamphlets to write an eighteen-page history of the Great Mutiny in Lucknow in 1857. He quoted his sources extensively. A British officer drove him around the city and its environs, following the route of Sir Colin Campbell's rescue forces. Mark Twain viewed the entire city in the light of the Great Mutiny. Modern Lucknow made no apparent impression on him, nor did nearby Cawnpore, to which he gave but a paragraph.

From Cawnpore they went to Agra, home of the Taj Mahal. As we have seen, elsewhere in the book and in his notes Mark Twain expressed disappointment in the Taj, because it had been over-described by so many romantic tourists. But now he wrote from a more conventional point of view:

> We are eager to see any celebrated thing—and we never fail of our reward; just the deep privilege of gazing upon an object which has stirred the enthusiasm or evoked the reverence or affection or admiration of multitudes of our race is a thing which we value. . . . For ever and ever the memory of my distant first glimpse of the Taj will compensate me for creeping around the globe to have that great privilege.[106]

Nevertheless, Mark Twain was glad that he had not read too much about the other marvels of Agra. They came to him as an impressive surprise. The great old mosques, forts, tombs, and other relics from the days of the Muhammadan Emperors filled him with awe at their surpassing grandeur. He knew that now there was nothing vicarious in his wonder and awe. The enthusiasm he felt for them was strictly his own.

Following the Equator hurries much too fast over the final weeks in Lahore, capital of the Punjab and dear to Kipling, Rawalpindi, which was far up near the Afghan border, and Delhi, which had been the capital of the old Moguls. What marvelous tales he might have told of these places! But Rawalpindi he just mentioned by name; of Lahore he wrote one paragraph, about riding an elephant through the crowded streets; and in Delhi he gave only a page to some nonsense about monkeys invading private homes. He had planned to go clear up to Peshawar, only a few miles from the Khyber Pass, but illness upset his schedule, and word came that his ship was sailing earlier than expected. It was in Rawalpindi, therefore, that he gave his final reading.

Only in Jaipur did Mark Twain pause to describe the native scene. Due to his illness, the party remained in Jaipur for the first half of March, and during his recuperation they became more familiar with this fine small city than with any other place in India. Even so, he spent twice as long describing two of his servants as he did describing the city.

Jaipur contained only fourteen Europeans. Enclosed by a turreted wall, it was unlike any other Indian city they saw. It was ruled by an enlightened Maharaja, Sir Sawa Madho Singh, who had introduced such things as an English sanitation system and school program. But the many civic improvements had not damaged the most colorful qualities of India. The roads of Jaipur were always a "streaming flood of brown people clothed in smouchings from the rainbow." And the quaintness of the houses, said Mark Twain, gave to the streets the unreal look of a painting or of a scene in the theater. The illusion was more pronounced than ever during a procession for which the spectators jammed terraces, balconies, rooftops, and every available cranny: "For color, and picturesqueness, and novelty, and outlandishness, and sustained interest and fascination," cried Mark Twain, "it was the most satisfying show I have ever seen, and I suppose I shall not have the privilege of looking upon its like again."[107]

This would have made a far better ending to the Indian portion of the book than did his final chapter, on the Indians' humorous misuse of the English language. To Mark Twain this was the sole country endowed with imperishable interest for all foreigners. India, he said, was the one land which, for the traveler, was worth more than all the rest of the globe combined. Nothing had been left undone by man or nature, he believed, to make India the most extraordinary place on earth:

> There is only one India! It is the only country that has a monopoly of grand and imposing specialities. When another country has a remarkable thing, it cannot have it all to itself—some other country has a duplicate. But India—that is different. Its marvels are its own; the patents cannot be infringed; imitations are not possible. And think of the size of them, the majesty of them, the weird and outlandish character of the most of them![108]

In *Following the Equator* Mark Twain did not wish to mar the "specialities" of India by detailing the annoyances of every-day life, as he had marred his picture of Europe in 1867. Fascinating though they were, these months in India were somewhat less of an "excursion through heaven" than he pretended. The caste system caused a series of headaches. Screaming servants woke him up at five o'clock on many mornings. He had his customary troubles with stupid cabdrivers and was overcharged, he was sure, by a Bombay doctor. His notebook also complained of the piteous, cringing salaams of the native servants, many of whom had hideous teeth, black and bleeding from chewing betel nuts. These servants also lied, stole, and deceived, he said, without any realization that they were doing wrong. Good and cheap cigars there were, but they could hardly compensate for the galling heat, insects, filth, and general discomfort, all of which contributed to the ill health which plagued him during much of his visit.[109]

Secretly, he was also less pleased with the British than his book would indicate. As colonial administrators they were far from perfect, he thought, particularly in regard to their own troops overseas. In one memorable passage of his notebook he scored England as the "home of pious cant; and cant of the most harm-ful sort." He was stunned to hear that more than half the hospital beds in India were filled with very bad cases of syphilis. Hearty young men came out from home to protect the Empire, he said, but pious old England made no provision for their natural pas-sions. As a result, those seventy thousand young men went home to marry fresh young English girls and to transmit a heritage of disease to their children and grandchildren. Mincing no words in his notebook, he asserted, "Clean women subject to rigid in-spection ought to be kept for these soldiers. Any other course is treachery to the soldiers."[110]

The Clemens party sailed from Calcutta on March 28. In ten weeks Mark Twain had given about twenty "At Home" lectures (as he called his readings) in at least ten different cities. Far down the east coast they stopped for a day in Madras (no record left) and then passed several more days in Colombo, where he gave two more readings. Finally they were far at sea on the "Wardha" under shady awnings, leading the lazy life which he loved best. These were truly, Mark Twain said, "days of heaven."

Not until April 15 did they reach the small island of Mauritius, south of the equator. They went ashore at Port Louis the next morning but wasted no time in taking the train up into the cooler, luxuriant hills to the town of Curepipe. Here they rested tranquilly for almost two weeks. Although Mauritius was a British colony, the French outnumbered the British, twenty thousand to eight thousand, and Mark Twain seems to have given no lectures here. He grumbled that the French had everything their own way on the Island and that the French way was seldom the good way. But despite the French and the rains, he found Mauritius pleasant enough in its small way, like a garden or a park. It was pretty and charming, but, unlike his beloved Hawaii, it lacked the sense of remoteness and mystery which were required to "exalt the spirit and move it to see visions and dream dreams."[111]

Perhaps it was the curious makeup of the Island which now set Mark Twain to thinking about the problem of European colonialism. The British and French were both far outnumbered by the natives, and all three groups were apparently outnumbered in turn by coolies brought over from India to work in the sugar factories and elsewhere. Mark Twain was glad that this potpourri was under British rule. What he could not understand was why Great Britain had permitted France to possess the much larger island of Madagascar. He hoped that it was due to no silly respect for France's prior claims:

> Dear me, robbery by European nations of each other's territories has never been a sin, is not a sin today. To the several cabinets the several political establishments of the world are clothes-lines; and a large part of the official duty of these cabinets is to keep an eye on each other's wash and grab what they can of it as

opportunity offers. All the territorial possessions of all the political establishments in the earth—including America, of course
—consists of pilferings from other people's wash. No tribe,
howsoever insignificant, and no nation, howsoever mighty, occupies a foot of land that was not stolen.[112]

This sort of land robbery, said Mark Twain, now had sanction
as the "law of custom" and had become a "European governmental frenzy." Africa had just been divided up among members
of the "gang," and already the nations were trying to "steal each
other's grabbings." There was only one rule, he said: "Get the formalities right—never mind about the moralities." Madagascar
saddened him, because at one time England could have saved it
from the "calamity of French civilization," but now it was too late.
With a note of wistful resignation in the face of history, Mark
Twain could only hope that all this colonial frenzy would turn
out for the best:

> The signs of the times show plainly enough what is going to
> happen. All the savage lands in the world are going to be
> brought under subjection to the Christian governments of
> Europe. I am not sorry, but glad. This coming fate might have
> been a calamity to those savage peoples two hundred years ago;
> but now it will in some cases be a benefaction. The sooner the
> seizure is consummated, the better for the savages. The dreary
> and dragging ages of bloodshed and disorder and oppression
> will give place to peace and order and the reign of law. When
> one considers what India was under her Hindoo and Mohamme
> dan rulers, and what she is now; when he remembers the miseries
> of her millions then and the protections and humanities which
> they enjoy now, he must concede that the most fortunate thing
> that has ever befallen that empire was the establishment of
> British supremacy there. The savage lands of the world are to
> pass to alien possession, their peoples to the mercies of alien
> rulers. Let us hope and believe that they will all benefit by the
> change.[113]

Exactly one month after their departure from Calcutta, the

Clemens family left Mauritius, and four days later they steamed
slowly into Delagoa Bay off the southern coast of Mozambique. It
was a stupendous bay, walled in by a 150-foot cliff, atop which
could be seen pretty clusters of homes. They spent the afternoon
on shore. When Mark Twain saw swarms of native women
straining to do the work of stevedores, he thought he could guess
the rest: "This is Portugal all over—insolence, piousness, poverty, impotence."[114]

Four days later, on May 6, the party landed in Durban, South
Africa. They felt that at last they were nearing home. Only one
more long ocean voyage, and they would be back in England,
where Susy and Jean were planning to meet them. The mild South
African winter, just beginning, was a welcome relief after eleven
months of unbroken summer heat. But Mark Twain must have
been bone-weary and brain-weary from sight-seeing. For novelty,
South Africa was also an anti-climax after India. About their
ten weeks there he wrote almost nothing in *Following the
Equator*. He wrote less than seventy pages in all, and some forty-
five pages of these were devoted to political turmoil.

The drama of the recent Jameson Raid fired Mark Twain's
imagination. He visited the British prisoners and paid a call on
President Kruger, but confessed that it was impossible, while on
the scene, to make much sense out of the British-Boer conflict. By
May, 1897, however, when he was writing this part of the book,
he felt he knew certain facts well enough to pass them on to his
readers.

Mark Twain gave two lectures in Durban. Then, leaving his
wife and daughter there in comfort and safety, he and Smythe set
off for a swing through the seething hinterland—Pietermaritzburg, Johannesburg, Pretoria, Bloemfontein, Queenstown, King
Williams Town—and finally back to the coast again at East London. From here they took a steamer south to Port Elizabeth, where
they rejoined the ladies about June 17.

Except politically, these six weeks were rather boring to Mark

Twain. His letters to Livy and his notebook speak of the pleasant weather, the fine scenery, and the divine air. As he rolled across the rising, sweeping veld for one full day on the admirable Cape Colony railroad, he was filled with enthusiasm, temporarily. "Verily," he wrote Livy, "it is as the clergyman said in his sermon yesterday, 'It is a hell of a country.' "[115]

He was not, however, interested in describing the country or even his own activities. Although his lectures went well, even with the slow Boer audiences, he was horribly tired of the slavery of the platform. On one occasion, though, he became so thrilled at being in the thick of the political storm in Pretoria and Johannesburg that he wrote to Rogers that he would like to "burn around" these interesting countries for another year and talk. His passing references to the cities describe them as being generally neat, clean, and attractive. About the Imperial Hotel in Pietermaritzburg, capital of Natal, he could not say enough good things. The landlord, the food, the comfortable rooms, the Indian chambermaid with soft eyes, the great Zulu porter, the sociable kitten— all were perfect. And Natal itself, he thought, must be the garden of South Africa.

Indeed, Mark Twain came to like South Africa, and it even crossed his mind that they might settle there for a while, instead of going back to Europe or America. The people were friendly, the climate was wholesome, the political situation was exciting. The great mining operations also fascinated him, even the Boer tobacco was excellent. Above all, he saw an honorable position open to him. From King Williams Town, therefore, he wrote an urgent letter to his wife:

> Livy dear, how would you like me to be U.S. Consul at Johannesburg for a year? Mr. Chapin wants to quit, & I suppose I could have the place for the asking. I might make a fortune, I might not. But a Consul there must have mighty good chances. I've never said anything to Chapin, but I would like you to telegraph me yes or no. If yes, I think I would stop at the Cape & write the book.[116]

Orange Free State, S.A.
Bloemfontein, June 7/96

King William's Town, June 8/96.

Livy dear, how would you like me
to be U. S. Consul at Johannesburg
for a year? Mr. Chapin wants to
quit, & I suppose I could have the
place for the asking. I might make
a fortune, I might not. But a Consul
there must have mighty good chances.
I've not said anything to Chapin, but
I would like you to telegraph me
yes or no. If yes, I think I would stop
at the Cape & write the book.

I had been awake 19 hours when
I went to sleep last night. I know I
shall feel tired to-morrow. You &
Clara are at East London by now.
I shall try to get a telegraphic greeting
to you. Sent two or three letters there
to be sent on board.

Good-bye sweetheart, I love you
ever so much   Saml

Mark Twain's letter to Livy, June 8, 1896.

Livy's answer was probably known to him even as he wrote the letter, but he wrote anyway. Soon he rejoined her and Clara on the coast for a week at Port Elizabeth. Then they all moved on to Grahamstown for five days, and from there to Cradock and Kimberley. The gold fields of Johannesburg interested the old Nevada miner, but the renowned diamond crater of Kimberley was the only sight which truly absorbed him in all of South Africa. For a chapter he reveled in the unusual methods and glamorous statistics of the diamond business. "It is worth while to journey around the globe," he said, "to see anything which can truthfully be called a novelty, and the diamond mine is the greatest and most select and restricted novelty which the globe has in stock."[117]

Nothing else managed to distract him for long from the current political conflict in South Africa. This was the first time he had ever been confronted by imperialism in the making, in the actual shooting stage. He was thrilled by the intrigue and violence, but he was not quite sure about the rights and wrongs of it all. In this genesis of the Boer War, he did not yet know which side to be on. But before the war was over, it would cause him a great deal of embarrassment and soul-searching.

Simply put, the Boer War was occasioned by the British colonials' rebelling against the Boer government. The Boers, proud of their Dutch and Huguenot origins, had been in South Africa for over two centuries and did not intend to give up any of their power. However, said Mark Twain, the Boers had themselves stolen this power from the black natives. Moreover, the Boers did not evidence the usual progress associated with white men. They were profoundly dull, ignorant, bigoted, unclean in their habits, lazy, and backward. The laws they passed were hostile to religious freedom, denied political rights to non-Boers, and were grossly unfair in taxing non-Boers. In short, said Mark Twain, the Boers were simply white savages with none of the blacks' native intelligence and cheeriness. Some of them even sold their daughters to the blacks!

> Did the nigger ask the *Boer* to come? It is human, it is Xian, for the strong to take from the weak; the Boers did it; they must expect their turn presently . . .
>
> Has always been a bitter hard master to the niggers & is feared & disliked & distrusted by them.[118]

It was not the blacks, however, who were now rebelling. It was a rival colonial group, behind which Mark Twain saw always the scheming hand of Cecil Rhodes. Having never met Rhodes, Mark Twain was free to denounce him. And denounce him he did—even though he was obliged to admire the Englishman's "gray-headed strategy" and his ability to plan things on a grand scale—for he was convinced that Rhodes was secretly engineering the entire revolt.

Had it not been for Cecil Rhodes, Mark Twain might immediately have sided with the British. The traditional sense of honor and fair play, however, seemed to have been left out of this particular Englishman. He and his "gang," said Mark Twain, had forsaken all scruple in robbing, murdering, and enslaving the harmless natives. This enslavement, moreover, was worse than the American slavery which had pained England so much; the British master in South Africa did not care for his slaves in their illness or old age. Rhodes's method of reducing the native population, said Mark Twain, was

> a return to the old-time slow-misery and lingering-death system . . . with its daily burden of insult, humiliation, and forced labor for a man whose entire race the victim hates. Rhodesia is a happy name for that land of piracy and pillage, and puts the right stain on it.[119]

When Rhodes was added to the human race, observed Mark Twain, he tripled its poverty. Restricted by the requirements of a book, Mark Twain fulminated in twelve or fifteen pages of private notes about this "bloody assassin," this "Satan in a new & unusually repulsive form." He called Rhodes a Cain, a Judas

Iscariot, a Kidd, a Tweed, and a Golden Calf and added that he would make an elegant duke: "He is greatly admired by the lower class of dukes & earls & such in Eng. & after his humiliating confession, which would have ostracized a tramp, he actually left the country in good odor with that element."[120]

According to Mark Twain, Rhodes was such an extraordinary personage that people dared to speak against him only in whispers. He himself, perhaps he realized, also spoke against Rhodes, if not in whispers, at least in modulated tones—in public. The whole South African world, he announced, seemed to stand in a kind of shuddering awe of Cecil Rhodes, as if he were able to make or destroy people with his breath. His power was incalculable, not only in Africa, but also throughout the entire Christian world. Mark Twain concluded wryly that Rhodes was

> the marvel of his time, the mystery of the age, an Archangel with wings to half the world, Satan with a tail to the other half.
> I admire him, I frankly confess it, and when his time comes, I shall buy a piece of the rope for a keepsake.[121]

Following the Equator ends as feebly as *A Tramp Abroad*. Mark Twain's final week was spent in Cape Town, where he gave three highly successful "At Homes," but he crammed all of Cape Town into one catch-all paragraph. Duty demanded that he at least mention that he saw such things as Table Rock, the Castle, the government buildings, and the bay view from the beautiful scenic drive along the mountains. But his heart was no longer in it. He had really wanted to end the book with India and had told his publisher so. At a later day, he explained, he would write a separate book about South Africa, "if there is material enough in that rather uninteresting country to make the job worthwhile."[122] Understandably, the publisher wanted the whole trip at once.

The Clemens party sailed from Cape Town on July 15, 1896— one year after they had begun their long tour in Elmira, New

York. During this year Mark Twain had given well over a hundred readings in over fifty cities and netted perhaps thirty thousand dollars. The sixteen-day voyage to Southampton was a delightful prospect. He might even get a few chapters of his travel book written, because herein lay his present hope for paying off his debts.

He hoped also to write most of the book in the peace of his re-united family. Fate, however, had in store for him a blow far more cruel than his financial failure. On August 18 his eldest daughter Susy—his favorite—died in their old Hartford home before Livy and Clara could reach her bedside. Unaware of the seriousness of her ailment, Mark Twain had remained in London, working. It was here that, broken and alone, he had the fatal telegram put into his hand. It would henceforth be his task to try to repair not only his financial affairs but his personal and spiritual life as well.

V

Internationalist

After the burial of Susy, the Clemens family reassembled in England. They hid themselves away in a secluded corner of Chelsea for an autumn and winter of mourning. Burdened with a sense of personal guilt for Susy's death, Mark Twain suffered torments which deepened his pessimistic outlook on life in general. He wanted to be left alone in his anguish. His guilt was imaginary, not real, but that made no difference to him.

It was during this period that he wrote *Following the Equator*, striving to mask the despair in his soul. Only his close friends knew his address, and he went out to dinner seldom—with Bram Stoker, the Chattos, Percy Spalding, Andrew Lang, Henry M. Stanley, Poultney Bigelow, and several others. It was a time to work without interruption and to try to forget.

On April 13 he thought he had finished the book, but apparently the publisher did not agree. Perhaps South Africa had been left out. At any rate, his notebook reads, "May 18, '97. Finished the book *again*—addition of 30,000 words." Thereafter, as if his penance were done, he began to go out more freely. He was shortly elected, together with Stanley, Nansen, and the Prince of Wales, an honorary life member of the Savage Club.

In the course of this year in England, Mark Twain was in a mood to find many faults with his hosts, but only in his private notebook. Much of his censure was rather trivial, such as his long diatribe against English tailors, his attack on the autocratic water company, and his complaint about the flimsy construction of English houses. He was also disgusted by the shameless "hugging and kissing" in the parks and in the underground. The post office, too, raised his dander, and once again he condemned the British penal code, this time for still imprisoning people for debt and for jailing a harmless kleptomaniac who pilfered nothing but mirrors.

The "colossal Comedy" of the Anglican Church also drew comment. He was still convinced that the Church of England fought against progress until progress arrived, then took the credit. The "unconscious arrogance" of the British people annoyed him more than usual, and it was the behavior of one of his neighbors which caused him to remark upon "adultery in high places." And most likely he had certain Londoners in mind when he observed, "There are no such vulgar people as the over-refined ones."[1]

Soon afterward, on the Continent, Mark Twain tried to organize his impressions of England in a forty-eight-page manuscript entitled "Travel-Scraps. I. London, Summer, 1896." His mood was less dour now. This time he concentrated on facts to prove the inadequacy of the telephone, telegraph, and postal services. He also devoted several pages to that "invention of Satan himself," the London underground. The bulk of the manuscript, however, spoke well of London and its citizens. The shopkeepers were simple and kindly, with "no hateful city ways," and so were the bus drivers—neat, courteous, and dignified. London did have many inconveniences, said Mark Twain, but "the spirit of accommodation was everywhere." Perhaps this spirit went hand in hand with the generosity of the English to charities. At any rate, he summed up, "I believe that London is the pleasantest & most satisfying village in the world. The stranger soon grows fond of it, & the native lives & dies worshiping it."[2]

The Clemenses did not leave for the Continent until after the

Queen's Jubilee, June 22, 1897, the date chosen to celebrate
Victoria's sixty-year reign. During the magnificent procession
and the other ceremonies, Mark Twain grew as excited as the
British. His syndicated report for newspapers in the United States
expressed pride in the history of old England and pride in the
rapid progress of modern England under her beloved Queen.
This advancement, he stressed, was not merely scientific but also
moral and social. He cited the modification of England's cruel
laws, the broadening of her liberties, the melioration of her working conditions. "But it is useless to continue the list—" he said,
"it has no end."[3]

In doing homage to Victoria, Mark Twain overlooked the
shortcomings of her subjects and of her realm, perhaps because,
despite these shortcomings and despite Cecil Rhodes, who was not
in the Jubilee parade, Mark Twain had determined to take England's part in the turmoil of international politics. It was fitting,
therefore, that he concentrate on her virtues. Early in 1897 he explained to Howells that England was sound-hearted and sincere,
and ought to be supported by the United States in her time of
trouble in South Africa:

> This has been a bitter year for English pride, & I don't like to see
> England humbled—that is, not too much . . . We are sprung
> from her loins, & it hurts me. I am for republics, & she is the
> only comrade we've got in that. We can't count France, & there
> is hardly enough *of* Switzerland to count.[4]

Extensive traveling had given Mark Twain a wider perspective
on world affairs. Petty bickering must be put aside. England, he,
along with Henry Adams, was beginning to admit, was America's
natural and most reliable ally against the tyrannies and oppressions of the rest of the world, particularly of Eastern Europe. The
English-speaking countries must join forces in order to maintain
world peace and assure the spread of liberty. He openly preached

the interweaving of the English and American flags, "flags which, more than any others, stand for freedom and progress in the earth—flags which represent two kindred nations, each great and strong by itself, competent sureties for the peace of the world when they stand together."[5]

It might be well to pursue this doctrine here, even though it will lead us down to the end of the Boer War in 1900. Until this date, whether he knew it or not, Mark Twain was a supporter of Colonial Minister Joseph Chamberlain's "Greater Britain" policy. Chamberlain argued that it was England's "great duty" to carry her civilization into heathen lands. Mark Twain's observation, as we have seen, convinced him that the British took peace and order with them wherever they went in the world. For once it did not seem to occur to him that most natives might prefer their old chaos and freedom to peace and order without freedom. "Take up the White Man's Burden—" cried Rudyard Kipling, "Send forth the best ye breed." Mark Twain's growing respect for the British made it easy for him to subscribe to this trusteeship theory. Jesting in earnest he said, "Since England and America have been joined together in Kipling, may they not be severed in Twain."[6]

This desire to see the interweaving of America's flag with England's caused Mark Twain to resent being praised for his Americanism or his patriotism. He was not for America; he was for the world. He was an internationalist. Patriotism was beginning to strike him as a passion born of selfishness and nurtured by violence. "From man's point of view," he said, "patriotism is the noblest thing there is; from God's it is the meanest."[7]

Needless to say, Mark Twain usually fell back in his emotions to man's point of view. In South Africa his natural sympathy was for the Boers, because they had got there first and because they were greatly outnumbered by the British. In his original notes for *Following the Equator* he even worked up a passage of statistics to show what poor soldiers the British were and to expose the Jameson Raid as an "immortal farce." Judiciously, he withdrew this passage.[8]

He also worked up thirty-four pages of notes for a story called "Affeland," a satire on "snivelization" in general and on imperial exploitation in particular. Cecil Rhodes was the prototype for the villain, who organized the Christian powers to take over Affeland, subject the natives, and rob them of their diamond mines. In this embittered sketch, the French were called the "M-links." Rather illogically, however, the monkeys of Affeland observed, "Humans are descended from *us*; there is nothing below them except the French."[9]

In his heart Mark Twain was incensed by "The Absent-Minded Beggar," a poem written by his friend Kipling to honor those brave Englishmen who were volunteering to fight the Boers. In 1899, employing some of Kipling's language and meter, he began his own "Absent-Minded Beggar":

> Duke's son, earl's son, son of the noovo rich,
> Bilk's son, snob's son, bastard son of a bitch,
>   None of 'm whine, they *all* jine,
>   Jine the cavalree,
> And hell they raise for God his praise
> In the Boer his counterree.
>   Pay, pay, goddam you, pay.[10]

Opinions of this nature Mark Twain did not express for publication, but merely to let off steam. He informed several friends that he was writing bitter articles in his head about the Boer War and planned to publish one of them anonymously in the *London Times*. He seems to have changed his mind. "I, like all other human beings," he said later, "expose to the world only my trimmed and perfumed and carefully barbered public opinions and conceal carefully, cautiously, wisely, my private ones."[11]

These were difficult and embarrassing years, the two he spent

in England during the late nineties. For fear of being surprised
into exposing a private opinion of the Boer War, he declined
most invitations. He was even changing his opinion about the
culture of the Boers now. It began to strike him as superior to that
of both England and America. The Boer's honest simplicity, kindliness, love for freedom, his fortitude, patience, and contentment
with a humble, peaceful life were preferable, thought Mark
Twain, to the insane excitements of the English and Americans,
with their "habit of imagining that a lot of artistic, intellectual
and other artificialities must be added, or it isn't complete."[12]

All this, however, did not alter Mark Twain's fundamental and
considered response to the international situation in general. The
continent of Europe was split into two armed camps with the
Dual and Triple Alliances. The two camps had at least two de-
sires in common: to see England humbled by the Boers in South
Africa—the Kaiser even sent a congratulatory telegram to President Kruger—and to see Spain humble the United States in Cuba
and the Philippines in 1898. Only England sympathized with
America's cause, even urging outright annexation of the
Philippines.

Mark Twain, who *in the beginning* considered America's stand
against Spain to be a noble stand, appreciated the loyalty of Great
Britain. In 1898, therefore, when he wrote in defense of the
Spanish-American War, he was gratefully silent about England,
although he arraigned the imperialistic crimes of Russia, France,
and Spain.[13] The war caused him to muse in his notebook, "Are
there any supremely illustrious Spaniards—call to mind at the
moment none but the Duke of Alva, Torquemada & Satan."[14]
Had he really forgotten his old hero, Cervantes?

Although he regretted that Chamberlain had "manufactured"
this conflict with the Boers,[15] Mark Twain announced that America must back the British. Most Americans did not want to. It
was a prickly situation for Mark Twain. Whenever someone
demanded his opinion face to face, it was his custom to reply that

his head was with the Briton but his heart was with the Boer. Later, in *What Is Man?*, he developed the thesis that one's intellect and feelings can act quite independently from each other. The Boer War provided one of those rare occasions on which his own intellect controlled his actions.

Mark Twain found himself in accord with the leading statesmen in both England and America. To his closest friends at home he sought to explain and to justify a position which, it would appear, was objectionable to them. In January, 1900, he confessed to Howells that the Boer War was a "sordid & criminal war, & in every way shameful & excuseless." But, he added, he could not express this opinion in public:

> For England must not fall: it would mean an inundation of Russian & German political degradations which would envelope the globe & steep it in a sort of Middle-Age night & slavery which would last till Christ comes again—which I hope he will not do; he made enough trouble before. Even wrong—& she is wrong—England must be upheld. He is an enemy of the human race who shall speak against her now.[16]

Stephen Leacock says, "This is the bunk, and he knew it."[17]

Two days later Mark Twain wrote essentially the same thing to Twichell. Even though he was coming to look with more and more favor upon the culture of the Boers, Mark Twain's dread of Eastern Europe convinced him that England must not fail in this war; "for her defeat and fall would be an irremediable disaster for the mangy human race."[18]

The Boer War was only simmering, in that summer of 1897, when Mark Twain covered the Queen's Jubilee for the papers. At this time he was tempted by an offer to return to the States for a lecture tour—125 readings for 50,000 dollars. The money looked good to a family still in debt. Livy was against the idea, however, so they went instead to Switzerland for the rest of the summer. Accompanying them were Mrs. Crane and their niece, Julia

Langdon. Two years would pass before they returned to England.

In a trifling sketch entitled "Letters to Satan: Swiss Glimpses," Mark Twain indirectly described part of the trip—the slow Channel steamer, the hotels, the trains in Holland. The sketch, which did not get as far as Switzerland, supposedly was written by a junior devil to His Grace Satan. The young devil is amused at human customs and inventions. He reports that it will no longer be necessary to grease the palm of Cecil Rhodes, since that worthy will serve Satan "just for the love of it." The whole European Concert, in fact, is secretly following Satan's plan by coddling the Sultan, defiling Greece, and massacring over one hundred thousand Christians in Armenia and Turkey. This sketch, written in 1897 but not published until 1923, concludes:

> If Your Grace would instruct me to add the Concert to the list of your publicly acknowledged servants, I think it would have a good effect. The Foreign Offices of the whole European world are now under your sovereignty, and little attentions like this would keep them so.[19]

The situation and time were not yet ripe for Mark Twain to launch a major attack on Western imperialism. He was at that time in Weggis, far from the political maelstrom, resting and writing for two months in a quiet house above the lake, a half-hour from Lucerne. He thought it the loveliest and most satisfactory place in the world, even though his absent-minded strollings caused him, on occasion, to be warned off for trespassing in a neighbor's wood. Meals were brought up to them from the pension below, on the lakeshore. The cost, he said, was modest, and the scenery, dominated by the towering Mount Pilatus, was beautiful beyond compare. They had several bicycles and a rowboat. Because no one knew they were there, no visitors marred the serenity. Sunday in heaven, said Mark Twain, was noisy by comparison.

Mark Twain wrote with enthusiasm, but none of the books

begun in Weggis was ever completed. One seems to have been a satire on Monarchy, with the scene laid in central Europe about 1725.[20] He found the Swiss people to be courteous and natural, but he could not really take them to his heart. They were too grave, too austere. They lacked vivacity, he noted, and were a bit repellent in their manner. Nevertheless, he declared, he would as soon spend the rest of his life in Weggis as anywhere else in the world. This was a glorious, refreshing summer, marred only by the first anniversary of Susy's death, and by his regret that the paradise of Weggis was wasted on the "ignorant, poor, good-hearted jabbering animals" who lived there.[21]

Not wishing to spend the winter in the Alps, the Clemens family moved on to Vienna late in September, 1897. Here they set a new record by visiting fifteen hotels before finding suitable rooms and settling down in the excellent Metropole on the banks of the Danube. Clara wished to study piano under the famed Leschetizky, and her father, despite his love for Weggis, was probably ready now for a more sociable existence. From long habit he was pretty much a summertime-writer. His notebooks during the long sojourn in Vienna contain scores of names and addresses, together with "at home" hours. The names are distinguished ones, and nearly all the European names are titled.

Mark Twain always took a frank pleasure in associating with the nobility and aristocracy. All over Europe they were among his warmest friends. His republican theories made slight impression upon his social practice, for his nature contained more than a little of the romanticism of Colonel Sellers, his American Claimant. In 1902 he wrote a long article, "Does the Race of Man Love a Lord?" His answer was a firm yes.[22]

In the privacy of his notebooks Mark Twain continued to scoff at certain aspects of hereditary peerage: "Dukes for sale. Prime line of damaged earls. Nobles within reach of the meanest millionaire. French lot going cheap. Branch houses in London &

Paris & Berlin."[23] And when the Empress of Austria was assassinated in Geneva in September, 1898, he secretly blamed the assassin less than he blamed the whole system of "Militarism, which burdens and impoverishes and maddens. Royalty is itself the Empress' murderer before the fact."[24]

So dramatic was this event that Mark Twain composed an article about it. "The Memorable Assassination" put the blame on the assassin, an Italian who allegedly had simply sought to make his mark in history. Mark Twain described the Empress Elizabeth as a woman beautiful in heart and mind and person. Her character, he wrote, contained every quality that invites affection and homage. "Her tastes, her instincts, and her aspirations were all high and fine," he said, "and all her life her heart and brain were busy with activities of a noble sort."[25]

In order to attend her funeral, Mark Twain came back to Vienna from his summer place in the country. He jotted down many notes for his article. Obviously, he was impressed by the universal grief which moved all Austria, but he seems to have been more preoccupied with the drama of the funeral procession itself. For color and costumery, he said, it beat the circus. Most of all, perhaps, he was thrilled to be living once more in the midst of a historic event. Having the news broken to him by a friend of the Empress, he told Twichell, seemed to make him a "part of it & personally interested." He was sure that the event would "still be talked of & described & painted a thousand years from now."[26]

Many English people were surprised and probably offended that Mark Twain should leave London for Vienna. A London newspaper found it remarkable that such a polished gentleman should be interested in a polyglot people not far from the gates of the East. When he returned to England two years later, the papers asked his opinion of the Emperor Franz Josef. Mark Twain's reply reminds one of his description of the Czar thirty years before. The Emperor, he said, struck him as

a very fine fellow altogether [with] a great deal of good, plain,
attractive human nature in him . . . He is a man as well as an
emperor—an emperor and a man. He has a sense of humor. One
is incomplete without that.[27]

Living under such kindly and charming rulers as those of
England and Austria helped to reconcile Mark Twain in his later
years to the monarchical system. Queen Elizabeth of Romania
even became a personal friend of his family. As a nation, however, Austria never won his affection as fully as did England, or
as Germany had in the old days. For food, servants, comforts, and
society Vienna was excellent, but in certain ways Austria did not
appear to be quite civilized. Perhaps it *was* too far East.

For one thing, Austria had not yet rid itself of the barbaric
custom of dueling. The duel in Austria was a solemn, often tragic
event in which the duelist risked his life. The Austrian duel,
Mark Twain emphasized, had little in common with the French,
in which the duelist flourished a blunt hairpin and did not even
risk his shirt.[28] Measures were being taken to outlaw the practice,
but in the nineties no important government official could decline
a challenge, from any motive whatever, without covering himself
and his family with shame and disgrace. Such a situation, Mark
Twain pointed out, was hardly conducive to wise, stable government.

Mark Twain attended parliamentary sessions in the winter of
1897–98 and was dismayed by the tumult and disorder. When
the Austrian House was legislating, he said, you couldn't tell it
from artillery practice. He was in the gallery on Thanksgiving
Day, a day on which, he reported, the "harried, bedeviled, and
despairing government went insane." In order to free itself from
harassment, the Majority party called in sixty soldiers, who
dragged away vociferous members of the Opposition. In a long
article for *Harper's Magazine,* March, 1898, he wrote:

It was an odious spectacle—odious and awful. For one moment
it was an unbelievable thing—a thing beyond all credibility; it

must be a delusion, a dream, a nightmare. But no, it was real—
pitifully real, shamefully real, hideously real . . .

It was a tremendous episode. The memory of it will outlast all
thrones that exist today.[29]

Again Mark Twain felt the excitement of participating, as it
were, in the drama of history. As usual, he overestimated the
lasting importance of the event. Analyzing the Austrian government, he discovered that Hungary was not represented at all in
the Parliament and that nearly all the voting power was controlled
by the great landed proprietors. So-called reforms were a farce.
The government supported a swarm of Catholic priests, he said,
whose function was to keep the populace obedient, docile, and
ignorant of politics. The government also deleted from the newspapers every word with a dangerous look and employed a "persuasive soldiery" to discourage protest gatherings. Skillful
methods had been devised, moreover, to prevent men of ability
from exercising their talents in political affairs.

In an unpublished paper called "Government by Article 14,"
Mark Twain explained how the Austrian crown preserved its prerogatives by simply ignoring its promises and continuing to do
business at the same old stand in the same old way. The results
were as seen. Legislative sessions were bedlam, with free-for-all
fights breaking out on the floor. In mingled pity and contempt,
Mark Twain said that he was reminded of the Arkansas legislature
of 1847.[30]

Also repugnant to Mark Twain was the persecution of the
Jews in Austria. For many years he had respected the Jews as the
intellectual aristocracy of the world. Their mistreatment throughout most of the Continent disturbed him deeply. In Austria it
seemed that even the most prominent and most religious men
hated the Jews, missing no chance to do them harm. Mark Twain
described this persecution in "Concerning the Jews," a second
long article for *Harper's*.[31] The whole trouble, as Mark Twain
saw it, was that the Jew caused envy and hatred by being a better

"money-getter." For this the Austrians and Germans could not
forgive him, nor could the French and Italians. England and
America, he added, gave the Jew an open field and survived,
aided by the Sunday-Sabbath holiday.

Mark Twain seems to have worked hard in Vienna, at least at
the start. He told Howells that he was writing eight or nine hours
at a stretch, even on Sundays. Except for a number of short stories,
however, nothing turned out well. His creative imagination had
lost its magic, and his organizing ability, never strong, had practically collapsed. Much of his writing, therefore, dealt with
trifles: their servants,[32] a brilliant young inventor whom the
Austrian government forced into schoolteaching to avoid military
draft,[33] and a burlesque account of his experiences at a nearby
health resort.[34]

Special mention should be made of "Diplomatic Pay and
Clothes," a *Forum* piece in which he took up the old cudgel he
had used in the sixties against the penny-pinching government
which had cheated his brother Orion in Nevada. It had also
cheated his friend Bayard Taylor in Berlin in the seventies. Years
of traveling had now made Mark Twain a cosmopolite, able to
compare the practices of his own government with those of other
nations. The comparison did not make him happy. In foreign relations, he said, the United States had long been reaping the
damage from a "couple of disastrous precedents." The first one
had to do with diplomatic clothes. He had no patience with what
he called the old "Republican Simplicity sham," which began
with Benjamin Franklin. We should show more consideration
for the customs of other nations, he said. We should confer military rank on our diplomats and should design "glaringly conspicuous" uniforms for them.

With greater assurance he attacked the other precedent—that
of "shabby pay to public servants." American diplomats were
not provided with salaries large enough to maintain their great
positions. He compared American diplomatic pay in various

capitals with English pay, which was two to four times as generous. He felt sorry for American ambassadors unless they were
wealthy men. Furthermore, he deplored the damage done to the
reputation of his native land. Having resided in numerous capitals, and having moved in diplomatic circles, Mark Twain knew
whereof he spoke. For example, he said, an ambassador to Paris
or Berlin paid only 17,500 dollars by rich America was a ludicrous
and incongruous spectacle:

> It is a billionaire in a paper collar, a king in a breechclout, an
> archangel in a tin halo . . . Oh, Republican Simplicity, there are
> many, many humbugs in the world, but none to which you need
> take off *your* hat![35]

Any damage done to the prestige of the United States certainly
did not reflect upon the Clemens family in Vienna. Mark Twain
was a privileged personage, as he had been everywhere since
starting his voluntary exile in 1891. His apartments at the Metropole were like a court, and his daily activities were chronicled
in the papers, as if he were a visiting monarch. It was in Vienna
that Clara met Ossip Gabrilowitsch, whom she married in 1909.
Clara seems to have turned the heads of many of Leschetizky's
male pupils, all of whom, said the old master, appeared to be
suffering from the same ailment—Delirium Clemens.

Fortunately, Mark Twain's financial woes were coming to an
end. *Following the Equator* was showing a faster first-year sale
than any of his other Chatto & Windus books except *A Tramp
Abroad*. In November, 1897, Mark Twain wrote to his financial
adviser, H. H. Rogers, to begin paying off the debts; by the end
of January the final payments were made. No longer did he have
to trouble the Vice-Consul about such small economies as contracting with a barber to come to the hotel at 8:30 each morning
to shave him and trim his hair for two dollars and fifty cents a
month. Mark Twain took pride in such small savings. Now at
last he and Livy were free of their spirit-crushing debt, and the
newspapers of the world hailed their victory.

The Clemenses were not yet ready, either emotionally or financially, to return to the States. First, they must learn to live without
Susy. Then, they must make certain of an income adequate for the
heavy commitments of Eastern society. So they stayed in Vienna
through 1898 and well into the following year.

Their second winter in Vienna was busier and more sociable
than their first. Mark Twain sought to collaborate with a Viennese
journalist in writing several plays for the Burg Theater, but they
good-naturedly gave up the project when understanding each
other proved too arduous. The Director-General of the Burg
Theater and the leading comedienne were disappointed, and so
was Mark Twain. His admiration for the Burg and its majestic
dramas was tremendous. New York, he announced, was sorely in
need of a Burg Theater, "that wonder of the world for grace and
beauty and richness and splendor and costliness."[36]

Money worries ended, Mark Twain wrote more easily now and
accepted more invitations to speak at banquets and for charities.
One speaking trip took his family down to Budapest for a week.
They had a great time, he reported, and found Hungarians to be
lovely people. He was especially thrilled to dine with Franz
Kossuth, a man of quiet dignity. Mark Twain liked him im-
mensely and kept saying to himself, "This is Louis Kossuth's
son."

He wrote to Howells that he was renewing his youth in Vienna
this year, making so many banquet speeches and attending foot-
ball matches. Indeed, he seems to have been the unchallenged lion
of the Austrian capital. He accepted the position easily. The distinguished visitors who gathered in his rooms were of many nations and ranks. His biographer observes:

> It was the winter in London of twenty-five years before over
> again. Only Mark Twain was not the same. Then he had been
> unsophisticated, new, not always at his ease; now he was the
> polished familiar of courts and embassies—at home equally with
> poets and princes, authors and ambassadors and kings.[37]

North Pole, the Prince of
Wales, & you. Now what do
you think of that?"

"Well," I said, "it must <del>take</del>
make the Prince feel pretty fine."

=

During 8 years, now, I have
filled the past — with some
credit, I trust — of self-appointed Ambassador
at large of the U. S. of America
- - - - without salary.

—

=

May 9, '98, Vienna. Visitors yesterday, Countess Wydenbruck-Ester-
hazy, Austrian; Nansen & his wife, Norwegians; Freiherr <del>von</del>
de Laszowski, Pole; his niece,
Hungarian; Madame x x x,
Hollander; 5 Americans & 3
other nationalities (French,
German, English.) Certainly
there is plenty of variety in Vienna.
To-day, the Nansens to luncheon.

A page of Mark Twain's 1898 notebook.

It was with justifiable pride, therefore, that Mark Twain was able to confide to his notebook at this time: "During 8 years, now, I have filled the post—with some credit, I trust—of self-appointed Ambassador at Large of the U.S. of America—without salary."[38] Mark Twain's ill fortune for these eight years had been America's good fortune, because it had provided America with an ambassador who was truly extraordinary, a roving ambassador of goodwill, an ambassador not only beloved for his humanity and his humor but also respected for his courage, his intelligence, his self-reliance, and his dignity. All these qualities were greatly needed in this period when old prejudices and party politics were dominating the scene. An Austrian commentator, recognizing this in 1898, observed:

> Mark Twain has a very keen understanding of the weaknesses of aging Europe; he unsparingly brings to light the contrasts between appearance and reality. There is a kernel of truth in even the most grotesque exaggeration and distortion. He is seldom superficial or lowers himself to the level of the mere joker.[39]

An example of Mark Twain's joking with a serious aim was his note to the editor of the *Review of Reviews,* when asked for his opinion on the Czar's proposal for universal disarmament: "Dear Mr. Stead,—The Tsar is ready to disarm. I am ready to disarm. Collect the others; it should not be much of a task now. Mark Twain."[40] As he explained to a friend, the disarmament movement would break itself on the selfishness of governments, which would never be persuaded to reduce their armaments, because these armaments were "not created chiefly for the protection of the nations but for their enslavement."[41] Although "peace by persuasion" would never work, he later told Mr. Stead, "peace by compulsion" might have a chance. He thought that a sliding scale of reduction in armaments might be plausible, also very economical.[42] The editor of the *Twainian* is surely correct in asserting that Mark Twain, were he living today, would approve of the United Nations but would insist that it have police power and "that the police power be effective."[43]

The social season being over in June, the Clemens family moved outside Vienna to the Villa Paulhof in Kaltenleutgeben. Mark Twain's work went better here, even though numerous friends and visiting Americans came out from the city to see him. Darkening the horizon was the new cloud of the Spanish-American War, a war in which America was generally thought by Europe to be acting with purely selfish motives. Mark Twain longed for assurance that this was not true. What a comfort it was to him, then, when Charlie Langdon and his son Jervis came to Austria with their personal assurance that the United States was merely trying to protect the helpless natives of Cuba and the Philippines from Spanish oppression. Not only did Congress disclaim any colonial intent, but also, in the words of a modern historian:

> America rushed into this war to "free Cuba," more nearly unanimous than in any war in her history. . . . This was a closer and more personal war to Americans than either world war; it was their own little war for liberty and democracy against all that was tyrannical, treacherous, and fetid in the Old World.[44]

Thus reassured, Mark Twain began to write his friends that this was actually a "good war with a dignified cause," and that we should have driven Spain out fifty years ago, "both for Spain's sake and the world's."[45] The violence of war repelled him as always, but this particular war he considered, at first, to be unique. It was the "worthiest one that was ever fought," he consoled Joe Twichell, whose son David had just been caught up in the military service. "It is a worthy thing to fight for one's freedom," he explained; "it is another sight finer to fight for another man's. And I think this is the first time it has ever been done."[46]

It is interesting to note, as an aside, that on Christmas Day in

1869 Mark Twain had published in the *Buffalo Express* a savage attack on the so-called Cuban patriot, whose struggles were wrenching hearts in the United States. This "patriot," he charged, would begin by shouting, "Down with the Spaniard," but, when captured, would gladly turn spy and traitor in order to save his own skin. If possible, he would then escape to the hills, from which he would raid and burn deserted plantations:

> Murder, theft, burglary, arson, assassination, rape, poison, treachery, mendacity, fratricide, homicide, parricide, and all sides but suicide, are instruments in his hands . . . I do not love the Cuban patriot or the Cuban oppressor either, and I never want to see our government "recognize" anything of theirs but their respective corpses.

His earnest hope, he said, was that these cruel, ignorant, swaggering "semi-devils" on both sides would continue to "eat each other up" until there was not enough left of "the last ragamuffin" to hold an inquest on.[47]

But this was long ago. In the 1890's, for as long as he resided in Europe, Mark Twain patriotically stuck to the view that this "righteous war" was in no way associated with the land robberies of the European nations. It angered him to hear other Americans speak apologetically about this war. Before whom, he asked, should they be ashamed? With a hot pen in 1898 he dashed off "A Word of Encouragement for Our Blushing Exiles," laying bare the atrocities of Russia, France, and Spain. "Is the Professional Official Fibber of Europe really troubled with our morals?" he asked. "Do not be ashamed; there is no occasion for it."[48] But he did not publish the piece.

This same year one of the giants of the century died—Bismarck. Once again Mark Twain paused to contemplate the relative importance of the true man of genius and the pipsqueak who inherits a throne: "I think a few monarchs have died here and there during the past year, I do not remember," he wrote. "It made a great silence. Bismarck has been dead five or six days now, but the reverberatings from that mighty fall still go quaking and thundering around the planet."[49]

Following their long summer retreat in Kaltenleutgeben, the Clemenses took a handsome suite in the new Hotel Krantz.* Never in Europe had the Clemens family been more comfortably situated. Solvent once again, they began to entertain as of old, until their drawing room became a salon which acquired the name of the "Second Embassy." This was appropriate, for no other American in Europe was given more lavish attention or was regarded as more typically representing his nation.

Now out of debt, Mark Twain even found himself on a wave of prosperity. Rogers was invaluable as financial adviser. He helped to negotiate with Harper & Brothers a contract which would assure Mark Twain and his heirs a very comfortable income. It gave Mark Twain pleasure to be able to decline ten thousand dollars for a tobacco endorsement, another ten thousand dollars for only ten lectures, and fifty thousand dollars simply for lending his name for five years as editor of a humor magazine. He was done with lecturing for pay and the other offers were too frankly commercial for him now.

It was not until the spring of 1899 that he met Franz Josef, although he was acquainted with most of the royal family. The Emperor seems to have regretted the delays and now arranged a meeting. As we have seen, Mark Twain found him altogether kindhearted, attractive, and well-suited to his office. It is the Emperor's personality," he said, "and the confidence all ranks have in him that preserve the real political serenity in what has an outside appearance of being the opposite."[50] His liking for Franz Josef, it appears, caused him to minimize the significance of that "odious spectacle" he had witnessed in Parliament eighteen months before.

* A bronze tablet by the main entrance now advertises Mark Twain's residence there during the winter of 1898–99.

A meeting which turned out less agreeably was that with the new American Minister to Austria. This was Addison Harris, of Indianapolis. His predecessor, now in St. Petersburg, had been perfect, said Mark Twain, but the new man was impossible. In an eleven-page paper Mark Twain listed the nine requirements for a minister and found that Harris failed on every count; for example, he spoke only English, his private income was too small, he seemed lacking in all the social graces. This last criticism was based on observations made when the Clemens family visited Harris one afternoon. Mark Twain's ego seems to have suffered because the new Minister had been in the Hotel Krantz for three weeks without paying his respects. Also, no tea or drinks were offered, there were no facilities for smoking, the ladies were seated far across the room, and Harris himself had nothing to say; he just slouched with his legs stretched out and his head on the back of his chair. Most shocking of all, perhaps, Harris was ignorant of the sensational Dreyfus Case. As for the Secretary of the Legation and the Naval Attaché, they were both well-meaning, vulgar asses. "I wonder," said Mark Twain, "where our Government fishes for its average foreign-service officials."[51]

In a letter to Howells shortly after this unhappy occasion, Mark Twain was less rough on—and doubtless more fair to—the new Minister and his aides. They were good men all, he admitted, but out of place. His point remained the same, however: "Our government has more talent for displacement than the new White Star ship; & her possible is 17,200 tons."[52]

In this same long letter of May 12–13, 1899, Mark Twain told his friend that he was finally able to put aside his "pot-boiler pen" and to write a book without reserves. It was a luxury, an intellectual drunk, he said, to show man "what a shabby poor ridiculous thing he is." After two false starts, the book was now under way. This was *The Mysterious Stranger,* but not until 1916 was one of these manuscripts published by his literary executor, who took astounding and unwarranted liberties with the text. Set in

medieval Austria, the book had as its villain Father Adolf, a
drunken Catholic priest—dissolute, profane, and malicious. Satan was thinking of introducing the Austrian brand of Christianity into hell. Mark Twain, it is apparent, was secretly reviving
some of his hot opinions from *Connecticut Yankee* days. His
notebook was quite specific in its indictment of the Church in
Austria:

> The Church impoverishes a people by propagating ignorance,
> superstition & slavery among them, & then godifies itself for its
> fine & noble work in furnishing crumbs of relief, procured by
> begging—not from its own coffers, but from the pockets of the
> paupers it has created.[53]

Mark Twain also resumed his attack on the undemocratic institutions of monarchy and hereditary aristocracy. He was not
writing for publication, it must be remembered—at least not in
his own lifetime. "Aristocracies are bred from villainies &
whores," he wrote, and they combine with monarchies and the
Church in "chocking the wheels of progress." But now he inveighed less against these three institutions themselves than
against the suspicion and cowardice of the people in allowing
them to exist. Human nature was his target now.

The Mysterious Stranger, as first published, gave only a
passing glance at imperialism in the person of an obnoxious
Portuguese sahib in India. The original manuscript was far more
sweeping and explicit in its censure. The omniscient young Satan
spoke of royal "land-thieves" in latter-day Europe and explained
that late in the nineteenth century England would finally lose her
reputation in a "single shameful little war," plundering tiny nations in order to enrich a handful of adventurers. He also foresaw
the Boxer Rebellion in the Orient:

> England, desiring a weak State's diamond mines, will take them
> —by robbery, but courteously. Desiring another weak State's
> gold mines, her statesmen will try to sieze [sic] them by piracy;

failing, they will manufacture a war and take them that way; and with them the small state's independence.

The Christian missionary will exasperate the Chinese; they will kill him in a riot. They will have to pay for him, in territory, cash and churches, sixty-two million times his value.[54]

The Mysterious Stranger was directed not specifically against Europe, in spite of the setting of this version, but rather against the so-called progress of Christendom. The young angel scoffed at this progress, showing it to be little but the advance from clubs to swords to guns. No spiritual development took place to curb the warfare, which became bloodier and bloodier with each century. Intensified by personal griefs and failures, the disillusionment of Mark Twain now dramatized itself in this story. Mark Twain had been a strong apostle of Christian progress, but now, again like Henry Adams, he shuddered in disbelief as he saw the way Western powers were behaving the whole world over. The morning newspaper, he told Howells in 1899, was comprised of

> the usual depravities and basenesses & hypocrisies & cruelties that make up Civilization, & cause me to put in the rest of the day pleading for the damnation of the human race . . . We all belong to the nasty stinking little human race, & of course it is not nice for God's belovéd vermin to scoff at each other . . .[55]

In May, a month after this letter was written, the Clemens family finally packed up and moved from Vienna. As their train pulled out, a great crowd of Austrian friends and well-wishers waved and cheered from the platform. It was a sentimental leave-taking, the end of a brilliant period in Mark Twain's career.

While stopping in Prague for a day or two, the family was invited by the Prince of Thurn and Taxis to visit his castle. Here they had an excellent view of the country life of the Bohemian nobility. From Prague they went to Cologne, then on to London, arriving at the end of the month.

Invitations immediately began to pour into their London apartments. The ensuing weeks were a gay round of the usual luncheons, teas, dinners, and informal speeches. More than ever Mark Twain was in demand by the bohemian clubs such as the White Friars and the Savage Club. "Mark Twain Evenings" are now historic occasions in many club annals. It was between seasons in London, however, and Jean's epilepsy was worse, so the parents took her to Sanna in Sweden for the supposedly miraculous treatments of Heinrick Kellgren, an osteopath.

They remained in Sanna from early July until late September. One of Mark Twain's first letters to Clara from "Hell (Sanna Branch)" delighted in cursing the heat, the food, the hotel, and particularly the flies. "Make your peace with Satan, & come along," he urged his daughter. "Leave your clothes behind: fly-paper is the only wear."[56] As time went on, though, the cures seemed to help his own rheumatism, and he rapidly became a convert to the new "Swedish movements" system. He forgot his complaints about living conditions in Sanna and began to write enthusiastic letters and even long articles (unpublished) in praise of Kellgren's miracles. By mid-August he was writing to his friends that Sanna was providing the most interesting summer that ever was, and by mid-September he was telling them that he did not want to leave—"for me it's leaving heaven. I've *never* spent such a delicious summer."[57] Despite the "mangy human race," apparently, Mark Twain found the world filled with "heavens" which he hated to leave.

But we know little about these two and one-half months in Sweden. Mark Twain's notebook is almost barren during this period, while his correspondence and miscellaneous writings deal mainly with osteopathy and the glorious sunsets. For the rest of his life he remembered these sunsets. For exquisite beauty and infinite change and variety, he said, they were far beyond anything he had ever imagined. They were, he believed, the ones that had been used in heaven the day before.

Back in London late in September, Mark Twain leased an

268

Hell, July 12/99
(Summer Branch), Sweden

Dear Spider:

This is the Daily itinerary:

8 to 10 a.m. .... coffee for the Sommers.

10 to 12 a.m. "Treatment" for the Sommers.

12 to 2. Rest & gossip & fight the flies.

2. Dinner for the Sommers.

3 till 8 p.m. Rest & gossip & fight the flies.

8. Supper & flies for the Sommers.

9 till 11. Flies, gossip & profanity.

11 p.m. Bed. Fellow candles. Flies.

to midnight — dirna, pale blue daylight all night (Lat. 61°N) Cool, twilight & pleasant, but the flies stand watch-- & watch, and prevent the dreamed all night. No mattress for protection.

Review — the size of a tiger's cage.

Earth-closet.

Not a bath- room in the whole settlement.

A great lake, but not near by.

Open fields all around the dammed up woods.

Have bought a swimming suit & swim in the lake.

It is 4.30 (a.m., & too sleepy but to write.

Make your peace with Satan, & come along. Leave your clothes behind; they're superfluous is the only wear.

Strosp by jing on the left-hand side of the montl- press the notes 3

Come. And tell Jean to come. Tell her it is cool & delicious here. Tell Livy that Livy can happen to think of, put after all, I can't let Livy come. There are no present cages. Livy can can, & keep up the watch — if you are minded here; but we never met expecting her till the 26th.

Slanted. With a power of love,
papa

apartment at Thirty Wellington Court, Albert Gate, in order to be near the local branch of Kellgren. He also had a study at the Chatto & Windus publishing house, although his writing now was mainly for speeches. For a time his notebook became little more than an engagement book, so continuous was the entertainment. And from every dinner party, Clara reports, her father returned full of praise for the English people, whom he now admired with all his heart and mind.

Meanwhile, Mark Twain's contempt for the French people showed no diminution. Following his world tour, he carefully skirted France in his peregrinations. Several times he wrote to Clara, hoping to dissuade her from going to Paris to study music. When he wrote that he had no race prejudices, bar one, it was hardly necessary for him to name that one. It is truly startling—at times in the most irrelevant stories and articles—to see how Mark Twain could hurl gratuitous insults at the French. Now, at the turn of the century, France had done two more things which aroused his anger: she had gone back on her solemn pledge to Joan of Arc—Joan's one little request!—and was collecting taxes in the village of Domrémy; and France was willfully deceiving herself in her unconscionable treachery to that young Jewish captain, Alfred Dreyfus. "From the beginning of the Dreyfus case to the end of it," he wrote, "all France, except a couple of dozen moral paladins, lay under the smother of the silent-assertion lie that no wrong was being done to a persecuted and unoffending man."[58] Again, in order to get the flavor of Mark Twain's Francophobia, perhaps the best procedure is merely to sample his private notebook:

There is a Moral Sense, & many nations have it. Also there is an Immoral Sense. The French have it. [1896] Money cannot do everything. It failed to find a man who could explain how the French lost their tails. [1897] Write a French novelette—let the family all assemble around the dying bed of mamma, & all its fathers be called & apportioned out as they belong. [1897] There

is nothing lower than the human race except the French. [1899]
There is but one love which a Frenchman places above his
country, & that is his love for another man's wife. [1899]
Lust reaches perfect expression only when a F gets his eye on
another man's centime. [1899][59]

Several of these ideas Mark Twain incorporated into stories
and treatises he wrote, but seldom published, in the late nineties.
Sometimes they made as little sense as when Philip Traum (young
Satan) remarked that the people were "mainly French" where
he came from. He was *not* from hell.

Apparently, however, the only manuscript which Mark Twain
wrote about the French during these years was "The New War-
Scare" (1898). This amusing paper described the minute princi-
pality of Monaco, whose population was largely French in origin.
Mark Twain made fun of the alarm caused in Europe by reports
that the Pope was planning to exalt Monaco to imperial dignity,
thus, allegedly, upsetting the balance of power on the Continent.
Monaco possessed, said Mark Twain, only 8 square miles, 13,000
inhabitants, 1 naval vessel, and an army of 14 generals and 181
privates. The privates were disbanded in time of peace. Monaco
was so diminutive, he said, that its palace stuck out across opposite borders. One of the chief attractions was the Suicide's Rest
near the casino of Monte Carlo: "Hundreds go there in season;
the majority to stay."[60]

By about 1900 it became possible for Mark Twain to censure
mankind without always singling out the French for special contempt. Perhaps he decided that mankind no longer deserved a
scapegoat. It also seemed to him that other nations, England and
America included, were now acting as badly as France and even
worse in many parts of the globe. South Africa, Cuba, the Philippines, and China preoccupied his thoughts about foreign matters. France dimmed in the background.

Fond as he was of the British, in spite of the Boer War, Mark
Twain was anxious to get back home by 1900. For three of the

past five years he had lived under the British flag. He had lived under it contentedly, but his roots were deep—deeper than Henry James's—and demanded nourishment from native soil. Early that year he wrote to Rogers that he was tired to death of his ever-lasting exile. And Livy was even more restless than he to return to old friends and familiar places. Too long they had been living out of trunks in rented rooms. They had been on the move since June, 1891.

They decided to end their wanderings in the spring. Jean's progress, however, was painfully slow, so they postponed their sailing. Her Kellgren treatments were continued. The British, of course, welcomed the delay, for they now considered Mark Twain almost as one of their own. In April the House of Lords invited him to address the Select Committee on the subject of copyrights, and the committee seems to have been greatly impressed by the maturity of his judgment. But then he did not go to amuse the lords.

Among Mark Twain's closest friends in London were Moberly Bell, editor of the *Times,* and Sir Henry Lucy of *Punch*. One of his new conquests of this season was the King of Sweden. Especially gratifying to Mark Twain was the pleasure of dining with William E. H. Lecky and spending the evening with that author of his long-standing favorite, *History of European Morals*. Lecky was Irish, and Mark Twain seemed to establish a fine rapport with the Irish and Scots whom he met this year. They were "darlings, every one," he told Twichell. "One would have to travel far to match their ease and sociability and animation and sparkle and absence of shyness and self-consciousness."[61]

In July the Clemens family moved to Dollis Hill House, just a stone's throw from London. This had been a favorite retreat of Gladstone, and they could easily understand why. The quiet wooded hilltop surrounded by wide lawns may have reminded them of their Hartford home. All four of them found it divinely beautiful and peaceful. Visitors streamed out all summer, generally to find the family under the spreading oak trees, reading, strolling, entertaining at tea, conversing, or sleeping. With the enthusiasm we have noted for other places, Mark Twain pronounced that Dollis Hill House came nearer to being a paradise than any other home he had ever occupied.

Once more the time came to forsake an earthly paradise. The packers and movers came out near the end of September to get things ready to ship to the States. To Mark Twain the men seemed to be vexingly slow in doing their job. It struck him as typical of the British, and he sat down to write a paper about how slow England was in adopting new ideas and getting things done. "In London you must not hurry the doer," he said, "you must give him time to turn around—time to turn around."[62] And to Joe Twichell he wrote in much the same way he had written many years before: "I cannot help feeling rather inordinately proud of America for the gay and hearty way in which she takes hold of any new thing that comes along and gives it a first rate trial."[63]

At the end of September they closed Dollis Hill House and returned to London for a week or so to await their sailing date. They put up at Brown's Hotel, one of the Family Hotels which Mark Twain called a specialty of London. It was a sort of ramshackle club, he said, whose once-spacious rooms had been split up into coops. In a friendly letter he had great fun belittling Brown's and its ilk:

> All the modern inconveniences are furnished, and some that have been obsolete for a century . . . Some quite respectable Englishmen still frequent them through inherited habit and arrested development; many Americans also, through ignorance and superstition. The rooms are as interesting as the Tower of London, but older I think. Older and dearer. The lift was a gift of William the Conqueror, some of the beds are prehistoric. They represent geographical periods. Mine is the oldest.[64]

The Clemens family finally sailed from England aboard the "Minnehaha" on October 6, 1900. Mark Twain swore that if he ever got ashore, he was going to break both his legs so that he couldn't get away again. As we shall see, however, still in his future were a sad trip to Italy and a joyous trip to England, where he chose to stay in—yes—Brown's Hotel. But his long self-imposed exile was ended, and, for a while, his travels were done.

VI

Oracle

MARK TWAIN had grown accustomed to enthusiastic receptions during his nine years of almost constant traveling abroad, but nothing had prepared him for the wild excitement which marked his homecoming. The whole nation had sympathized with him in his troubles and bereavements. Now it gloried with him in his world triumphs. When he landed in New York on October 15, 1900, the public and the newspapers sought to outdo each other in paying homage to a conquering hero.

In a short time the new Clemens residence on West Tenth Street became one of the most conspicuous homes in the country. Magazines and syndicates begged Mark Twain for manuscripts, offering fifty cents and even a dollar a word for whatever he would send them. No banquet or public event in New York City could count on complete success unless he said a few words, or at least sent a message to be read. It was all an exhilarating experience for the aging author whose desperation had driven him to Europe almost a decade before.

Fortunately, his health was blooming. And, to his credit, he did not lose his head in the tempest of adulation, an adulation in which he may have noted a new and finer quality than before. He was still the beloved humorist, of course, but he had been tried by fire. He was older now and wiser. He had been to far places, seen strange things, and talked as an equal with the great men and women of many nations. Almost inevitably, as his biographer points out, Mark Twain came to be respected as a sort of Solon presiding over a court of final opinions.

Although he was used to being asked for his opinions, Mark Twain was not used to having these opinions taken quite so seriously. In one way he was not well suited to this new role. Never had he been a systematic thinker. His schooling and background had not been of the quality to equip him with the kind of knowledge required for feeling at home in the world of ideas. Because his opinions had originally been formed by the rough-and-ready liberalism of the Frontier and had proven susceptible to the influences of the settled East and then of the sophisticated Old World, Mark Twain found it hard to achieve a consistent philosophy of life.

Systematic thought or not, the essence of Mark Twain the man was not very different in the last years of his life from what it had been in the sixties. Then he had been known as a moral censor for San Francisco; now he became moral censor for the world. His role was much the same. The abuses to be exposed were on a vastly larger scale, but they were the same in nature. Not the Chinese laundryman but all of China concerned him now:

> It is all China, now, and my sympathies are with the Chinese. They have been villainously dealt with by the sceptred thieves of Europe, and I hope they will drive all the foreigners out and keep them out for good.[1]

Travel, reading, and informed associations had deepened Mark Twain's insight, but nothing had been needed to deepen his compassion or broaden his love for the common man. Damn the human race though he did in these late years, his predominant attitude toward the race was one of sympathy. Of this his friends were sure. Joe Twichell said so. Mark Twain's head told him that mankind was not worth saving—he wished he had it in the ark with an auger!—but his heart kept trying to save it. As Howells put it, Mark Twain's was "as mild a misanthropy, probably, as ever caressed the objects of its malediction."[2]

The profound, imaginative fellow-feeling of Mark Twain, indeed, may have been his greatest artistic asset. With Walt Whitman he could honestly say, "I was the man, I suffered, I was there." For this reason there was an extremely personal quality to his compassion for the Chinese, the Filipinos, and the blacks of the Belgian Congo. The spectacle of self-interested strength taking advantage of weakness all over the globe aroused his fury to a degree unapproached since his *Connecticut Yankee* days.

Now that he was back in his homeland, Mark Twain's passion burst forth in a number of hotly worded magazine articles and pamphlets, plus a stack of manuscripts which he never published. If the people wanted to know his opinion, by God, he would let them know. Less than ever now in his late years did he care how people would react to this opinion. His travels had proved to him that people were people no matter where they lived. Nothing would dissuade him from championing the weak and oppressed of the earth.

The word was soon out that Mark Twain was an anti-imperialist. Like a man who defends his own children from public criticism, he had tried, while living in Europe, to look favorably upon America's war with Spain. Now that he was home, he took a fresh look at America's activities overseas. His discovery was that America actually meant to annex the Philippines. This caused a crisis in his thinking:

> When the United States sent word to Spain that the Cuban atrocities must end she occupied the highest moral position ever taken by a nation since the Almighty made the earth. But when she snatched the Philippines she stained the flag.[3]

He must have been embarrassed by his earlier stand. He must have been ashamed at having been taken in by the pious utterances of President McKinley. He may have thought it his duty as a

humorist and realist to have seen through the sham, to have discerned America's *real* motive. At any rate, he became furious, for
he had been deceived. Now that his eyes were opened at last, it
was up to him to set things straight.*

First, he joined the Anti-Imperialist League, even permitting
his name to be used as vice-president. Then he began to write.
The main task, as he saw it, was to convince Americans that their
new Empire was corroding the virtues of their old Republic. He
was enraged by what he termed "majority patriotism," which
preached, "My country, right or wrong." This, he said, was merely
an adoption of the pernicious gospel that "The King can do no
wrong." "We have thrown away the most valuable asset we
have—" he cried, "the individual right to oppose both flag and
country when he (just *he* by himself) believes them to be
wrong."[5]

The Boss in Camelot had preached this same doctrine. Mark
Twain believed that the true patriot must speak his innermost
convictions and refuse to accept the "shop-worn product" which
usually passed for patriotism. "Only when a republic's life is in
danger," he said, "should a man uphold his government when
it is in the wrong. There is no other time."[6] In 1900 America's
life was in no danger, so he felt free to speak out. To his countrymen he seemed transformed into a vigorous reformer as he ex·
plained his new attitude regarding imperialism:

> I left these shores, at Vancouver, a red-hot imperialist. I wanted
> the American eagle to go screaming into the Pacific . . . I said to
> myself. Here are a people who have suffered for three centuries.
> We can make them as free as ourselves. . . . But I have thought
> some more since then, and I have read carefully the Treaty of
> Paris, and I have seen that we do not intend to free, but to sub-

* *History has not confirmed Mark Twain's fears. Fifty years later
the Filipinos were a free people again. Samuel Eliot Morrison asserts:
"Seldom has there been so successful an experiment in the now despised 'colonialism' or 'imperialism' as American rule in the Philippines."*[4]

jugate the people of the Philippines. We have gone there to
conquer, not to redeem . . . And so I am an anti-imperialist. I
am opposed to having the eagle put its talons on any other land.[7]

Mr. Dooley may have been right, essentially, when he observed, "American paypole didn't know and didn't care, whether
the Philippines wuz islands or a brand of canned goods." But
Mark Twain both knew and cared. His resolve to take arms
against the popular cause of Christian imperialism could not
have been easy. Only a few years before he had been its staunch
advocate in India and other backward lands. Awestruck by the
mirage of "progress," he had been victim to a persuasive illusion
of the age. Now he began to see the chasm between the Christian
ideal and the so-called Christian practice. Two of his most cherished illusions were slipping away, one after the other—the first,
that Western colonization was truly a blessing to savage lands;
the second, that his democratic homeland was untainted by the
European frenzy of land-grabbing.

Parting with these illusions was painful. Mark Twain's bitterness deepened as he watched the United States begin to participate
in the "European game." She was losing her unique quality, he
maintained, and was betraying the ideals of her founders. He explained this in *Eddypus,* a sort of universal history which he began to write a few years later. Our democracy, he said, was established with the noble intention of befriending all oppressed
peoples; then it became contaminated by foreign evils until it
began to steal land from weak countries and to assassinate their
liberties. "This endeared it to the monarchies and despotisms,"
he said, "and admitted it to their society as a world power."[8]

During the next few years Mark Twain spent many hours fill-
ing his tablets with fulminations against America's new imperialism. He sometimes turned to verse, beginning one satire, "Co-
lumbia the sham of the Ocean," and another:

> Rally round the flag, boys, rally once again
> Shouting the burglar cry of Boodle.[9]

Eventually he settled on a meter and composed a twenty-line "Battle Hymn of the Republic (Brought down to date)." It begins:

> Mine eyes have seen the orgy of the launching of
>   the Sword;
> He is searching out the hoardings where the
>   stranger's wealth is stored;
> He hath loosed his fateful lightnings, and with
>   woe and death has scored;
>   His lust is marching on.[10]

The most elaborate and effective of these poems is "My Last Thought" (1901). In this poem of eighty-two lines, a dying leader begs forgiveness for leading his country into Cuba and the Philippines:

> I erred through weakness, not intent. For I
> Was overborne by sordid counsels,
> Base ambitions . . .

His final glimpse of the American flag is tragic:

> O, not as it was in its great old days!
> The Stars are gone, a Skull and Bones
> Are in their place . . .[11]

The fighting in the Philippines distressed Mark Twain more than any other imperialistic activity of the time. "Oh, the Philippine mess!" he exclaimed on New Year's Eve, 1900. "McKinley's war is as discreditable as Chamberlain's. I wish to God the public would lynch both those frauds."[12] The public, he realized, would do no such thing, since each country approved of its own war. This approval, he said, showed that the old-fashioned standard of honor was shrinking pretty fast everywhere.

In the autumn of 1901 Mark Twain began to take an extraordinary interest in the Filipino leader, Aguinaldo. He read and marked a biography of Aguinaldo, as well as other documents

1900 -1?

1903

Battle Hymn of the Republic.

(Brought down to date.)

Mine eyes have seen the orgy of the launching of the Sword;

He is searching out the hoardings where the stranger's wealth is stored;

He hath loosed his fateful lightnings, & with woe & death has scored;

His lust is marching on.

I have seen him in the watch-fires of a hundred circling camps,

They have builded him an altar in the Eastern dews & damps;

I have read his doomful mission by the dim & flaring lamps —

His night is marching on.

I have read his gospel writ in burnished rows of steel:

"As ye deal with my pretensions, so with you my wrath shall deal;

Let the faithless son of Freedom crush the patriot with his heel;

Lo, Greed is marching on!"

are guarding her retreat; *

We have legalized the strumpet &

Greed

He is mercing out commercial souls before his judgment seat;

O, be swift, ye clods, to answer him! be jubilant my feet!

Our god is marching on!

In a sordid slime harmonious, Greed was born in yonder ditch,

With a longing in his bosom — for others' goods an itch —

As Christ died to make men holy, let men die to make us rich —

Our god is marching on.

X In Manila the Government has placed a certain

industry under the protection of our flag.

Anti-imperialist poem written about 1901-1903.

about the Philippines. "Humanity," "Keeper of pledges," "Magnetism," "Fortitude," "purity of his motives"—such marginal notes as these attest his admiration for the little patriot, whom he saw as sharing the noble ambitions of Joan of Arc, William Tell, and George Washington. In a long paper (unpublished) he vilified American troops for hounding Aguinaldo through the hills and for butchering not only the native troops but also women and children.[13]

When Aguinaldo was finally captured by means of pledging him safe-conduct, Mark Twain could no longer hide his fury. In the *North American Review* of May, 1902, he broke into print with a caustic "Defense of General Funston," the general who had perpetrated the deceit. The article was savage and courageous, for it attacked a military hero in the hour of his triumph. It quoted accounts of Funston's treachery and vividly described the inhumanity of American troops. It also decried General Smith's infamous command to take no prisoners, but to kill and burn— to kill all above the age of ten and to make Samar a howling wilderness. Small comfort to the two generals that Mark Twain urged his readers not to blame them, since they were simply mechanisms dominated by inherent dispositions which they did not select.

Mark Twain wrote more, much more, about American aggression in the Philippines and those connected with it. "Oh, 'Patriotism,'" he cried in one paper, "I wouldn't allow a son of mine to march the flag into dishonor tho the entire nation demanded it . . . Dirty commercialism is the only principle left to X^n nations."[14] In another manuscript he prophesied that the seizure of the Philippine Islands was the first step toward monarchy in the United States.[15] And in 1903 he withheld from publication, at the very last minute, a fierce and perhaps libelous attack on the character of Leonard Wood, who was up for promotion to the rank of Major-General for his work in the Philippines.[16]

In the most powerful of these unpublished papers Mark Twain

summed up the entire Philippine situation in two paragraphs. He told how the United States had coaxed a confiding little nation into a trap, closed the trap, then "pacified some thousands of the islanders and buried them." America captured the Islands, he said, by means of benevolent assimilation, which was merely the "pious new name for the musket."

> And so, by these Providences of God—the phrase is the government's, not mine—we are a World Power; and are glad and proud, and have a back seat in the family. With tacks in it. At least we are letting on to be glad and proud; it is the best way. Indeed, it is the only way. We must maintain our dignity, for people are looking. We are a World Power; we cannot get out of it now, and we must make the best of it.[17]

The year that Mark Twain ended his exile was also the year of the Boxer Rebellion, in which Chinese nationalists sought to drive out all foreigners. Mark Twain wished them well. He believed that the Chinese had a right to determine who should be allowed in their own country. "In America I am a Boxer," he said, "and why should I not be if I lived in China?" On this issue, too, he asserted himself vigorously, unlike many literary people. He had a strong fear that the Chinese situation might end in tragedy. "When the crash comes," he said, "it will be best for England, best for America and best for the world that the union jack and the stars and stripes should wave together."[18]

Because he felt this abiding need for Anglo-American cooperation, Mark Twain agreed to introduce young Winston Churchill to his first big New York audience. This was on December 7, 1900. The young English newsman was fresh from fighting the Boers and from imprisonment in South Africa. His cockiness did not appeal to Mark Twain, nor did the colonial policy for which he stood. Nevertheless, Mark Twain made the best of it, emphasizing how nearly alike the English and Americans were in character. Then, with an irony which must have grated on Churchill, he demonstrated how the two nations worked together in foreign policy. They forced China to admit foreigners she did not want; they did not charge China the Germans' "fancy rates" for "extinguished missionaries"; and they both looked on sweetly while France and Germany helped Russia to rob the Japanese. Finally, as England had sinned in South Africa, the United States had sinned in the Philippines:

> We have always been kin: kin in blood, kin in religion, kin in representative government, kin in ideals, kin in just and lofty purposes; and now we are kin in sin, the harmony is complete, the blend is perfect, like Mr. Churchill himself.[19]

It is interesting to note that Mark Twain's anti-imperialism gave him second thoughts about Warren Hastings, whose conquest of India he had extolled in *Following the Equator*. Tammany Hall, he said, was modeled on the East India Company and motivated by the same principle: avarice. Both organizations were "always ready to lie, forge, betray, steal, swindle, cheat, rob." Boss Croker, however, was less corrupt than Hastings, who "stands alone in desolate and awful isolation—in a black solitude of perjury, treachery, heartlessness, shamefulness and an indifference to guiltless suffering, pain and misery properly described as fiendish."[20]

Mark Twain had lost his faith, not only in the professed motives of Christian colonization, but also in the superiority of Western civilization itself. As he explained in *What Is Man?*, both men and nations were simply impersonal mechanisms whose primary function was to secure their own satisfaction and comfort. They could not help being the way they were. The fault was God's, he said, who made man at the end of the week, when He was tired.

Most of all Mark Twain was galled by the sly hypocrisy of the imperialistic nations, particularly in manipulating the missionary. Ever since his Hawaiian months of 1866 he had admired those missionaries who endured poverty and exile in order to teach, heal, and succor their fellow men. But more and more now he observed the link between the missionary and the gunboat. Eventually, he viewed the average missionary as the advance guard, perhaps unwitting, of Western rapacity. Some of them, he thought, such as the Spanish friars in the Philippines, who used the confessional to make women betray their husbands, were in fact secret agents of the army. In a brief satire called "The Fable of the Yellow Terror," he tried to link the missionary with armed force.[21] And for New Year's Eve, 1900, Mark Twain wrote "A Greeting from the Nineteenth to the Twentieth Century":

> I bring you a stately nation named Christendom, returning bedraggled, besmirched, and dishonored, from pirate raids in Kiao-Chow, Manchuria, South Africa, and the Philippines, with her soul full of meanness, her pocket full of boodle, and her mouth full of pious hypocrisies. Give her soap and a towel, but hide the looking-glass.[22]

Mark Twain even took to the platform on behalf of China. As always, he wished the Boxers success. America did not let the Chinese come here, so the graceful thing would be to allow China to decide who should go there. In a long letter written for the *London Times,* but not mailed, he suggested that China might let the businessman stay but not the missionary, who frequently caused trouble. He caused trouble and was hated, said Mark Twain, because it was his duty to insult the natives' own religion, to tell them that their gods were false and that, as a result, their dear deceased were in hell.[23]

In his notebook Mark Twain wrote: "True Irreverence is disrespect for the other man's god."[24] Every missionary of every creed, he said, was an embodiment of this irreverence, and so his symbol ought to be a polecat, an animal which does no bodily harm but whose presence is unendurable. To Mark Twain there

was an especially bitter irony in the fact that American missionaries went to China, whose civilization, he believed, was markedly
superior to America's. China was one of the few places he had not
visited, but he had been reading about it with interest. He marked
up his little book in which a Chinese official gave his views of
Western culture. Here is a passage typical of the many he marked:

> Among you no one is contented, no one has leisure to live, so
> intent are all on increasing the means of living . . . We measure
> the degree of civilization not by accumulation of the means of
> living, but by the character and value of the life lived.

At the end of Chapter Four Mark Twain wrote sadly,

> He makes us out a pretty poor lot. Well, the fact is, that is what
> we are. It is the fault of our civilization. If we could only get
> rid of it! God speed the American Board in its conspiracy to un-
> load it onto China.[25]

About the American Board of Foreign Missions he was being
facetious. Early in 1901, in two articles for the *North American
Review,* he had openly attacked America's exploitation of China
under the guise of Christian missions. At least, that is the way
he saw it. The articles created a storm, almost every paper in
England and America commenting on them editorially. They left
no thinking person unawakened. Abusive letters and newspaper
attacks flooded the Clemens home, but distinguished men on
both sides of the Atlantic hailed the brave articles. As Mark
Twain observed in his notebook: "Do right and you will be conspicuous." He was convinced that he was right.

The first of these articles, "To the Person Sitting in Darkness,"
began with an assault on the Rev. Mr. Ament of the American
Board. Ament had been sent to China to assess indemnities for
damage done to church property by the Boxers. He was reported
to have claimed compensation for each native Christian killed
and to have levied fines amounting to thirteen times the amount

of the indemnity. The newspapers quoted Ament as saying that these fines were moderate compared to those collected by the Catholics, and that the Chinese took advantage of people who were too gentle. He preferred the mailed fist of the Germans. The "blood-money" demanded by Ament, said Mark Twain, would condemn innocent peasants to starvation, yet America was proud of Ament for representing the old American spirit—that of the Pawnees.

Mark Twain then launched into his most spectacular appraisal of Western imperialism in general. He spoke of it as great bales which were marked for export with conspicuous labels: LOVE, JUSTICE, LIBERTY, EQUALITY, and so on. But the people sitting in darkness were beginning to grow suspicious. Business was being ruined by carelessness. The Kaiser, the Czar, Chamberlain, and the French were now exporting the Actual Thing with the outside cover left off. Mark Twain gave examples: the burnings and slayings by Britain in the Transvaal, Russia's robbing Japan of her hard-earned spoil at Port Arthur, Germany's demand for outrageous indemnities for two missionaries killed in a Shantung riot. "Would Germany do this to America," he wondered, "to England, to France, to Russia? Or only to China, the helpless—imitating the elephant's assault upon the field mice?"[26]

The Person Sitting in Darkness, said Mark Twain, no longer knew what to think of those Civilized Powers which came with the banner of the Prince of Peace in one hand and a loot-basket and butcher knife in the other. Why did Western soldiers frequently boast of taking no prisoners and of giving the wounded "the long spoon" (the bayonet)? And now President McKinley was beginning to play this European game, instead of ordering Dewey to sail away from Manila as soon as he had destroyed the Spanish fleet and to set up guarantees regarding life and property.

> The more we examine the mistake, the more clearly we can see that it is going to be bad for Business. The Person Sitting in

Darkness is almost sure to say: "There is something curious about this—curious and unaccountable. There must be two Americas: one that sets the captive free, and one that takes a once-captive's new freedom away from him, and picks a quarrel with him with nothing to found it on; then kills him to get his land."[27]

Like modern historians, Mark Twain now saw imperialism, at its best, as merely the logical extension of capitalism and its principles to international affairs. To Joe Twichell he complained that the United States had "gone to hell" in the few years since 1896 or 1897. And all too many missionaries, he said, were tools of the government, sent abroad to bully better men into adopting a culture inferior to their own.

It was cold comfort to him to discover that a cable error had been responsible for the report that the American Board demanded compensation of thirteen times the actual damage. A decimal point had been misplaced, making 1.3 read 13. To some people this made a vast difference, but not to Mark Twain. The principle was precisely the same, he argued in a second article, "To My Missionary Critics." His original attack on the missionaries had been poorly received, even by many who had approved his support of the Filipinos. His mail was bombarded with clippings, and there were demands that he apologize to Ament. More than once he was likened to his own delightful sea captain, Ned Wakeman, who insisted on hanging the man first, then holding the trial.[28] But Mark Twain was not about to apologize, as he explained sarcastically and rather tediously. He still believed that the American Board was doing less in a spiritual way than it was in spreading a lust for money and power. That may not have been its intention, he admitted, for the average missionary was "pretty nearly all heart." However, he added, "Sometimes the headpiece of that kind of man can be of an inferior sort, and error of judgment can result—as we have seen."[29]

In his own judgment, Mark Twain was not by nature a con-

tentious man. He confessed that he found it "policy" always to
tune his opinions to his neighbor's pitch. In the summer of 1905
he wrote a paper (unpublished) called "The Privilege of the
Grave" in which he explained his own "fine discretion" in keeping certain of his opinions out of print:

> Sometimes my feelings are so hot that I have to take the pen &
> pour them out on paper to keep them from setting me afire in-
> side; then all that ink & labor are wasted, because I can't print
> the result. I have just finished an article of this kind, & it satis-
> fies me entirely. It does my weather-beaten soul good to read it,
> & I admire the trouble it would make for me & the family. I will
> leave it behind & utter it from the grave. There is free speech
> there, & no harm to the family.[30]

Sometimes, as we have just seen, he was so incensed that he
could not wait for the "privilege of the grave." He had to speak
out openly in defense of helpless peoples against the mad money-
lust of Europe and America. "This lust has rotted these nations,"
he said; "it has made them hard, sordid, ungentle, dishonest,
oppressive."[31] On the other hand, a great deal that Mark Twain
wrote about imperialism and the missionaries still has not been
published. There is, for example, "Journey to an Asterisk," a
chapter of fifty-six pages, which he planned as part of *Captain
Stormfield's Visit to Heaven*. On a tiny asteroid in space the captain discovered Lilliputian monarchs dividing up savage lands
and civilizing them with Bibles, bullets, and taxes. "And the way
they did whoop-up Morals, & Patriotism, & Religion, & the
Brotherhood of Man was noble to see . . . I couldn't see that they
differed from us, except in size."[32]

Also unpublished are pages on "that criminal industry" of
foreign missions. The familiar charges were levied, with the
stress on the missionary's effort to beguile small children to forsake their parents' religion, thereby breaking their parents' hearts.
Mark Twain begged Joe Twichell to call his daughter back from
the mission field in Turkey.[33] He did not print his rather mild

anti-imperialist dialogue,"The Devil and the Offensive Stranger,"[34] or his attack on the alleged warmongering of Theodore Roosevelt.[35] Curiously, the anti-imperialist section of *The Mysterious Stranger* appeared in *Harper's Monthly* right in the midst of the most violent anti-war rioting. In vivid fashion the story explained the process by which a "loud little handful" of people could seduce a nation into a dishonorable war of aggression and ultimately deceive the citizens into believing it to be a just war.

Mark Twain's most virulent and sweeping indictment of imperialism has still been published only in part. "The Stupendous Procession" is a thirty-three-page manuscript written on the last day of 1901. Although Mark Twain got as far as making corrections on a typescript, the paper seems to have been too outspoken for Livy to allow publication. In it he describes an international parade of floats passing in bloody review: England, Russia, Spain, France, Germany, and the United States. England has mutilated Negroes fast in chains. France displays a guillotine with Zola under the axe and a mutilated Dreyfus following on foot. A mailed German fist holds a Bible aloft beneath a banner with the motto, "For God and Swag."[36] The major part of the procession depicts American crimes in Cuba and the Philippines, as well as the corruption of Tammany Hall. There being nothing new in the charges Mark Twain makes in this manuscript, it is enough here simply to inspect the figures which lead the procession. First comes the Twentieth Century, "A fair young creature, drunk and disorderly, borne in the arms of Satan." Behind her disreputable Guard of Honor comes Christendom:

> A majestic matron in flowing robes drenched with blood. On her head a golden crown of thorns; impaled on its spines the bleeding heads of patriots who died for their countries—Boers, Boxers, Filipinos; in one hand a slung-shot, in the other a Bible, open at the text, "Do unto others," etc. Protruding from pocket bottle labeled "We bring you the blessings of civilization." Necklace—handcuffs and a burglar's jimmy.[37]

A great deal more moving and more artistic than this rambling tirade is the brief "War Prayer" which Mark Twain dictated about three years later and also kept unpublished. This deals with the basic issue of warfare, together with the blindness and hypocrisy of the Christian religion. The setting is a church service. A great war is raging, and the preacher raises an eloquent prayer to God, appealing for victory on the battlefield. Suddenly, an aged stranger, clad in a long robe, ascends the platform. At God's request, he says, he will put into words the "unspoken part" of the preacher's prayer. In part he says:

> "O Lord our God help us to tear their soldiers to bloody shreds with our shells; help us to cover their smiling fields with the pale forms of their patriot dead; . . . help us to wring the hearts of their unoffending widows with unavailing grief; . . . for our sakes who adore Thee, Lord, blast their hopes, blight their lives, protract their bitter pilgrimage, make heavy their steps, water their way with tears, stain the white snow with the blood of their wounded feet!"[38]

The congregation thinks the old man insane, for there is no sense in what he says.

After 1902 Mark Twain saw little to be gained by pursuing his attack on American imperialism. The international furor was ended for a while. His nature was too volatile, perhaps, and his reaction to imperialism too emotional for him ever to present his case in the garb of a major satirical work. Still, his essays had a power which stirred consciences wherever they were read. Despite his political disagreement, Rudyard Kipling was moved in 1903 to write to his American publisher: "I love to think of the great and godlike Clemens. He is the biggest man you have on your side of the water by a damn sight, and don't you forget it. Cervantes was a relation of his."[39]

Amid the cyclone of controversy Mark Twain had felt far from godlike. For this reason he was particularly grateful to Yale University and the University of Missouri for conferring honorary degrees upon him at this time. In a way, these honors seemed to be institutional stamps of approval.

It was probably about 1901 that Mark Twain founded his pleasant little international club. He called it the Juggernaut Club and kept it going until at least 1906. Its members were selected from unknown girls and women who had written him charming letters from abroad. There was only one member to a country. He, and only he, corresponded with them all and knew their identity. Notably, even France and Russia were represented, the Russian girl being only thirteen. The French member was twenty-nine, the Bulgarian forty-three, the Indian sixty. As founder and president of the club, Mark Twain tried to practice the principles set down in its Constitution, which opens with a quotation from J. G. Burnet's *The Gods of India:*

> The god Juggernate (or Juggernaut) is the only deity among the two million gods of India who has no preferences, no partialities, no prejudices, no resentments, & sets no man higher than another, nor lower. He is the common friend of the human race; in his presence, master & slave, prince & peasant, banker & beggar, stand upon one level; at his temple's threshold rank & caste dissolve away . . .[40]

The god Juggernaut, obviously, was Mark Twain's kind of god.

Life was more relaxed and pleasant for Mark Twain now that international crises were temporarily out of the headlines. He overlooked his recent attacks on Germany and made a trip down from Riverdale-on-the-Hudson to New York City in order to attend the Mayor's dinner for Prince Henry of Prussia. It may be no mere coincidence that only two months later, in the *North American Review* for April, 1902, there appeared a long paper, "Does the Race of Man Love a Lord?" As we have seen, he maintained that snobbery is an inborn defect and that we all love to get "some of the drippings of Conspicuousness." He himself was no exception.

The Clemens family was in better health in the spring of 1902

than it had been for some time. Mark Twain thought it safe now
to accept Rogers' invitation to go yachting in the Bahamas. He
asked whether he might go as a Sunday-school superintendent at
half rate. This would be a stag party on the "Kanawha," which
had often whisked them up and down the Hudson River. On
March 13, he left New York by train for Florida, and about a
week later the yacht was lying off Miami, waiting for a storm to
subside.[41]

As always, Mark Twain was well supplied with guidebooks.
His curiosity about new countries remained lively. The record
of this cruise is contained almost exclusively in the short, happy
letters he sent to Livy. The letters comment frequently on the
brilliant colors of the sea and on the "delightful holiday." They
tell of swimming at Nassau and Hog Island, of reading and
writing on deck. One letter describes a call at lonesome little Rum
Cay to look up a native woman who had been seamstress in the
Rogers household for twenty-two years. This call, they were told,
would be the talk of the Cay for months.

One night they had a party on board in Havana harbor, only
fifty yards, said Mark Twain, from the sunken "Maine." This
was no sight-seeing expedition; the seven men were marvelously
congenial, enjoying nothing more than sitting around smoking,
talking, and playing draw poker, as they cruised among the lush
Islands. Of the places visited or the natives, Mark Twain made
almost no mention. He did remark in passing, however, that
Kingston was an interesting town and that Jamaica provided the
most prodigal exhibition of tropical scenery that could be imagined. On April 3, the "Kanawha" sailed from Nassau to Jack-
sonville and thence up the coast in easy runs. This two-week floating poker party was unlike any of Mark Twain's earlier trips
outside the States. It was precisely the holiday he needed from his
literary battles.

It was while the Clemens family was vacationing that summer
in York Harbor, Maine, that illness struck them again. They

managed to get Livy back to Riverdale, but their second winter there was a nightmare, especially since Jean caught pneumonia just before Christmas and nearly died. Forbidden to see his wife, Mark Twain often sat outside her door or pushed little notes under it. Finally, he wrote in his notebook: "Dec. 30. 2:40 P.M. Saw Livy five minutes by the watch.—The first time in more than three months. A splendid five minutes."[42] Then in February he himself went to bed with bronchitis.

Early in July they managed to get to the beloved Quarry Farm in Elmira, but they knew they could not endure another winter in the cold and snow. Plans were made to sail for Italy in the fall. It is perhaps curious that they did not try Bermuda, that balmy island paradise he had fallen in love with in 1877. Mark Twain himself was to return to Bermuda frequently for his health between 1907 and 1910, but he never took Livy there.

The decision may have been hers. They all remembered their two sunny winters in Florence ten years before. This was where they would go. On October 24, 1903, therefore, they sailed for Genoa on the excellent "Princess Irene." A trained nurse went with them, also Katie Leary, who had been in their service since 1880. Ten days after sailing they reached Gibraltar, thence on to Naples, Genoa, and finally into the hills of Florence.

This turned out to be a dismal winter in Florence and both a maddening and heartbreaking one for Mark Twain. Not only did they seem to have heavy fogs and rain almost every day, but also they were less fortunate than before in their choice of a villa. The vast Villa Reale di Quarto was a palace built by Cosimo I four hundred years before. Its view out over Florence to the Chianti hills was magnificent, but there was a funereal aspect to its gardens. There was no "home feeling," said Mark Twain, in the eighty bare-floored, barnlike rooms, the top twenty of which were not even furnished. None of the royal occupants had installed modern conveniences.

Compounding their misery was their landlady, the Countess

Massiglia. American-born, once divorced for infidelity, the Countess was now living on the estate with a handsome "master," while her noble husband was in the Orient. By springtime Mark Twain confessed that his prejudices against the Villa Quarto had fallen away, but time served merely to increase his loathing for the Countess. He dipped his pen once more in hell and wrote dozens of scorching pages about her alleged treachery, rascality, foul language, and wanton malignity. All winter he drove around the hills of Florence searching for another villa to lease. He was dissuaded with difficulty from suing the Countess for fifty thousand pounds. Never in his life, perhaps, had he spent so much time reviling a person of no consequence to the world.

The Italians, said Mark Twain, also hated the Countess Massiglia, because, contrary to ancient custom, she had driven all the peasant families from the estate. The ancestral hearthstone was sacred to the Tuscan. It belonged to him by right of venerable usage and loyal service. Mark Twain denounced this treachery of hers to the Tuscan peasant, whom he knew and loved. On occasion, he said, the Tuscan might lie or pilfer, but he was the salt of the earth:

> He is courteous, obliging, warm-hearted . . . a manly man &
> ignorant of what servility is; he is quite unconsciously dignified
> in his manner & bearing; he is of sweet & winning nature, & he
> easily puts a spell of affection upon the foreigner who comes to
> know him.[43]

Mark Twain's temper was not helped by the fact that Livy's health was failing rapidly. He blamed the Countess, in part, because she had limited their heat and water and service. It helped Mark Twain to discover a tangible villain to flay, especially during those days when he was permitted to see Livy for only a moment or two. He also tried to keep busy writing about more agreeable things than their landlady—about the delightful Villa Viviani in which they had lived from 1892 to 1894, about "Italian without a Master" and "Italian without Grammar."[44] He probably hoped to recapture the hilarious mood of his "Awful German Language." But these were not months for traveling, for describing the foreign scene, or for discussing international politics. These were seven months during which all his thoughts and energies were centered on his fading wife.

Finally, on June 5, 1904, Livy died at the Villa Quarto. A tidal wave of sympathy from all over the globe overwhelmed Mark Twain. On June 7 he noted, "Fifty-four lamenting cablegrams have arrived—from America, England, France, Austria, Germany, Australia. Soon the letters will follow. Livy was beloved everywhere."[45] He did not consider the cablegrams as tributes to him. To avoid returning to America on the ship which had brought them over, he and the four ladies booked passage on the "Prince Oscar" later in June. They sailed from Naples on the 28th. The simple marker which he ordered for Livy's grave bore only her name and dates, followed, interestingly, by a single line in German:

Gott sei dir gnädig, O meine Wonne!

Aging in years and broken of heart, Mark Twain was sure that never again could anything persuade him to cross the Atlantic. As we shall see, he was mistaken. But before his next trip, he threw himself into the arena of international politics for several more battles. First he attacked Nicholas II of Russia, whose atrocities were outraging most of the civilized world. To the continuing oppression of the Czar's Polish subjects was now added the massacre of the Jews in Moscow. "The Czar's Soliloquy" was the lead article of the *North American Review* of March, 1905.

Even though the satire is scathing, Mark Twain pictures the Czar as a man of spirit and intelligence. While gazing in the mirror at his skinny, spider-legged image, the Czar gives voice to three of Mark Twain's old convictions: that people worship clothes, that true patriotism means loyalty only when the govern-

ment is worthy, and that all thrones can be founded and over-
thrown only by violence. No great title, he realizes, means much
without the clothes to support it. If he were to go naked into the
street, he might be offered a kopek to carry someone's suitcase.

Cruel and heartless though he is, the Czar echoes Mark Twain's
contempt for the human race. For centuries, he says, the swarming Russian millions have meekly allowed his family to rob them
and trample them underfoot. They are too stupid to do anything
but suffer and die for the sole purpose of making the royal family
comfortable. Only in recent years have they showed any signs
of waking up from their "immemorial slave-lethargy." What an
irony, he laughs, that the civilized world insists that a ruler can
be deposed only by legal means!

> We do as we please; we have done as we pleased for centuries.
> Our common trade has been crime, our common pastime murder,
> our common beverage blood—the blood of the nation. Upon our
> heads lie millions of murders. Yet the pious moralist says it is a
> crime to assassinate us. We and our uncles are a family of cobras
> set over a hundred and forty million rabbits, whom we torture
> and murder and feed upon all our days; yet the moralist urges
> that to kill us is a crime, not a duty.[46]

In closing, the Czar describes several of his recent atrocities
which have stunned the outside world. He marvels that his own
nation can continue to worship him as a deity—worship *him,*
"this thing in the mirror—this vegetable . . . Is the human race
a joke? Has it no respect for itself."[47] He puts on his clothes.

Mark Twain's hatred for the Czar and his disapproval of
America's activities in China and the Philippines seem to have
persuaded the Russian Communists that spiritually he was at one
with them. In recent years they have sought to attribute his immense popularity in Russia today to a current of subconscious
communism, which they say runs through his writings. When
they cannot avoid confronting Mark Twain's explicit praise of
the whole capitalistic system with its powerful, free labor force,

the communist spokesmen simply shrug off this praise as one of his "blindspots."[48]

Mark Twain's hatred of the Russian government was mingled with fear, just as his hatred of the French people was mingled with contempt. He seldom spoke now of the people of Russia or the government of France. His knowledge of Russia being limited, he viewed her as a sprawling, barbaric empire, vast and dark. Her alliance with France reinforced his conviction that England and America must band together to preserve the peace. When the Czar killed the Constitution of Finland, Mark Twain observed: "I am not as young as I was. I realize it when I put the Finland tragedy & the Hague Comedy [Dreyfus Trial] together & find that I want to cry when I ought to laugh."[49]

Following the Boxer Rebellion in 1900, the Russian troops refused to withdraw from Manchuria. This led within a few years to an open clash with Japan, which attacked the Russian fleet at Port Arthur and defeated it. Mark Twain was overjoyed. It seemed obvious to him that Japan was going to smash the Russian forces in the Far East. Because the war was not popular with the people of Russia, Mark Twain was sure that this crisis would enable them to wring important liberties from the Czar.

In a satirical piece which he called "Flies & Russians," Mark Twain sought to appeal to the peasant's pride, although no peasant in Russia would have read the article, even if it had been published. The average Russian, he said, was one of nature's miscarriages—a combination of the rabbit, mollusk, idiot, and fly. "The making of flies & Russians—just as they are, I mean—could not have been intentional," he said. And yet how magnificently the Russians did fight in Manchuria! If only some intelligence could be injected into them! "Then," he added, "these humble & lovable slaves would perceive that the splendid fighting-energy which they are wasting to keep their chipmunk on the throne would abolish both him & it if intelligently applied."[50]

President Roosevelt's intervention in this war seemed inexcusable to Mark Twain. In the Treaty of Portsmouth the Russians won favorable terms. Mark Twain was infuriated, for the terms now left the Czar once more free to "resume his medieval barbarisms with a relieved spirit and an immeasurable joy." As for Russian liberty, it had had its last chance, said Mark Twain, and because of Roosevelt it had lost it:

> I think nothing has been gained by the peace that is remotely comparable to what has been sacrificed by it. One more battle would have abolished the waiting chains of billions upon billions of unborn Russians, and I wish it could have been fought.[51]

When asked to dine with the emissaries to Portsmouth, Mark Twain sent a polite note of regret. The invitation came from a close friend, George Harvey of *Harper's Magazine* and the *North American Review*. Mark Twain also wrote a reply which was less polite and which he did not mail. This note made it clear that he had no respect for the treaty-makers; with a stroke of the pen they had "annulled, obliterated, and abolished every high achievement of the Japanese sword."[52]

Mark Twain proved right about the Czar's being free to resume his barbarisms. Government storm troopers restored the autocracy, and within a week some three thousand Jews were murdered. Mark Twain was wrong, however, as he probably knew, in stating that the treaty had destroyed the last chance to overthrow the Czar. Another chance presented itself in the following year, 1906, and the royal family was finally ousted during World War I.

With the Russian revolutionary movement of 1906 Mark Twain himself had an embarrassing connection. He met and admired the celebrated revolutionary Tchaikovsky, who came to America to raise money for the cause. The grizzled old Russian, he said, still had a Vesuvius in him, strong and active. Tchaikovsky hoped to arouse a conflagration of sympathy among Americans. "But honesty," said Mark Twain, "obliged me to pour some cold water down his crater."[53] He informed Tchaikovsky that Americans had lost their ancient sympathy for oppressed peoples. Not much money would be raised, he said, except from wealthy Russian Jews.

Unable to speak at a revolutionist meeting—he was speaking that night on behalf of the blind—Mark Twain sent a letter to be read aloud. It was his hope, he announced, to see the end of government by butcher knife in Russia and to see the day when Czars and Grand Dukes were as scarce in Russia as he hoped they were in heaven.

With Howells he went to call on the chief of the revolutionaries, Maxim Gorky, who had just arrived in New York. Enthusiastically, the two Americans worked on a literary dinner to be given in Gorky's honor. The whole movement was gaining considerable momentum when Gorky was suddenly evicted from his New York hotel. The woman registered as his wife was found to be Madame Andreieva, a Russian actress. She was a revolutionary leader herself. Her relationship with Gorky was respected in Russia, but not in the United States. As Gorky and his mistress were turned out of a succession of hotels, the papers rang with headlines and the revolutionary movement in America ground to a halt. Mark Twain joined respectable society in repudiating the Russian leader, remarking sadly, "Custom is custom: it is built of brass, boiler-iron, granite; facts, reasonings, arguments have no more effect upon it than the idle winds have upon Gibraltar."[54] Apparently, Mark Twain wished to go on with the dinner, since it was purely "literary"; but even this idea was allowed to die.

Early in December, 1906, Mark Twain was reminded of Russia by a newspaper report of a famine in the Volga River valley. Girls were allegedly being sold into white slavery and peasants were taking their wives to the cities, where they forced them to earn money in brothels. Mark Twain clipped the report for inclusion in his autobiography. This was further proof, he said, that life in Russia was still more awful and cruel and pitiful than life in the Middle Ages. It was flattery, he thought, to speak of Russia as being medieval. He recalled the purpose of his *Connecticut Yankee:* to demonstrate the superiority of modern civilization. "That advantage is still claimable and does creditably and handsomely exist everywhere in Christendom—if we leave out Russia and the royal palace of Belgium."[55]

Belgium had become a new *bête noire* because the atrocities of Leopold II in the Congo had become an international scandal. For a number of years Mark Twain's friends had heard him fulminate against the Belgian King. Reformers now urged him to speak out publicly. The favorable response given to his "Czar's Soliloquy" encouraged him to attack Leopold in much the same fashion. So he began to read missionary reports, send for congressional documents, and even collect photographs taken in the Congo.

The result was *King Leopold's Soliloquy,* an illustrated booklet published in 1905 by the Congo Reform Association. *Harper's Monthly,* to his disappointment, had turned it down, perhaps because its chief editor was a Catholic, he thought, but more likely because Leopold had "bought up the Harper silence, along with hundreds of other papers."[56] At any rate, he gave the article outright to the Congo Reform Association, which sold it for twenty-five cents a copy. Mark Twain said that he had ordered a copy sent to every Protestant minister in the United States and that it would be sent to the Catholic priests later on. King Leopold was making his anti-Catholic fever run high once more. For some reason, his notion was to make the Congo first a religious issue in the United States, then a political issue. This was far from his usual practice. But now his prejudice convinced him that the American Catholics would "cast a solid vote for Leopold, slavery, robbery, mutilation, starvation, murder & American dishonor." The Protestants, who outnumbered them sixty-eight million to twelve million, would overwhelm them, however: "When our people find that Leopold's ardent backer is the Church of Rome;

that our missionaries in the Congo are not allowed full rights . . .
—they will get excited, & the Congo question will become a
political one."[57]

When Mark Twain wrote *King Leopold's Soliloquy,* he believed that the United States had a treaty obligation to oversee the
management of the Congo. He also failed to distinguish between
Leopold's personal *domaine de la couronne* and that part of the
Congo which was administered by the Belgian Parliament. Ver-
bose and repetitious though it is, this soliloquy presented quite an
accurate picture of conditions in the Congo, which were truly
horrifying. It describes charred corpses, dismembered bodies, de-
sexed men, women put to torture so that their men would work
harder. The description is supported both by photographs (some
apparently doctored) and by accounts written by eyewitnesses
such as government officials and missionaries.

King Leopold himself is shown to be an arrogant, inhuman
fiend, bloodier than the Czar. In twenty years, he says, he has
reduced by butchery the Congo population from twenty-five million to fifteen million. Personal gain is his only motive, but what
of that? He is an Emperor and is divine. Leopold is incensed at the
carpings of the "race of tadpoles . . . these meddlesome American
missionaries! the frank British consuls! these blabbering Belgian-
born traitor officials!" Why don't they mention the good things
he does, such as spending more money on art than any other
monarch of his time? Instead, he complains, they all take pictures of women chained together by the neck and of men and boys
with their hands chopped off. The Kodak, he sighs, has been a
calamity to his Congo business.

Leopold is proud of having taken in the President of the United
States with his pious act. Let Americans call it a pirate flag in the
Congo, he cries; all the same, they were the first to salute it. But
now there are too many "blabberers" trying to spoil his lucrative
venture. Effusively kissing the crucifix, he murmurs:

Yes, they go on telling everything, these chatterers! They tell
how I levy incredibly burdensome taxes upon the natives—taxes
which are pure theft; taxes which they must satisfy by gathering
rubber under hard and constantly harder conditions, and by
raising and furnishing food supplies gratis—and it all comes
out that, when they fall short of their tasks through hunger,
sickness, despair, and ceaseless and exhausting labor without
rest, and forsake their homes and flee to the woods to escape
punishment, my black soldiers, drawn from unfriendly tribes,
and instigated and directed by my Belgians, hunt them down
and butcher them and burn their villages—reserving some of the
girls. They tell it all: how I am wiping a nation of friendless
creatures out of existence by every form of murder, for my
private pocket's sake, and how every shilling I get costs a rape,
a mutilation or a life.[58]*

As a satire this obviously leaves much to be desired. With
Mark Twain's name on the cover, however, it did bring certain
facts before the masses for the first time. It also seems to have
stirred United States officialdom into action. In December, 1905,
Robert Bacon of the State Department wrote to Mark Twain,
asking for suggestions on how the United States might act effec-
tively in the Congo. Within the next two months Mark Twain
went to Washington. He came away from his State Department
conference with an altered view of the role which his own country
ought to play in the Congo theater.

Prior to this conference Mark Twain had thought that the
United States had legal, as well as moral, obligations to the Con-
golese. He had called his own government the "official godfather
of the Congo Graveyard."[60] Now he learned that the United

* The soliloquy was reprinted in 1961 in East Berlin by the Seven
Seas Press. In a long introduction, Stefan Heym charges that Mobuto
and Tshombe are heirs of Mark Twain's cannibal chief N'Cusa and
that "the current King Leopolds hide behind the flag of the United
Nations."[59] New photographs allegedly show natives being mal-
treated by modern Belgian and UN troops.

States was not one of the fourteen nations pledged to oversee Leopold's activities in Africa. To him this made a great deal of difference. He was sorry for much of what he had said in *King Leopold's Soliloquy*. Certain parts, he felt, had value as an exposure of Leopold, but other parts were "pernicious," because they mistakenly charged the United States with unfaithfulness to duty. His government was right in refusing to act. For it to intervene in the Congo, even in concert with other nations, would be "undiplomatic intrusion." He had written a Congo speech for Carnegie Hall, but he now declined to give it, since it would stir up the people to no purpose. "Our government could intervene in the form of a prayer or protest," he observed, "but so could a Sunday-school."[61]

Mark Twain's booklet, despite pressure from bankers to suppress it, gave momentum to the anti-Leopold movement. Soon the Belgian Parliament could ignore the international outcry no longer. In 1908 it finally took Leopold's private domain into its own control. A cartoon in the *New York World,* April 3, 1906, shows Mark Twain unbalancing the Czar's throne with a giant pen. A more appropriate cartoon in 1908—and perhaps there was one somewhere—might have pictured him snatching the Congo from under the butcher knife of King Leopold II.

Although Mark Twain stopped trying to shame his government into taking action in the Congo, he continued his private railing at Leopold himself. One manuscript calls him "the most elaborate & limitless villain that has ever worn a human skin . . . the monumental miscreant of all the ages." Even Leopold's own handpicked commissioners, it says, come back from their inquiry holding their noses. For ages after all the Caesars, Washingtons, and Napoleons have been forgotten, Mark Twain believed, the stench of Leopold's name would offend the nostrils of mankind.[62]

As 1906 progressed, Mark Twain's interest moved into new areas and back into old ones. He was now busily dictating his autobiography to a stenographer and editing parts of it for the

North American Review. He was also engrossed in his theological writings, and was trying to ready his philosophical treatise, *What Is Man?*, for the press. Then, in the midst of this, the Philippine problem flared up once more.

This shameful war, it appeared, was not ended after all. Guerrillas were still holding out in the hills. General Leonard Wood had just cabled about a glorious victory, but to Mark Twain it was anything but glorious. It was slaughter, mass murder. A tribe of Moros, six hundred men, women, and children, had been trapped within the crater of an extinct volcano and wiped out at leisure with artillery fire. For two days in March, 1906, Mark Twain interrupted his dictations about his boyhood in order to revile General Wood, Governor of the Islands, as he had reviled General Funston in 1902. He was unable to detect any of the heroism and gallantry of American troops which had been praised in Wood's report. These troops, charged Mark Twain, were simply "uniformed assassins." Once again they had dishonored the American flag. In blistering sarcasm he summed up the so-called brilliant feat of arms:

> There, with six hundred engaged on each side, we lost fifteen men killed outright, and we had thirty-three wounded—counting that nose and that elbow. The enemy numbered six hundred —including women and children—and we abolished them utterly, leaving not even a baby alive to cry for its dead mother. *This is incomparably the greatest victory that was ever achieved by the Christian soldiers of the United States.*[63]

The following month Mark Twain turned to a happier international matter—that of setting up a group of men to entertain foreign authors who were visiting New York City. Perhaps he remembered the Gorky fiasco. He had also just received an invitation from Howells to come to lunch with H. G. Wells, "the man from Mars and other malign planets, and an awfully nice little Englishman." He found that Howells had invited ten men, and he knew that his friend could ill afford such hospitality. Several days later, therefore, he suggested to Howells, "Let us insitute a gang next Fall, made up of nice publishers & nice literary folk, whose function it shall be to entertain at luncheon the visiting literary stranger, the expense to be distributed among the gang."[64] He offered fourteen nàmes to help get the "gang" started and had his secretary jot down a memo so that he would not forget to follow up the idea.

Whether or not such a group actually was organized at this time, Mark Twain continued to do his part in entertaining visitors from abroad. Now his daughters Clara and Jean acted as hostesses when needed. His warmhearted welcome of such visitors was one more example of his love for individuals, regardless of his growing contempt for mankind in general. He himself, moreover, and his family had been entertained too nobly abroad and in too many foreign places for him to neglect these pleasant duties when at home.

But these gestures of friendship toward individuals from overseas did not curtail his denunciation of international arrogance or oppression wherever he saw it. At a banquet late in 1906, he heard a smug boast, "We are of the Anglo-Saxon race, and when the Anglo-Saxon wants a thing *he just takes it.*" This "mephitic remark," he was ashamed to see, caused a delighted outburst of enthusiasm among the audience. Again he was so angry that he interrupted his dictations to condemn America for importing the whole spirit of patriotism and imperialism from monarchical Europe.[65]

During these late years, any glaring flaw in man's nature was likely to remind Mark Twain that modern civilization was preparing its own doom. Civilization often seemed to be "progressing" only by means of such things as the Inquisition, the Terror, witch-burnings, lynchings of the innocent, and "slobbering hypocrisies, reeking, dripping, unsavory."[66] Progress of this sort, he believed, led to the destruction of civilization, but such was the pattern of history. Civilizations rose and fell and rose again. Nothing happened which had not happened before and would not happen again. This he called the Law of Periodical Repetition.[67]

In the cycle of history Mark Twain saw the United States sweeping toward the monarchical system. Not only was it natural for men to love a lord, as he put it, but also English novels had taught Americans to worship hereditary privilege and many other undemocratic things. Sometimes this made him angry, sometimes glad. The issue did not appear as black and white to him as when he was writing *A Connecticut Yankee*. His democratic heritage persuaded him that succumbing to the monarchical system would cause the collapse of the United States, whereupon the globe would sink once more into a moral and mental midnight. On the other hand, his travels and experiences during the nineties persuaded him differently. Most of the time he had resided in the monarchies of England, Austria, and Germany, where he had not found the population miserable or oppressed. Instead, the masses showed a genuine affection for their royal families.

These royal families, moreover, and their nobility had been exceedingly kind to him, a visiting democrat. More or less in the course of things, Mark Twain came to regard kingship less as outlawry and more as just the highest of all social distinctions. For such overbearing pipsqueaks as the Prince of Montenegro he had only contempt, but he realized that no institution should be judged by its lowest form of development. Everything considered, he came to the conclusion that the average man could not long be satisfied with the drab nature of republics and democracies. "The inspirations of his character," he said in 1907, "will always breed circumstances and conditions which must in time furnish him a king and an aristocracy to look up to and worship."[68]

And there was that other point, which he had made clear in his old Gondour essay. Did the average man have sufficient wisdom to govern himself, to vote wisely? Should not the administration of a country be delegated to those of highest training, culture, and intelligence? Echoing the sentiment of the early Federalist, Mark Twain now made the maxim: "The Majority is always in the wrong."[69]

For these reasons he more or less resigned himself to the coming of the monarchical system to the United States. As a matter of fact, he thought it had already been firmly established in the dictatorship of the Republican party. Roosevelt had named Taft, he said; Taft would name his successor; and so on. "The monarchy is here to stay. Nothing can ever unseat it. From now on, the new policy will be continued and perpetuated . . . "[70] How interested he would have been to see Roosevelt split the party a few years later! Monarchy had become acceptable to him by this time, for he had lost his confidence in the judgment and character of the masses. Bernard De Voto went so far as to assert, "Mark Twain will vote for the monarchy. He is not only marching in the procession, he is carrying a banner."[71]

Most of what Mark Twain wrote after the death of his wife in 1904 did not see print during his lifetime, nor was it meant to. He knew that he could speak more honestly from the grave. The years went smoothly, tranquil summers being spent in Dublin, New Hampshire, after sociable winters at Twenty-One Fifth Avenue. Soon these winters were broken up by voyages to Bermuda. At Christmas, 1906, he took Joe Twichell back to that island heaven they had visited in 1877 and to which they had promised to return. It was a sentimental journey. Bermuda was as fresh and clean and full of bloom as they remembered it, and the British still ran it with their customary good taste and judgment. The daughter of their former landlady entertained them as guests in her mother's memory. The two men walked and drove

around the Island, luxuriating in its climate and serenity. The
tropical paradise awakened in Mark Twain an affection which
he did not permit to sleep again.

As he talked about Bermuda on his return to New York, Mark
Twain was reminded of its flowers, its smooth, glistening roads,
its excellent hotels. The Island's charm, he said, lay partly in
its climate and beauty, partly in the kindliness of its inhabitants,
and partly in its pervading atmosphere of contentment and well-
being. It was important to him that there were no signs of poverty
or wretchedness. He loved the European ease and "serenity"—
a favorite word—without the Old World's discomforts or grinding misery. Again he credited British influence:

> There is no rush, no hurry, no money-getting frenzy, no fretting,
> no complaining, no quarrelling, . . . no graft, no office-seeking,
> no elections, no legislatures for sale; hardly a dog, seldom a cat,
> . . . nobody drunk, no W.C.T.U., and there is a church and a
> school on every corner. The spirit of the place is serenity, repose,
> contentment, tranquility—a marked contrast to the spirit of
> America.[72]

Early in May, 1907, Mark Twain received a completely unexpected and profoundly soul-warming invitation. Oxford University wished him to come over to accept the honorary degree of
Doctor of Letters. To his old friend Moberly Bell of the *London
Times* he wrote, "Although I wouldn't cross an ocean again for
the price of the ship that carried me, I am glad to do it for an
Oxford degree."[73] Mark Twain took this honor as the highest
mark of esteem bestowable by men of culture. It healed, he confessed, a "secret old sore" which pained him year after year when
American universities, except for Yale and Missouri, overlooked
him and gave honorary degrees to relative unknowns. "I take the
same childlike delight in a new degree," he said, "that an Indian
takes in a fresh scalp, and I take no more pains to conceal my joy
than the Indian does."[74]

Invitations began to pour in by cablegram, as societies and dignitaries of England sought to outdo one another in honoring Mark Twain. He was seventy-one now and at first hoped to avoid a maelstrom of activity. The English persisted, however, so Mark Twain gave up and hired a young English secretary named Ralph Ashcroft, who was familiar with the social life of London. Ashcroft would serve as traveling companion, courier, press secretary, social secretary, amanuensis, and major domo.

On June 8, 1907, forty years to the day since Mark Twain had sailed on the Mediterranean cruise which brought him to fame, the two men sailed from New York on the "Minneapolis." Mark Twain must have been sad to think that Livy, who had been through so much with him, was unable to share this moment of triumph. Return passage was booked on the same ship for June 29. But he told reporters that the "boys" in London might persuade him to stay longer. They did. They would not let him go until July 13. During these twenty-five days in England, Ashcroft kept a scrapbook, an oversized volume pasted solid with clippings about Mark Twain's visit. News items by the hundred are interspersed with scores of photographs and sketches. When the long celebration was finally over, Mark Twain was so brimming with glorious memories that he was compelled to dictate them for his autobiography all through the summer and into the fall.[75]

Mark Twain's arrival in England began auspiciously at Tilbury, when the stevedores gave him a round of cheers which went straight to his very marrow. George Bernard Shaw happened to be at the pier, meeting Archibald Henderson, who wrote a biography of Mark Twain in 1910. Shaw was eager to meet Mark Twain. He had long admired him, he said, as America's leading satirist —a man who, like himself, was obliged to say serious things in jest. Later the two men lunched together, discussing their views of mankind. Shaw must have been impressed, for he henceforth asserted that America had produced only two great geniuses, Poe and Mark Twain. To the latter he wrote:

I am persuaded that the future historian of America will find your works as indispensable to him as a French historian finds the political tracts of Voltaire. I tell you so because I am the author of a play in which a priest says, "Telling the truth's the funniest joke in the world," a piece of wisdom which you helped to teach me.[76]

In London, Mark Twain had reserved rooms in quiet, old-fashioned Brown's Hotel, about whose inconveniences he had made so much fun back in 1900. He had hoped for a peaceful retreat. According to the London papers, however, his arrival transformed the hotel into a combination royal court and post office. Among the pile of invitations already accumulated were cards of honorary membership to the Athenaeum, the Garrick, and a dozen other London clubs. The attentions paid him on previous visits had not prepared him for the quality and magnitude of the welcome accorded him now. Writers, editors, statesmen, scientists, titled socialites—all vied in showing their affection for the world's best-loved personality. Mark Twain's resolutions to seclude himself were soon forgotten. He was caught up, as he probably hoped to be, in a steady succession of breakfasts, luncheons, teas, and dinners. When it was all over, Ashcroft typed out a memorandum which he called "What Happened."[77] It mentions more than forty names—distinguished names, most of them—which read like a *Who's Who in England*. Most of these people were Mark Twain's old friends.

Four days after his arrival Mark Twain attended the King's Garden Party at Windsor Castle. Edward and he were acquainted from Nauheim in the early nineties. They spoke often of those days. Although there were over eight thousand guests at the party, many newspapers reserved their largest type for the name of Mark Twain. And the descriptions of the grand affair suggest that Mark Twain was as prominent in the throng as any member of the royal family.

No sooner was he back in America than Mark Twain began to

describe his experiences in England: "I may say with truth that I lived many happy lifetimes in a single week, in those days. Surely such weeks as those must be very rare in the world; I had seen nothing like them before; I shall see nothing approaching them again."[78]

It is evident that England enjoyed those weeks fully as much as Mark Twain did. No one alive was more colorful newspaper copy than he. His every word and action were reported in the press, which also delighted in concocting bits of humor about him. When the Ascot racing cup was stolen just at the time of his arrival, the papers cried: "Mark Twain Arrives: Ascot Cup Stolen." The same joke was worked after the disappearance of certain state jewels and other regalia. Mark Twain relished the fun as much as anyone and helped to keep it going.

The day following the King's Garden Party there occurred another event which made a deep impression on Mark Twain. It took place at the residence of Archdeacon Wilberforce, a gentleman who had accidently taken Mark Twain's hat after a luncheon back in 1899. At that time the two men had exchanged amusing notes. On the present occasion, the Archdeacon escorted Mark Twain into his library and introduced him to a Bristol merchant. The merchant, who struck Mark Twain as a man of integrity, was said to be clairvoyant. With great care Wilberforce now unwrapped a curious vessel of silver, ancient in appearance, and placed it reverently in Mark Twain's hands. This, said the Archdeacon, was the genuine Holy Grail. It was a moment of drama for Mark Twain. Although the Holy Grail was simply a poetic legend to him, he was moved by the sincerity and faith of his host. His romantic imaginings raced back to Christ on the cross, to old Nicodemus, to the stainless Sir Galahad and his quest, to the princely Crusaders who laid down their lives in efforts to find the Holy Grail. "I am glad I have lived to see that half-hour—" said Mark Twain, "that astonishing half-hour. In its way it stands alone in my life's experience."[79]

Another highlight of Mark Twain's visit was the elaborate luncheon given in his honor on June 25 at the Savoy Hotel by the Pilgrims, a distinguished club with branches on both sides of the Atlantic. Their invitation was one of the first he had accepted before sailing from New York. At the top of their elegant program appeared a verse about two great nations standing "as one in honoring Twain." The underlying seriousness of the poem's praise animated all the good fellowship which ensued. Augustine Birrell, for example, introduced Mark Twain as a "true consolidator of nations," whose humor destroyed national prejudices. By reason of his love for truth and honor, said Birrell, Mark Twain had made the world better by his presence. In reply, Mark Twain announced that this flood of affection from the Pilgrims and from citizens all over the Island made him feel that, whenever he stood under the British flag, he was not a stranger, not an alien, but at home. No longer, we can see, did Mark Twain have to tread softly in England, as he had done when the Boer War was in progress. Then his head and heart had been in conflict with each other. Now they functioned harmoniously in his love for the British.

The British returned this love officially at Oxford on the morning after the Pilgrims' luncheon. The Sheldonian Theater had been packed with students and other spectators since an early hour. They applauded with vigor as the Prime Minister, the sculptor Rodin, Rudyard Kipling, General Booth of the Salvation Army, and other distinguished guests were honored. When Mark Twain was summoned forward, they went wild. Such a cyclone of shouting and applause greeted him, said the newspapers, that it seemed as if it might be impossible to make the presentation. "Most amiable and charming sir," Chancellor Curzon finally managed to say in Latin, "you shake the sides of the whole world with your merriment." The Missouri boy who had been forced to quit school at twelve was now a Doctor of Letters, Oxford.

The next couple of days in Oxford found Mark Twain be-

sieged by crowds wishing to photograph him, shake his hand, exchange a greeting, or simply catch a glimpse of his shaggy
white head and give him a cheer. At the great Oxford Pageant, the
historical characters waved to him and called out as they passed
the box where he sat with Lord Curzon and his old friend Kipling.
One of the newspapers dubbed it "Mark Twain's Pageant." Of
the many dictations he made about these weeks in England, the
only one Mark Twain gave for publication was his description
of these two unforgettable events at Oxford.[80]

Shortly after his Oxford triumph, Mark Twain was guest of
honor at the dinner given at the Mansion House for the Savage
Club by the Lord Mayor of London. Having delayed his departure, he was also able to attend the Fourth of July dinner of the
American Society at the Hotel Cecil. Here he responded to the
Ambassador's toast with remarks designed to salve the old wounds
of the Revolutionary War. Ignoring Great Britain's colonial
policy, he spoke of the British colonists themselves and of their
love for liberty. England had also, he pointed out, led the way
in freeing slaves. Americans ought to love and revere the great-
hearted mother of their race, for she was truly "the venerable
Mother of Liberties, the Champion and Protector of Anglo-Saxon
Freedom."[81]

Punch magazine had already honored Mark Twain with a
front-page illustration. It showed Mr. Punch himself drinking a
toast to his guest's long life and perpetual youth. Now the fun-
loving staff of the magazine gave Mark Twain a party which
seems to have delighted him more than any other event in London.
He spent the last two days of August dictating an account of the
joyous occasion.

The morning after the *Punch* dinner Mark Twain set off for
Liverpool in the Prince of Wales's private railroad car. He had
tried to decline the Liverpool invitation, but that city would not
be put off. So, on July 10, he found himself guest of honor at the
Lord Mayor's reception and banquet in the Town Hall. Although

too tired to come early and sit through the long dinner, Mark Twain appeared in time to respond to his toast.

This was Mark Twain's farewell address to England. It was longer than his usual after-dinner speech and was perhaps the most sentimental speech of his entire career. From the heart he spoke of his gratitude to England for the honor and affection she had showered on him. In conclusion, taking an image from *Two Years Before the Mast,* he acknowledged that he was only the scrubby little coastal sloop the "Mary Ann," but that England's welcome had swelled his conceit until he forgot this and felt like the "Begum of Bengal," that majestic Indiaman, 142 days out from Canton, laden with spices, homeward bound.

During his last two days in London, Mark Twain made as many personal calls as time allowed. This time he was certain that he would never be back. He must thank those who had been kind to him and say good-bye to old friends, some of whom he had known since his first visit in 1872. When he finally boarded the "Minnetonka," on July 13, he was surrounded to the last by a throng of reporters, photographers, friends, autograph-hunters, and well-wishers. They gave him a rousing, sentimental farewell. The *London Times* reported that the ship had trouble getting clear, so thickly was the water strewn with the bay-leaves of his triumph: "For Mark Twain has triumphed, and in his all-too-brief stay of a month has done more for the cause of the world's peace than will be accomplished by the Hague Conference. He has made the world laugh again."[82]

In New York, later that year, Mark Twain was asked to speak at a function honoring an English Bishop, who had brought over a valuable King James Bible for presentation. He told the Bishop that the government of the United States was gradually becoming more like England's. "Sometimes you call your system a monarchical republic," he said; "ours is a republican monarchy. There is no real difference. . . . The Party only is hereditary now, but the leadership of it will be hereditary by & by, in a single family."[83]

In this speech he reiterated his thanks to England for its recent
hospitality and confessed that, like all other human beings, he
himself had a reverence for rank, no matter how much he might
scoff in public. Again he stated his theory about envy of the conspicuous. An American girl, he insisted, would rather marry a
title than an angel.

Privately, Mark Twain believed that it was generally a mistake
for an American girl to marry a title—or any foreigner. He had
seen these international marriages fail too often when he was
residing on the Continent in the nineties. Now it was reported
that Gladys Vanderbilt, sister of the Commodore, was about to
marry Count Szchenyi of Austria. He saw great unhappiness
ahead for her. American girls, he thought, should draw the line
with Englishmen, Scotsmen, and Irishmen:

> When they marry a foreigner of any other nationality the chances
> are nine to one that they will regret it—if the foreigner be a
> Frenchman, an Italian, a German, a Russian or a Turk; and
> when he is an Austrian, a Hungarian, or a Bohemian, of noble
> degree, the chances are ninety-nine to one that in time the girl
> will wish she hadn't made the venture. In other foreign countries
> she takes her husband's rank; in the last three mentioned she has
> no rank at all, and is a nobody. He attends court functions, the
> ambassadorial functions, and the dinners, luncheons, and teas,
> of the nobility, while she abides lonely and homesick in her
> palace and rocks the baby.[84]

There was, of course, a great deal of truth in this admonition.
Nevertheless, two years later he gladly allowed his daughter Clara
to take that one chance in nine, and she won. She had a long and
happy marriage with Ossip Gabrilowitsch, the Russian pianist
and conductor whom she had met in Vienna.

In January, 1908, Mark Twain sailed again to Bermuda in
order to escape the foul New York weather, which threatened him
with another bronchial attack. The highlight of this trip was the
lasting friendship he formed with Margaret Blackmer, age twelve,

and her somewhat older friend, Elizabeth Wallace. He roamed
the Island with them, sometimes on foot, more often in a small
donkey-cart. Often he just sat on the veranda with Margaret,
helping her to memorize famous dates of history. Never did he
talk down to Margaret. Always he addressed her with courtesy
and a kindly deference of manner. Margaret and Betsy were made
charter members—he called them Angel-fish—of his new club,
the Aquarium, most of whose members were about Margaret's
age. The small Angel-fish took the place in his heart of the grandchildren he never had in his lifetime. The children adored this
courtly, white-haired gentleman who always considered their
opinions with dignity and seemed, magically, to understand their
secret selves. Several years later Betsy wrote:

> As the ship sailed away bearing the sweet little girl, Margaret,
> and the sweet old man, Mr. Clemens, we felt that the island had
> grown suddenly smaller, that the colors had faded, and that
> there was a chill in the air.[85]

Mark Twain had been back in New York only a short time
when he discovered that his friend Henry Rogers was in poor
health. Nothing would do but that Rogers return with him immediately to the balmy Island. Betsy was thrilled to have him
back again so soon; he had been gone just two weeks. She took him
on an all-day picnic to the far end of the Island and escorted him
to Prospect Park to hear the military band and to admire the
scarlet uniforms. She may also have accompanied him on his drive
out to investigate a newly discovered cave—a cave which he described in a letter to another Angel-fish. It was 150 steps down
underground, he wrote, was 250 feet long, and contained a brilliant lake surrounded by great shining stalactites. He supposed
it was the "most beautiful cave in the world."[86] He also told of
a "screaming good time" during the afternoon spent on board a
British cruiser in the bay.

These outings, however, were not the rule. As a matter of fact,

Betsy reported, the cave did not interest Mark Twain very much. He used to tell her that he had probably seen the biggest city in the world, the highest mountain, the greatest cathedral, etc., so why should he trouble himself in his old age to see second-rate curiosities? Most of the time, Mark Twain and Rogers contented themselves with short walks and short drives under the shady trees. They avoided most of the social functions, preferring to sit peacefully on the veranda sharing fine talk or else teasing each other for the amusement of the listeners who would gather. When they wished to escape the ever-present cameras and curious people, they would retire to Mark Twain's room. Here they would play hearts. Frequently a few Angel-fish and other close friends were invited in to hear Mark Twain read aloud, generally from the poetry of Rudyard Kipling. The two old men were privileged persons; they could do as they wished. They did not wish to be sightseers in Bermuda in 1908.

In time they felt they should return home. Early that summer Mark Twain dismantled his house at Twenty-One Fifth Avenue and moved into his newly constructed mansion on a hilltop in Redding, Connecticut. So contented did he become with his new surroundings and local interests that Bermuda failed to entice him the following winter. "Innocents at Home" was his first name for the estate, but he soon changed it to "Stormfield." There were many visitors at Stormfield and much entertaining, with Clara and Jean and his secretary Isabel Lyon as hostesses. It was here, in the autumn of 1909, that Clara was wed to Ossip Gabrilowitsch.

On November 19 Mark Twain sailed once more to Bermuda. Rogers had died that spring, so he took along his neighbor, biographer, and billiard partner, Albert Bigelow Paine. The two men had comfortable rooms at the Hamilton Hotel, but Mark Twain seems to have spent most of his time at Bay House, the home of William H. Allen, American Vice-Consul. Helen Allen was an Angel-fish and accompanied the two men almost everywhere. And Bay House was a quiet place where family and servants surrounded Mark Twain with the sort of affection he had grown used to in his own home.

Paine tells us that Mark Twain prolonged his visit to Bay House from day to day and from week to week. Helen frequently took dictation in the morning and generally acted as Mark Twain's secretary. In the afternoon there were drives and strolls— short ones, because his heart was beginning to give him pain. Most of the days were glorious and were spent soaking up the natural beauties of the Island. It was at Bay House that Mark Twain spent his seventy-fourth birthday.

On December 18 the two men left Bermuda. Mark Twain was not well, but he was anxious to get home for Christmas with Jean. That winter Clara and Ossip were on a concert tour in Europe, and Jean was gaily making all the Christmas preparations by herself. But her father had been back in Stormfield for only a day or two when suddenly Jean died, on the day before Christmas. Although stunned by Jean's death, Mark Twain was also now freed of the dread that he might die first and leave her, an epileptic, behind, unloved and untended in a world which had forfeited his respect. "O, Clara, Clara dear," he wrote, "I am so glad she is out of it and safe—safe!"[87]

Once Jean was safely laid to rest, Mark Twain took his physician's advice and returned to sunny Bermuda. Paine did not go this time. Instead, Mark Twain took Claude, the butler, to be his valet. He tired easily now, and his chest pains were sometimes alarming. The two men sailed on January 5, 1910, and were in Bermuda two days later.

This time Mark Twain went directly to Bay House. Claude came over from the hotel twice a day to inquire if his services were needed. The Allens gladly took turns acting as his secretary, and Helen continued to accompany him on his drives, when he paid calls and when he simply admired the scenery. At the end of January he wrote to Paine that there was not a fault in the life he was leading, tranquil contentment all day and every day without a break.

These letters to Paine, who was keeping Stormfield open for him, provide our best record of these three months in Bermuda. They were not exciting months; excitement was not desired. Mornings, it appears, Mark Twain followed his old habit of reading and writing in bed—even receiving visitors. He had given up all attempts, however, to write or dictate for publication. Conversing and reading were his chief amusements, although special invitations from those he loved best occasionally persuaded him to drive off to a military lecture or to join a motor-launch excursion. Miniature golf on the Bay House lawn was among his more strenuous activities; one photograph shows him playing with Woodrow Wilson.

Most soothing of all, the Island was isolated from many of those things which annoyed or enraged Mark Twain elsewhere. To his absent Bermuda Angel-fish Betsy Wallace he wrote that she ought to be there now. The weather was divine, he said, and he had just watched the sun painting the waters along the North Shore. The sight never staled. Then he added:

> There are no newspapers, no telegrams, no mobiles, no trains, no tramps, no railways, no theatres, no noise, no lectures, no riots, no murders, no fires, no burglaries, no politics, no offenses of any kind, no follies but church, and I don't go there. I think I could live here always and be contented.
>
> You go to heaven if you want to—I'd druther stay here.[88]

Late in March, Paine received a letter which alarmed him for the first time. Mark Twain suddenly announced that he had booked passage home on April 23 and might have to leave sooner if his chest pains did not mend their ways considerably. He did not, he said, want to die in Bermuda. Hastening to Bermuda, Paine found Mark Twain gay, full of plans, and quite himself. Passage had been moved up, however, to April 12. Not until several days before that date did Mark Twain have his next heart attack. It seemed miraculous that he survived it, but the following night he was discovered marching up and down the veranda in his dressing gown. He thought a little exercise might do him good even though this was against strict orders.

The next morning a special tugboat came to the Bay House landing, and sailors carried Mark Twain aboard in a chair. Thus he was transferred to the ship. Paine said that he would never forget the homeward voyage. For two days Mark Twain struggled for breath, apologizing to Paine for being unable to "hurry this dying business." Strong arms and gentle hands got Mark Twain back into his own bed in Stormfield, where he wished to be. And Clara, his one remaining daughter, managed to come to his side from Europe. Gradually, his heart weakened, although his mind remained clear most of the time.

Finally, on April 21, 1910, the end came peacefully, and, to use his own words, he "arrived at the dignity of death—the only earthly dignity that is not artificial—the only safe one."[89] Three days later, while the entire world mourned as seldom before, Mark Twain's body was laid to rest beside his loved ones in Elmira, for two decades the birthplace of his undying characters.

CONCLUSION

In his introduction to *The Heidenmauer,* James Fenimore Cooper pointed out that the man who travels a great deal learns much about mankind, but that also "he is sure to be a loser in the charities that sweeten life." Association with people who dispense services to travelers they will never see again, said Cooper, reveals man's selfishness in its least attractive form. Mark Twain, as we have seen, was exposed to this unattractiveness abroad for a dozen years or more, and mainly at just the time (in the nineties) when he could have used a few more "charities" to sweeten his life.

In his early years he had embarked on his tours with zest. Hawaii, the Mediterranean countries, then the British Isles were sought out with hope and with delight. Unfortunately for his serenity of soul, Mark Twain was no antiquarian like Irving or scholar-adventurer like Longfellow. Before his eyes there swam no dreamy haze to obscure the bleak and the ugly. All too clearly he saw in Europe what Franklin and Jefferson had seen long before: the cruel chasm between opulence and poverty, the physical and spiritual oppression of the masses.

In his early years Mark Twain was not as well oriented politically as John Neal or Cooper had been, and he was less sophisticated socially. Patriotic though he was, he was also not so aggressively nationalistic. Oddly, he loathed the country which Cooper loved best—France. But not until late in life did he come to share Cooper's disillusionment in the workings of popular government as demonstrated in America.

Like Emerson, Melville, and others, he condemned the annoyances of travel and life abroad. He shared their disgust for those wandering sentimentalists who wallowed in the European past until their souls were easily warped out of their own natural orbits. Although forever charmed by the romance of the truly old, Mark Twain was a pragmatist of the present. And he was a voracious sightseer, at first, like Bayard Taylor. He wished to sample everything. Unlike Taylor, on the other hand, he had not predetermined to enjoy it all or to give the glamorous report so popular at the time. By instinct he joined Melville in frank denunciation of Old World beggars, fleas, dogs, swindlers, shams, and pervading filth and misery. These everyday matters helped to convince him that the worship of the past, the worship of dead institutions, was noxious.

As the years passed, however, like Hawthorne, he became less and less sure that Europe represented only corruption, superstition, backwardness, and feudal decay. He shared both Hawthorne's love for Europe's tranquillity and historical associations and Hawthorne's outrage at socioeconomic crimes, chief of which was the Italian Church. Like both Lowell and Adams, he passed through a period of intense Anglophobia but emerged with a warm admiration for the English gentleman. This admiration, shared also with Irving, Cooper, Emerson, and others, led him to the ultimate conviction that the security of the world resided in the stability of England and in her friendship with the United States. Although he was proud of his homeland, Mark Twain was not the first thoughtful American to grow more and more dubious about young, impudent, self-assertive America.

Mark Twain's observations about the foreign scene seldom achieved the analytic orderliness of Emerson's or Howells', nor did they rise to the philosophical heights of Adams'. The foreign experience, moreover, did not mean very much to him as a creative artist, as it did to Howells and obsessively to Henry James. For many years he tended to see Europe and the rest of the world in remoteness, as it were, with slight relevance to America socially, culturally, economically, or politically. Not until after his 1895–96 trip around the world did he begin to think in truly international terms. The Boer War, the Spanish-American War, the Boxer Rebellion, the Russo-Japanese War, the atrocities of King Leopold and the Czar—these great events almost obliged him to think of mankind as a whole.

The Western nations were behaving with particular violence and avarice when Mark Twain made his triumphal return in 1900 to the United States. Corruption, slaughter, treachery were rampant the world over. Christian civilization, even that of America, seemed to be no benign improvement over the barbarism of backward lands. So it was that Mark Twain began to share Melville's and Adams' hatred of so-called Christian imperialism in the Pacific and elsewhere. In the words of Van Wyck Brooks, "He, at any rate, the most sensitive, the most humane of men, rode forth to the encounter now, the champion of all who, like himself, had been in bondage."[1]

During her late years Mark Twain's mother wondered innocently why her famous son was so concerned with setting the world aright. It did not occur to Jane Clemens that perhaps he had inherited her spirit of humanity and that, like her, he was a "born sponsor of causes."[2] To many Americans in 1900 it seemed that the genial humorist had suddenly been transformed into a reformer and critic of the most vigorous kind. But such was not the fact. From his earliest days as a reporter for the California newspapers, Mark Twain had never ceased to level the lance of satire at man's flaws. The arena and the flaws had simply grown larger; that was all. Now they were worldwide. Stephen Leacock recognized this when extolling Mark Twain as the greatest literary figure that America had ever seen, and the most authentically American. "More than that," he said, " I think that Mark Twain, by the spirit that animates all his books—his hatred of tyranny and injustice, his sympathy with the oppressed individual, did more than any other writer towards making the idea of liberty a part of the American heritage."[3]

This "idea of liberty" lay at the instinctive heart of Mark

Twain. It was more a part of his *Weltansicht* than he himself may have realized, since he lacked the discipline ever to formulate his beliefs into a design. With a mind even less analytical than the minds of most artists, he was never quite at home in the realm of ideas. Consequently, many of his attitudes, not being grounded in solid principles, were subject to oscillations. The spontaneous Frontier radicalism which he brought East in 1867 proved extremely susceptible to cultivated influences.

Before these influences had grown strong, however, Mark Twain managed to inspect the venerated sights of Europe from a frankly Western American point of view. And his report, which he said went right on selling like the Bible, had an emancipating influence on the American soul. This would have delighted Fenimore Cooper. Even Howells praised *The Innocents Abroad* for helping to liberate the East from its timid anxiety about foreign opinion; he commended the West for "its ignorant courage or its indifference to its difference from the rest of the world."[4]

Although the ensuing years saw Mark Twain become, in many respects, a candidate for gentility, he steadfastly refused to judge the nations of the world either by the splendor of their pasts or by the refinement of their upper classes. By their fruits he wished to know them. And these fruits were the health, the happiness, the comfort, and the freedom of the masses. In spite of the theoretical pessimism of his late years, Mark Twain's feeling for his fellow man remained one of deep compassion. In practice he could not seem to remember his theory that the human race was too degenerate to be worth saving. He would damn it, then turn around and fight to save it wherever it was in deepest trouble.

It is true that to a certain extent the Philistinism of the Gilded Age did become articulate in Mark Twain. He was a frank modernist. He continued to deplore the lethargy of foreign countries in keeping up-to-date scientifically, so as to make the material conveniences of life available to their citizens. As we have seen, however, during the late eighties he came to believe that the average European suffered less by reason of material deprivation than he did from the oppression of such dominant institutions as the established church, monarchy, and hereditary caste system.

This view, in turn, underwent modifications during the nineties. Just as residence in Hartford and association with people of cultivated taste had long before reconciled Mark Twain's rude Western nature to most of the standards of genteel society, so now did his long residence abroad and his association with the regnant figures of Europe serve to allay his contempt for the undemocratic society and institutions of the Old World. In this respect, as Ludwig Lewisohn has pointed out, he was the average American of his time who twisted the tail of the British lion and dreamed of being rich enough and famous enough to have his wife and daughters presented at court. Because his early republican ideals were not bedded in firm principles, Mark Twain continued to react emotionally to conditions abroad, just as he had reacted to Napoleon III and the Czar in 1867. And it must be acknowledged that this tendency made him almost childishly incurious at times until near the turn of the century, dimming his awareness of nascent political and economic forces. Justin Kaplan goes so far as to say that Mark Twain, to a certain extent, became not only an expatriate from his own country but also, to a much greater extent, "an expatriate from his own times."[5]

This incuriosity, however, did not resemble the apparent indifference of such men as Irving, Longfellow, and James to the current problems of Europe. If Mark Twain lacked the cool perspicacity of the political scientist, it was not because he sentimentalized the traditions or cultural refinements of Europe but simply because he was temperamentally and intellectually incapable, until about 1898, of the concentration required to analyze sociopolitical forces. After 1898, in particular, he was right about a great number of things. Writing in 1940, George Hiram Brownell praised his insight and his gift of prophecy:

> Mark Twain, as of 1898, was probably the most internationally-minded thinker then alive . . . in the light of European developments during the past four decades, it seems evident that Twain's keen power of observation of affairs, in those [European] countries had thus early detected in them the genesis of the wars that have since occurred—all brought about by minorities led by the Prussian nobility, Hitler, Stalin and Mussolini.[6]

Coley B. Taylor recalls how Mark Twain used to shock his neighbors in Redding, Connecticut, in 1908 and 1909 with dire prophecies of a great world war just over the horizon. The good people thought his mind was weakened with age and grief. But, as Paul Carter points out, Mark Twain's prediction of a great war was not the offspring of a warped brain: "He had not wandered over Europe with closed eyes; he was voicing no willful prophecies; he backed his opinions with his observations."[7]

Observation and instinct helped Mark Twain to be right about many things. A great deal that he cried out against has now vanished from the earth, and a great deal that he cried out for has since become the order of the world. Like a nineteenth-century Cervantes he cried out for a long time against those romancers who infatuated people with the false grandeurs and specious beauties of the Old World, thereby setting back the clock of progress. Then, because he could perceive so many of the abuses of foreign civilization mirrored in his own native land, Mark Twain grew more humble in his attitude toward Europe, less defiantly American. It began to strike him, in the last analysis, that the abuses of foreign culture were attributable less to undemocratic institutions than simply to the frailties and shortcomings of human nature in general. And from this unhappy conviction grew his bitter attacks on the nature of man himself and ultimately on the Creator who made man the way he was.

Bitterness is ever a tone of the great idealists. So glorious is their vision of what life can be that they burn with fury at what it actually is. Mark Twain could fulminate with the Swifts and Byrons of history, and for the same reason: man's senseless inhumanity to man along the road to liberty and happiness.

If fulminations, however, and embittered cursings were truly the dominant tone of Mark Twain, he would not remain one of the most beloved authors in the world. His greatest books, as everyone knows, are animated chiefly by a humor, an honesty, and a warm compassion which seem to be worldwide in appeal. It was with these qualities that he served as a valuable mediator between the Old World and New World civilizations. To be sure, like Irving and Longfellow, he played his part in interpreting the foreign scene for his countrymen. His primary function, however, was not the importing of European culture into the United States but rather the interpreting of American culture in a broadly human fashion which could be appreciated by all nations of the world. Speaking always in the American idiom, he buttressed international amity by representing national ideals in universal terms and by illustrating, in both his life and his letters, the indivisibility of the human race. As other American writers had drawn America toward Europe, Mark Twain drew Europe and the rest of the world toward America. Never has the United States been blessed with another self-appointed Ambassador-at-Large so dedicated to mankind and so beloved.

NOTES

NOTES TO PREFACE

1. Limited to the European scene and to printed material are Günther Möhle's *Das Europabild Mark Twains* (Bonn, 1940), and Robert Gilkey's unpublished dissertation "Mark Twain Voyageur et son Image de l'Europe" (Paris, 1951). Dewey Ganzel, *Mark Twain Abroad: The Cruise of the "Quaker City"* (Chicago and London, 1968), restricts itself to the 1867 trip but makes excellent use of Mark Twain's unpublished manuscripts, plus the writings of his fellow travelers.

2. Mark Twain Papers, Notebook #32, p. 20. References to the Mark Twain Papers Notebooks are to the typescripts whose pages are numbered. All material quoted from Mark Twain Papers, General Library, University of California, Berkeley, is copyright © 1969 by, and used with the permission of, the Mark Twain Company.

NOTES TO FOREWORD

1. Cushing Strout, *The American Image of the Old World* (New York, 1963), p. 19.

2. Ferner Nuhn, *The Wind Blew from the East* (New York, 1942), p. 14.

3. Richard Beatty, *Bayard Taylor, Laureate of the Gilded Age* (Norman, 1936), p. 206.

NOTES TO CHAPTER 1

1. *Roughing It. The Writings of Mark Twain,* Author's National Edition (New York, 1913), VIII, 192. Hereafter, this collection is called *Writings*.

2. *Ibid.,* VIII, 128.

3. Letter to Orion, November 28, 1853, in *Mark Twain's Letters,* ed. Albert B. Paine (New York, 1917), I, 29.

4. *Writings, op. cit.,* VIII, 135.

5. *The Forgotten Writings of Mark Twain,* ed. Henry Duskis (New York, 1963), p. 280.

6. Letter to Olivia Langdon, January 24, 1869, in *The Love Letters of Mark Twain,* ed. Dixon Wecter (New York, 1949), p. 60.

7. *Mark Twain's Letters from Hawaii,* ed. A. Grove Day (New York, 1966). His great national scoop at this time was interviewing survivors of the shipwrecked "Hornet" in Hawaii.

8. *Mark Twain's Notebook,* ed. Albert B. Paine (New York, 1935), p. 16. Hereafter, this work is called *Notebook.*

9. Mark Twain Papers, Notebook #4–5, Part I, pp. 6q–6r. References to the Mark Twain Papers Notebooks are to the typescripts whose pages are numbered. All material quoted from the Mark Twain Papers is copyright © 1969 by, and used with the permission of, the Mark Twain Company. Hereafter, this collection is called MTP.

10. *Ibid.,* Notebook #4–5, Part I, p. 30.

11. *Ibid.,* Notebook #4–5, Part I, p. 10.

12. Ivan Benson, *Mark Twain's Western Years* (Stanford, 1938), p. 146.

13. *Writings, op. cit.,* VIII, 218. This chapter contains a glowing tribute to the missionaries, as does his letter to the *New York Tribune,* January 9, 1873, and his lecture of February 7, 1873.

14. *Notebook, op. cit.,* pp. 27–28.

15. MTP, Notebook #4–5, Part II, p. 14.

16. Albert B. Paine, *Mark Twain: A Biography* (New York, 1912), III, 1601, from Mark Twain's first lecture, October 2, 1866.

17. Louis J. Budd, *Mark Twain: Social Philosopher* (Bloomington, Ind., 1962), p. 33. *See* "Information Wanted" in *Sketches New and Old, Writings, op. cit.,* XIX; *see also* Mark Twain's letters to the *Daily San Francisco Alta California* and the *New York Tribune,* January 21, 22, 1868.

18. Walter F. Frear, *Mark Twain and Hawaii* (Chicago, 1947), p. 500.

19. *Ibid.,* p. 354.

20. *Mark Twain's Travels with Mr. Brown,* ed. Franklin Walker and G. Ezra Dane (New York, 1940), pp. 44–45. This volume contains all the lectures of this series.

21. *Notebook, op. cit.,* p. 40.

22. For further information about these lost letters, *see* Dewey Ganzel, *Mark Twain Abroad: The Cruise of the "Quaker City"* (Chicago and London, 1968), pp. 48–49, 261–282.

23. *See* Leon T. Dickinson, "Mark Twain's Innocents Abroad" (Doctoral Dissertation, University of Chicago, 1945), p. 7. *See also, Mark Twain to Mrs. Fairbanks,* ed. Dixon Wecter (San Marino, 1949), p. 22.

24. *See* Leon T. Dickinson, "Mark Twain's Revisions in Writing *The Innocents Abroad,*" *American Literature,* XIX (May, 1947), pp. 139–157.

25. *Mark Twain to Mrs. Fairbanks, op. cit.,* p. 110.

26. Note by Isabel Lyon, dated July 9, 1936, in the Berg Collection, New York Public Library; photostat in MTP.

27. In our own century, criticism of this tenor has been carried on by numerous writers, among whom a few of the best known are Stuart P. Sherman, Van Wyck Brooks, Edgar Lee Masters, Granville Hicks, Gamaliel Bradford, F. O. Matthiessen, Constance Rourke, and Arthur H. Quinn.

28. Henry Seidel Canby, *Turn West, Turn East,* (Boston, 1951), p. 81.

29. Theodore Witmer, *Wild Oats Sown Abroad* (Philadelphia, 1872), pp. 129, 146.

30. Samuel Fiske, *Mr. Dunn Browne's Experiences in Foreign Parts* (Boston, 1857), pp. 121–122.

31. *Ibid.,* p. 220.

32. John W. De Forest, *Oriental Acquaintance; or Letters from Syria* (New York, 1856), p. 80.

33. James De Mill, "The Dodge Club," *Harper's Monthly,* XXX (1867), pp. 410, 705–706.

34. Richard C. Beatty, *James Russell Lowell* (Nashville, 1942), p. 116.

35. MTP, unpublished letter of April 20, 1869.

36. R. W. B. Lewis, *The American Adam* (Chicago, 1955), p. 144.

37. Stephen Leacock, *Mark Twain* (New York, 1933), p. 46.

38. Note dated Hartford, November 6, 1886; photostat in MTP.

39. MTP, Notebook #7, p. 14.

40. *Writings, op. cit.,* I, 113.

41. *Ibid.,* VII, 157.

42. *Ibid.,* I, 116.

43. *Ibid.,* I, 170.

44. *Ibid.*, I, 331–332.

45. V. F. Calverton, *The Liberation of American Literature* (New York, 1932), pp. 319–328.

46. *Mark Twain to Mrs. Fairbanks, op. cit.*, p. 46.

47. Russell Blankenship, *American Literature as an Expression of the National Mind* (New York, 1931), p. 465.

48. Stuart Sherman, "Mark Twain," *The Nation*, XC (May 12, 1910), p. 479.

49. *Writings, op. cit.*, I, 307.

50. *Ibid.*, I, 149.

51. H. R. Haweis, *American Humorists* (London, 1883), p. 186.

52. *Writings, op. cit.*, II, 15.

53. *Ibid.*, I, 321–322. This tear jug is now in Berkeley with the MTP.

54. *Ibid.*, I, 177–178.

55. *Ibid.*, II, 20–21.

56. Granville Hicks, *The Great Tradition* (New York, 1933), pp. 40–41.

57. Sherman, *op. cit.*, p. 479.

58. *Writings, op. cit.*, I, 198.

59. *Ibid.*, II, 107.

60. *Ibid.*, I, 202, 203.

61. *Ibid.*, II, 271.

62. *Ibid.*, I, 278.

63. *Ibid.*, II, 30–31.

64. *Ibid.*, II, 313.

65. *Ibid.*, II, 310.

66. *Ibid.*, II, 378.

67. The Webster Collection owns at least thirty-five items Mark Twain brought back from this trip, among them marble from the Parthenon, cedar from King Godfrey's Tree, limestone from a Jericho well. A complete list of items is in the MTP.

68. MTP, DW #15 contains an unpublished typescript of material supposedly rejected from *The Innocents Abroad.*

69. *Writings, op. cit.*, I, 325–326.

70. *Traveling with the Innocents Abroad; Mark Twain's Original Reports from Europe and the Holy Land,* ed. Daniel M. McKeithan (Norman, 1958), p. 57.

71. Arthur H. Quinn, *American Fiction: An Historical and Critical Survey* (New York, 1936), pp. 244–245.

72. *Writings, op. cit.*, I, 226.

73. *Ibid.*, I, 204–205.

74. *Ibid.*, I, 315.

75. *Ibid.*, I, 316.

76. *Ibid.*, II, 185–186.

77. *Notebook, op. cit.*, p. 78.

78. *Traveling with the Innocents Abroad, op. cit.*, p. 141.

79. *Writings, op. cit.*, II, 123.

80. Thomas Bentzon in *Revue des Deux Mondes*, quoted from a clipping pasted in the back of Mark Twain's 1872 scrapbook, in MTP.

81. Letter to the *Alta California*, December 14, 1867, reprinted in the *Twainian* (September-October, 1947), p. 4.

82. *Writings, op. cit.*, I, 176, 173.

83. Quoted in De Lancey Ferguson, *Mark Twain: Man and Legend* (Indianapolis, 1943), p. 123.

84. *Writings, op. cit.*, I, 172.

85. *Buffalo Express*, November 19, 1870. Mark Twain was co-owner and co-editor of the paper at the time.

86. *Ibid.*, March 8, 1870.

87. *Traveling with the Innocents Abroad, op. cit.*, p. 69.

88. *Writings, op. cit.*, I, 218.

89. *Ibid.*, I, 329.

90. *Ibid.*, I, 327.

91. *Ibid.*, II, 382.

92. Haweis, *op. cit.*, p. 167.

93. *Writings, op. cit.*, I, 343.

94. *Traveling with the Innocents Abroad, op. cit.*, p. 87.

95. *Writings, op. cit.*, II, 26.

96. Letter from Naples to Frank Fuller, August 7, 1867; typescript in MTP.

97. *Writings, op. cit.*, I, 268–269.

98. *Notebook, op. cit.*, p. 93.

99. *Traveling with the Innocents Abroad, op. cit.*, p. 251.

100. MTP, Notebook #8, p. 50.

101. *Writings, op. cit.*, II, 358–359.

102. *Ibid.*, II, p. 384.

103. "Curious Relic for Sale," *Galaxy* (October, 1870), reprinted in Mark Twain, *Life As I Find It*, ed. Charles Neider (Garden City, N.Y., 1961), pp. 56–57.

104. *Writings, op. cit.*, II, 386–387.

105. *Ibid.*, II, 391–393.

106. MTP, DW #14.

107. *Writings, op. cit.,* II, 440.

108. *Mark Twain to Mrs. Fairbanks, op. cit.,* p. 59.

109. *Writings, op. cit.,* II, 362–363.

110. The book is inscribed "S. L. Clemens/Hartford 1877." It is now in the MTP.

111. *Writings, op. cit.,* I, 241–243.

112. *Ibid.,* II, 436.

113. Ganzel, *op. cit.,* p. 321.

114. Interview in the *New York World,* October 14, 1900, reprinted in *The Travels of Mark Twain,* ed. Charles Neider (New York, 1961), pp. 23–24.

115. "Current Literature," *Overland Monthly,* I (July, 1868), p. 101.

116. Quoted in George M. Pierson, "The M-Factor in American History," *American Quarterly,* XIV (Summer, 1962), p. 277.

117. Canby, *op. cit.,* p. 80.

118. Beatty, *op. cit.,* pp. 121–122.

119. From one of her articles written for Greeley's *New York Tribune,* 1847–49, quoted in *Discovery of Europe,* ed. Philip Rahv (Boston, 1947), pp. 166–167.

120. The best discussion of these roles and others is in John C. Gerber, "Mark Twain's Use of the Comic Pose," *Publications of the Modern Language Association of America,* LXXVII (June, 1962), pp. 297–304.

121. *Writings, op. cit.,* II, 346–347.

122. *Cambridge History of American Literature* (New York, 1921), III, 9.

123. John Macy, *The Spirit of American Literature* (New York, 1913), p. 251.

124. Sidney Brooks, "Mark Twain in England," *Harper's Weekly,* LI (July 20, 1907), p. 1054.

125. *Writings, op. cit.,* II, 444.

126. *Mark Twain's Speeches,* ed. Albert B. Paine (New York, 1933), pp. 29–30.

NOTES TO CHAPTER 2

1. Van Wyck Brooks, *The Ordeal of Mark Twain* (New York, 1920), p. 114.

2. *Mark Twain to Mr. Fairbanks,* ed. Dixon Wecter (San Marino, 1949), p. 108.

3. *Buffalo Express,* September 30, 1869.

4. Letter of November 28, 1870, to Elisha Bliss, *Mark Twain's Letters to His Publishers 1867–1894,* ed. Hamlin Hill (Berkeley, 1967), p. 42. In the same volume *see also* Mark Twain's fascinating letter to Riley on December 2, 1870, urging him to quit his job, setting forth terms of the agreement, etc.

5. The best discussion of this subject is Kenneth R. Andrews, *Nook Farm, Mark Twain's Hartford Circle* (Cambridge, Mass., 1950).

6. Albert B. Paine, *Mark Twain: A Biography* (New York, 1912), I, 465. Hereafter, this work is called *Biography.*

7. Mark Twain Papers, DV #69, carbon copy. All the material quoted from the Mark Twain Papers is copyright © 1969 by, and used with the permission of, the Mark Twain Company. Hereafter, this collection is called MTP.

8. *Ibid.,* December 3, 1873, typescript.

9. *The Love Letters of Mark Twain,* ed. Dixon Wecter (New York, 1949), p. 177.

10. William Dean Howells, *My Mark Twain* (New York, 1910), pp. 46–47.

11. *Mark Twain to Mrs. Fairbanks, op. cit.,* p. 166.

12. MTP, unpublished letter of October 25, 1872.

13. *Ibid.,* P #90.

14. *Ibid.,* DV #69, unpublished "Diary Notes Made in England 1872," pp. 103–111. Hereafter, this collection is called *Diary Notes.*

15. *Ibid.,* p. 112.

16. *Ibid.,* pp. 197-198.

17. *Ibid.,* pp. 175–192.

18. *Ibid.,* pp. 164–165.

19. MTP, P #176.

20. *Mark Twain's Sketches,* Authorized Edition (New York, 1874), p. 8.

21. *Ibid.,* p. 29.

22. MTP, letter to Livy.

23. MTP, DV #69, p. 149.

24. *Ibid.,* p. 118.

25. Howard Baetzhold, "Mark Twain: England's Advocate," *American Literature,* XXVIII (November, 1956), p. 332.

26. For a discussion of this subject, *see* my article, "Mark Twain's Revisions of *The Innocents Abroad* for the British Edition of 1872," *American Literature,* XXV (March, 1953), pp. 43–61.

27. MTP, DV #134. "To the English Reader" is the original for this Preface.

28. *Biography, op. cit.,* I, 484.

29. These letters are reprinted under the title "O'Shah" in *Europe and Elsewhere,* ed. Albert B. Paine (New York, 1923), pp. 31–86.

30. *Ibid.,* p. 68.

31. *Ibid.,* p. 81.

32. *Mark Twain to Mrs. Fairbanks, op. cit.,* pp. 174–175; letter of July 6, 1873, from London.

33. *Ibid.,* pp. 172–173.

34. For an account of this deliberate action see the *New York Times,* December 15, 1935, Section II, p. 2.

35. *Mark Twain's Letters,* ed. Albert B. Paine (New York, 1917), I, 207–208. Paine says here that this is the "only letter remaining from this time." Hereafter, this collection is called *Letters.*

36. Unpublished letter of January 3, 1873; photostat in MTP.

37. Unpublished letter of December 21, 1873, to Fitzgibbon, in the Berg Collection, New York Public Library. For information on Mark Twain's lecturing, *see* Fred W. Lorch, *The Trouble Begins at Eight* (Ames, 1968).

38. MTP, unpublished letter to Livy, November 24, 1873.

39. *Ibid.,* unpublished letter of December 25, 1873.

40. *Mark Twain's Notebook,* ed. Albert B. Paine (New York, 1935), p. 130. Hereafter, this work is called *Notebook.*

41. *Mark Twain to Mrs. Fairbanks, op. cit.,* p. 209.

42. Mark Twain, *Rambling Notes of an Idle Excursion* (Toronto, 1878), p. 61.

43. *Ibid.,* p. 57.

44. *Ibid.,* p. 48.

45. MTP, Notebook #11, p. 24. References to the MTP Notebooks are to the typescripts whose pages are numbered. Paine says that this story is first mentioned in the notebooks on November 23, 1877 (*Notebook, op. cit.,* p. 129), although his biography attests that about four hundred manuscript pages of the novel were written that summer.

46. *Letters, op. cit.,* I, 319–320.

47. *Mark Twain's Letters to Mrs. Fairbanks, op. cit.,* p. 222.

48. MTP, typescript of letter to Bayard Taylor, December 14, 1878.

49. *Mark Twain-Howells Letters,* ed. Henry Nash Smith and William Gibson (Cambridge, Mass., 1960), I, 236.

50. *Biography, op. cit.,* II, 666–667.

51. MTP, unpublished letter dated August 20, 1878.

52. *The Writings of Mark Twain,* Author's National Edition (New York, 1913), IV, 272. Hereafter, this collection is called *Writings.*

53. MTP, DV #4. This file contains manuscripts probably written for *A Tramp Abroad* but discarded and never published.

54. *Writings, op. cit.,* I, 272.

55. MTP, Notebook #14, p. 13.

56. *Ibid.,* Notebook #26, p. 6.

57. *See* Albert E. Stone, Jr., "The Twichell Papers and Mark Twain's *A Tramp Abroad," Yale University Library Gazette,* XXIX, 4 (April, 1955), pp. 151–165.

58. MTP, typescript of unpublished letter to Bayard Taylor, June 10, 1878.

59. *Ibid.,* DV #4.

60. *Ibid.,* Notebook #12, p. 4.

61. *Notebook, op. cit.,* pp. 135–136.

62. *Writings, op. cit.,* III, 87.

63. *Ibid.,* III, 78.

64. *Ibid.,* III, 242.

65. *Ibid.,* IV, 243–246.

66. MTP, Notebook #13, p. 21.

67. *Ibid.,* Notebook #12, p. 32.

68. *Writings, op. cit.,* III, 240.

69. MTP, Notebook #12, p. 16.

70. MTP, Notebook #13, p. 34.

71. *Writings, op. cit.,* IV, 173.

72. *Ibid.,* IV, 100.

73. *Ibid.,* IV, 50.

74. *Letters, op. cit.,* p. 351.

75. *Writings, op. cit.,* IV, 45.

76. *Ibid.,* IV, 230.

77. *Ibid.,* IV, 94–95.

78. Stone, *op. cit.,* p. 159.

79. *Writings, op. cit.,* IV, 255.

80. These observations are all from MTP, Notebook #13, pp. 9–30.

81. *Mark Twain–Howells Letters, op. cit.*, I, 248–249.

82. *Writings, op. cit.*, IV, 271.

83. MTP, DV #4 is the manuscript upon which these two paragraphs are based.

84. *Ibid.*, Notebook #14, p. 7.

85. *Notebook, op. cit.*, p. 153.

86. *Biography, op. cit.*, II, 641–642.

87. MTP, DV #4.

88. *Letters from the Earth*, ed. Bernard De Voto (New York, 1962), pp. 181–189. This volume, compiled by De Voto in 1940, contains a number of pieces considered too outspoken to be published earlier.

89. MTP, DV #4.

90. *Ibid.*, DV #4.

91. *Ibid.*, Notebook #13, p. 1.

92. *Ibid.*, Notebook #14, p. 22.

93. *Ibid.*, Notebook #14, pp. 25–26.

94. *Ibid.*, Notebook #14, p. 28.

95. *Ibid.*, Notebook #12, p. 49.

96. *Ibid.*, Notebook #14, p. 15.

97. *Ibid.*, Notebook #14, p. 23.

98. *Ibid.*, Notebook #14, p. 16.

99. *Ibid.*, Notebook #14, p. 29.

100. *Ibid.*, Notebook #14, p. 28.

101. *Ibid.*, Notebook #14, p. 14.

102. *Ibid.*, Notebook #13, p. 29.

103. *Notebook, op. cit.*, p. 154.

104. *Ibid.*, p. 154.

105. *Ibid.*, p. 154.

106. *Ibid.*, p. 140.

107. *Ibid.*, p. 150.

108. MTP, Notebook #14, p. 42.

109. *Notebook, op. cit.*, pp. 156–157.

110. MTP, P #276, "Mark Twain and England." This is the typescript of an article in the *Hartford Courant*, May 14, 1879, written before his 1879 visit.

111. *Ibid.*, P #276.

112. For an excellent description of the requirements of subscrip-

tion book publishing, *see* Hamlin Hill, "Mark Twain: Audience and Artistry," *American Quarterly*, XV (Spring, 1963), pp. 25–40.

113. *Mark Twain–Howells Letters, op. cit.*, I, 250.

NOTES TO CHAPTER 3

1. Quoted in Henry Adams, *The Education of Henry Adams* (Boston, 1924), pp. 190–191.

2. "General Note" at the end of *The Prince and the Pauper, The Writings of Mark Twain*, Author's National Edition (New York, 1913), XV, 315. Hereafter, this collection is called *Writings*.

3. Mark Twain Papers, DV #114–116. All material quoted from the Mark Twain Papers is copyright © 1969 by, and used with the permission of, the Mark Twain Company. Hereafter, this collection is called MTP.

4. Stephen Leacock, *Mark Twain* (New York, 1933), pp. 83–84.

5. *See* Arthur L. Vogelback, "*The Prince and the Pauper*: A Study in Critical Standards," *American Literature*, XIV (March, 1942), pp. 48–54.

6. *Writings, op. cit.*, XV, 167.

7. *Ibid.*, XV, 39–40.

8. *Ibid.*, XV, 165.

9. *Ibid.*, XV, 253.

10. *Mark Twain's Letters*, ed. Albert B. Paine (New York, 1917), I, 432. Hereafter, this collection is called *Letters*.

11. A copy of the patent is in MTP. Two of the playing boards are in *ibid.*, P #181, together with Mark Twain's drawings. *Ibid.*, DV #157 is a fifty-seven-page manuscript of 1883 in which he listed events and worked out instructions for the game. *See also, ibid.*, Notebook #17, pp. 10–22 (references to the MTP Notebooks are to the typescripts whose pages are numbered), *and* Albert B. Paine, *Mark Twain: A Biography* (New York, 1912), II, 751–754. (Hereafter this latter work is called *Biography*.)

12. *Writings, op. cit.*, IX, 213.

13. MTP, DV #141, a copy of the "Tourist Chapter." The original is in the Rogers Memorial Room at Harvard University and bears the pencil note by James R. Osgood, the publisher, "I should suggest omitting this chapter. JRO to p. 101." Incidentally, Mark Twain was an excellent speller, but "seize" and "siege" always gave him trouble.

14. *Writings, op. cit.*, XV, 347.

15. S. B. Liljegren, "The Revolt against Romanticism in American Literature as Evidenced in the Works of S. L. Clemens," *Essays and Studies in American Language and Literature* (Upsala, 1945), p. 35.

16. MTP, Notebook #18, p. 4.

17. *Ibid.*, marginalia in Daniel F. Beatty's *In Foreign Lands from Original Notes* (1878). The book was given Mark Twain by the author. Mark Twain noted that he read it on January 5, 1884.

18. *Ibid.*, letter of March 4, 1884, to Karl and Josephine Gerhardt, a charming young couple whom he was sponsoring at art school in Europe.

19. *Ibid.*, DV #111.

20. In 1885 he dictated an interesting account of this episode. It appears in *Mark Twain's Autobiography*, ed. Albert B. Paine (New York, 1924), I, 20–24.

21. MTP, Notebook #19, p. 32.

22. *Ibid.*, pp. 36–37. Compare *Mark Twain's Notebook*, ed. Albert B. Paine (New York, 1935), p. 185. (Hereafter, this latter work is called *Notebook*.)

23. MTP, Mark Twain's copy was translated by Bayle St. John (London, n.d.).

24. *Writings, op. cit.*, I, 86.

25. *Ibid.*, I, 200.

26. *Ibid.*, I, 375.

27. *Ibid.*, II, 117.

28. MTP, Notebook #21, p. 32.

29. *Ibid.*, Notebook #21, p. 32.

30. *Ibid.*, Notebook #21, p. 46.

31. *Ibid.*, unpublished letter of January 3, 1885.

32. *Ibid.*, P #91.

33. "International Copyright," *Life as I Find It*, ed. Charles Neider (Garden City, N.Y., 1961), pp. 214–215. This first appeared in *Century Magazine*, February, 1886.

34. MTP, Notebook #22, p. 64.

35. *Notebook, op. cit.*, pp. 195–202.

36. *Ibid.*, pp. 207–210.

37. *Mark Twain to Mrs. Fairbanks*, ed. Dixon Wecter (San Marino, 1949) p. 258.

38. John B. Hoben, "Mark Twain's *A Connecticut Yankee;* A Genetic Study," *American Literature*, XVIII (November, 1946), p. 212.

39. MTP, Notebook #23, I, 2, summer, 1888.

40. *Ibid.,* Notebook #23, I, 11–12.

41. *Ibid.,* Notebook #24, pp. 26–27.

42. *Ibid.,* Notebook #24, pp. 38–39.

43. *Ibid.,* P #200, DV #75, nine pages.

44. *Ibid.,* DV #16, eight pages.

45. *Ibid.,* P #200.

46. *Ibid.,* DV #128 (6), four pages.

47. *Ibid.,* DV #15, ten pages.

48. *Ibid.,* DV #14.

49. *Ibid.,* P #102a. Much of this paper was incorporated into Chapter 10 of *The American Claimant* (1892).

50. *Mark Twain's Speeches,* ed. Albert B. Paine (New York, 1933), p. 151.

51. MTP, P #102b, twenty-nine pages.

52. *Ibid.,* P #91.

53. *Ibid.,* DV #313, "The Curse of McAllister: A Defense." McAllister was the "creator & recognized Grand Lama" of the Four Hundred.

54. *Ibid.,* DV #80, thirty-five pages.

55. *Ibid.,* DV #344, thirty-two pages. Paine dated it "Probably '89" and filed pp. 24–32 separately as P #41.

56. *See, Mark Twain's Letters from Hawaii,* ed. A. Grove Day (New York, 1966), pp. xii–xvi, for A. Grove Day's and Fred Lorch's belief that much of the satire in *A Connecticut Yankee* was taken from an unpublished novel that Mark Twain had written about Hawaii in 1884.

57. *See,* O. H. Moore, "Mark Twain and Don Quixote," *Publications of the Modern Language Association of America,* XXXVIII (June, 1922), pp. 324–346.

58. *Notebook, op. cit.,* p. 198.

59. Cited by Bernard De Voto, *Mark Twain's America* (Boston, 1932), p. 212n.

60. William Dean Howells, *Harper's Monthly,* XXX (January, 1890), pp. 319–321.

61. *Notebook, op. cit.,* p. 199.

62. *Ibid.,* p. 210.

63. *Writings, op. cit.,* XVI, 106.

64. *Ibid.,* XVI, 161.

65. *Ibid.,* XVI, 161.

66. *Biography, op. cit.,* III, 1656.

67. William Dean Howells, *My Mark Twain* (New York, 1910), p. 80.

68. *Writings, op. cit.,* XVI, 217.

69. *Ibid.,* XVI, 65–66.

70. *Letters, op. cit.,* II, 519–520.

71. *Writings, op. cit.,* XVI, 402.

72. An excellent discussion of the complex character of Hank Morgan can be found in Roger B. Saloman, *Twain and the Image of History* (New Haven, 1961), Chapter 6.

73. *Writings, op. cit.,* XVI, 131.

74. *Ibid.,* XVI, 219.

75. MTP, DV #72, twelve pages.

76. *Writings, op. cit.,* XVI, 67.

77. De Lancey Ferguson, *Mark Twain: Man and Legend* (Indianapolis, 1943), p. 238.

78. *Writings, op. cit.,* XVI, 142.

79. *Ibid.,* XVI, 116.

80. *Ibid.,* XVI, 167.

81. *Ibid.,* XVI, 144.

82. *Ibid.,* XVI, 220.

83. *Ibid.,* XVI, 276.

84. Bernard De Voto asserts that the book contains a "complete statement of the Mugwump beliefs." De Voto, *op. cit.,* p. 275.

85. *Letters, op. cit.,* II, 524. Louis J. Budd points out that much of the Yankee's "say" against Church and State repeats in a catchy idiom the arguments of the agnostic Robert Ingersoll and of Andrew Dickson White, Henry C. Lear, and John W. Draper: Louis J. Budd, *Mark Twain: Social Philosopher* (Bloomington, Ind., 1963), pp. 116–117.

86. *Letters, op. cit.,* II, 525–528. Part of this famous and revealing letter is missing.

87. Clara Clemens, *My Father: Mark Twain* (New York, 1931), p. 289.

88. MTP, note on the back of a letter begun to a Mr. Blake and dated "Hartford, Apl. 3/91."

89. *Ibid.* This two-page manuscript is among the *The American Claimant* papers in Box 14. Paine's notation reads "Claimant?"

90. *Writings, op. cit.,* XXI, 123.

91. *Ibid.,* XXI, 105. In 1893 Mark Twain developed this idea in his humorous satire "The Esquimau Maiden's Romance."

92. *Letters, op. cit.,* II, 537.

93. MTP, a three-page typescript dated July, 1890.

94. *Ibid.,* DV #128 (7).

95. *Ibid., Notebook* #26, p. 4.

96. *Biography, op. cit.,* III, 1639.

97. Walter F. Taylor, *The Economic Novel in America* (Chapel Hill, 1942), p. 139.

98. Stuart Sherman, *On Contemporary Literature* (New York, 1917), p. 41.

NOTES TO CHAPTER 4

1. Mark Twain Papers, unpublished letter of February 13, 1869, from Ravenna, Ohio. All material quoted from the Mark Twain Papers is copyright © 1969 by, and used with the permission of, the Mark Twain Company. Hereafter, this collection is called MTP.

2. *Mark Twain's Notebook,* ed. Albert B. Paine (New York, 1935), p. 218. Hereafter, this work is called *Notebook.*

3. MTP, Notebook #25, p. 33. References to the MTP Notebooks are to the typescripts whose pages are numbered. Howells received this report from London.

4. *Ibid.,* Notebook #25, p. 45. The bracketed word is for one Mark Twain omitted.

5. Reprinted in *Europe and Elsewhere,* ed. Albert B. Paine (New York, 1923), pp. 94–112.

6. *What Is Man? And Other Essays,* Authorized Edition (New York, 1917), p. 226.

7. Albert B. Paine, *Mark Twain: A Biography* (New York, 1912), II, 923. Hereafter, this work is called *Biography.*

8. *Europe and Elsewhere, op. cit.,* p. 121.

9. Reprinted in Mark Twain's *Life as I Find It,* ed. Charles Neider (Garden City, N.Y., 1961), p. 231, where it is misdated 1895. The poem, entitled "A Love Song," first appeared in the *Medical Fortnightly* (St. Louis), May 15, 1892.

10. *Europe and Elsewhere, op. cit.,* pp. 126–127.

11. Clara Clemens, *My Father: Mark Twain* (New York, 1931), pp. 93–94.

12. *The Writings of Mark Twain,* Author's National Edition (New York, 1913), XXI, 483–501. Hereafter, this collection is called *Writings.*

13. *What Is Man? And Other Essays, op. cit.,* p. 194.

14. Paine retitled it "Down the Rhône" in *Europe and Elsewhere, op. cit.,* pp. 129–168. *See* my discussion in "The Innocents Adrift Edited by Mark Twain's Official Biographer," *Publications of the Modern Language Association of America,* LXXVIII (June, 1963), pp. 230–237. The original manuscript is MTP, P #138.

15. Mark Twain, *Letters from the Earth,* ed. Bernard De Voto (New York, 1962), pp. 218–220.

16. *See* my article, "The Innocents Adrift," *op. cit.,* p. 234.

17. In "Down the Rhône" Paine deleted all mention of the British, just as he managed to eliminate Harris and the other imaginary companions. He killed, indeed, the most interesting and revealing half of Mark Twain's manuscript.

18. MTP, HNS file, a twenty-one-page manuscript. Portions are printed in *Biography, op. cit.,* II, 930–931.

19. The fullest discussion of his reputation there is Edgar H. Hemminghaus's *Mark Twain in Germany* (New York, 1939).

20. MTP, DV #329.

21. John T. Krumpelmann, *Mark Twain and the German Language,* Louisiana State University Studies (Baton Rouge, 1953), p. 14.

22. Clara Clemens, *op. cit.,* p. 100.

23. William Dean Howells, *My Mark Twain* (New York, 1910), pp. 67–68.

24. Henry W. Fischer, *Abroad with Mark Twain and Eugene Field* (New York, 1922), pp. 42–43, 121, 209.

25. *Notebook, op. cit.,* p. 222.

26. *Writings, op. cit.,* XXI, 504.

27. MTP, P #73. This manuscript is complete, signed, and dated January, 1892.

28. *Europe and Elsewhere, op. cit.,* p. 180.

29. *Ibid.,* p. 185.

30. MTP, 1891–92 Scrapbook, p. 36; quoted from a typed translation in the same book.

31. *Notebook, op. cit.,* p. 225. He listed more than a dozen hateful things about this hotel.

32. *Europe and Elsewhere, op. cit.,* p. 187. He never printed this piece.

33. *Writings, op. cit.,* XX, 18.

34. *Ibid.,* XX, 91.

35. Quoted in my "Letters from Mark Twain to William Walter

Phelps, 1891–1893," *Huntington Library Quarterly*, XXVII (August, 1964), p. 379.

36. *Mark Twain to Mrs. Fairbanks*, ed. Dixon Wecter (San Marino, 1949), p. 269.

37. *Notebook, op. cit.*, p. 241.

38. Albert E. Stone, Jr., "Mark Twain's *Joan of Arc:* The Child as Goddess," *American Literature*, XXXI (March, 1959), p. 5.

39. *Mark Twain's Letters*, ed. Albert B. Paine (New York, 1917), II, 624; letter of April 29, 1895, the day after the novel was completed, to H. H. Rogers. Hereafter, this collection is called *Letters*.

40. George Bernard Shaw, Preface to his *Saint Joan* (New York, 1924), p. vi.

41. Vernon T. Parrington, *Main Currents in American Thought* (New York, 1930), III, 100.

42. *Writings, op. cit.*, XVIII, 160.

43. *Ibid.*, XVIII, 148.

44. Paine, in *Biography, op. cit.*, II, 987, mistakenly says that Mark Twain did not make a second trip in 1894. In MTP are several letters written by Mark Twain on Players Club stationery in New York and dated July and August, 1894. Also a letter of July 4, 1894, explains to Clara that he delayed his sailing date in Europe because of rioting consequent upon the assassination of the French President.

45. MTP, unpublished letter. How Orion, who was really poor and lived poorly, must have winced at that!

46. *Ibid.*, typescript of unpublished letter of November 6, 1894.

47. Clara Clemens, *op. cit.*, p. 106.

48. Fischer, *op. cit.*, p. 48. Plans for the book are discribed pp. 47–54.

49. MTP, unpublished letter of July 4, 1894.

50. *Ibid.*, DV #317.

51. *Writings, op. cit.*, XX, 157.

52. *Ibid.*, XXII, 145–146.

53. *Ibid.*, XX, 171. These are the words in which Mark Twain himself summarized the French argument. This second essay he published only in the London edition of *Tom Sawyer, Detective* (1896).

54. MTP, unpublished letter of March 21, 1895.

55. *Ibid.*, unpublished letter of May 19, 1896.

56. *Letters, op. cit.*, II, 676.

57. MTP, Notebook #28b, p. 56.

58. *Ibid.*, unpublished letter of July 2, 1897.

59. *Biography, op. cit.*, II, 1054.
60. *Writings, op. cit.*, V, 44–46.
61. *Ibid.*, V, 95.
62. *Ibid.*, V, 167.
63. MTP, Notebook #28b, p. 51.
64. *Writings, op. cit.*, V, 150.
65. *Notebook, op. cit.*, p. 254.
66. MTP, P #84, part of the original manuscript plus Livy's notes.
67. Clara Clemens, *op. cit.*, pp. 148–161.
68. *Writings, op. cit.*, V, 166.
69. From the *Melbourne Age*, September 27, 1895. This is in MTP, together with many other clippings about his lectures and interviews during the tour.
70. *Writings, op. cit.*, V, 216.
71. *Ibid.*, V, 275.
72. *Ibid.*, V, 274.
73. *Ibid.*, V, 336.
74. *Notebook, op. cit.*, p. 254.
75. MTP, Notebook #28b, p. 18.
76. *Writings, op. cit.*, VI, 16.
77. *Notebook, op. cit.*, p. 256.
78. *Writings, op. cit.*, V. 339.
79. MTP, Notebook #28b, p. 16.
80. *Notebook, op. cit.*, p. 248.
81. *Writings, op. cit.*, VI, 18.
82. *Ibid.*, VI, 23.
83. Clara Clemens, *op. cit.*, p. 153. One of their guides in Bombay was a young man named Virchand A. Gandhi, but it was wishful thinking for Paine to call him "Our good Mahatma of later years." *Notebook, op. cit.*, p. 272.
84. *Writings, op. cit.*, VI, 37.
85. *Letters, op. cit.*, II, 633; to Joe Twichell.
86. *Writings, op. cit.*, VI, 202.
87. *Ibid.*, VI, 217.
88. *Ibid.*, VI, 153.
89. MTP, Notebook #28*b*, p. 46. "Xian" stands for "Christian. His punctuation, too, shows signs of haste.
90. *Writings, op. cit.*, VI, 179.
91. *Notebook, op. cit.*, p. 278.
92. MTP, Notebook #29, I, 13–14.

93. *Ibid.*, Notebook #30, p. 39.

94. *Notebook, op. cit.*, p. 300.

95. *Writings, op. cit.*, VI, 269.

96. *Ibid.*, VI, 59.

97. Quoted in Coleman O. Parsons, "Mark Twain: Sightseer in India," *Mississippi Quarterly,* XVI (Spring, 1963), p. 78. To this article I am indebted for a number of details.

98. *Writings, op. cit.*, VI, 65.

99. *Ibid.*, VI, 71.

100. *Ibid.*, VI, 95.

101. *Ibid.*, VI, 98.

102. *Notebook, op. cit.*, p. 276.

103. *Writings, op. cit.*, VI, 204.

104. *Ibid.*, VI, 209.

105. *Ibid.*, VI, 242.

106. *Ibid.*, VI, 203–204.

107. *Ibid.*, VI, 294.

108. *Ibid.*, VI, 83.

109. Almost all of these unflattering comments were excluded from Paine's edition of *Notebook, op. cit.*

110. Surprisingly, Paine did print this: *ibid.*, p. 280.

111. *Writings, op. cit.*, VI, 328.

112. *Ibid.*, VI, 321–322.

113. *Ibid.*, VI, 324.

114. *Ibid.*, VI, 334.

115. MTP, typescript of unpublished letter of June 7, 1896.

116. *Ibid.*, unpublished letter of June 8, 1896.

117. *Writings, op. cit.*, VI, 392–393.

118. MTP, Notebook #30, pp. 24–25.

119. *Writings, op. cit.*, VI, 386.

120. MTP, P #84. Above the word "ostracized" Mark Twain wrote "discredited."

121. *Writings, op. cit.*, VI, 404, 405.

122. MTP, typescript of unpublished letter of March 26, 1897.

NOTES TO CHAPTER 5

1. These two paragraphs are based on Mark Twain Papers, Notebooks #29–#32a. References to the Mark Twain Papers Notebooks

are to the typescripts whose pages are numbered. All material quoted from the Mark Twain Papers is copyright © 1969 by, and used with the permission of, the Mark Twain Company. Hereafter, this collection is called MTP.

2. *Ibid.*, DV #82. This bears Paine's notation, "Written in Vienna." Portions appear in *Mark Twain's Autobiography*, ed. Albert B. Paine (New York, 1924). Hereafter, this work is called *Autobiography*.

3. "Queen Victoria's Jubilee," *Europe and Elsewhere*, ed. Albert B. Paine (New York, 1923), p. 205.

4. *Mark Twain-Howells Letters*, ed. Henry Nash Smith and William Gibson (Cambridge, Mass., 1960), II, 665.

5. Albert B. Paine, *Mark Twain: A Biography* (New York, 1912), II, 1064; speech of 1898. Hereafter, this work is called *Biography*.

6. Quoted in the *London Daily Graphic*, June 13, 1899.

7. MTP, Notebook #32b, p. 54. About 1906 he began a paper on the subject of patriotism as "Moral Cowardice," *ibid.*, DV #128 (13).

8. *Ibid.*, P #84.

9. *Ibid.*, P #100, apparently written about 1899.

10. Quoted in my *On the Poetry of Mark Twain with Selections from His Verse* (Urbana, 1966), p. 34.

11. *Mark Twain in Eruption*, ed. Bernard De Voto (New York, 1940), p. 317.

12. Letter to Joe Twichell in *Mark Twain's Letters*, ed. Albert B. Paine (New York, 1917), II, 695. Hereafter, this collection is called *Letters*.

13. "A Word of Encouragement to Our Blushing Exiles," in *Europe and Elsewhere*, *op. cit.*, pp. 221–224.

14. MTP, Notebook #32, p. 19.

15. *See* his 1899 article "My First Lie, and How I Got Out of It," *The Writings of Mark Twain*, Author's National Edition (New York, 1913), XXIII, 148. Hereafter, this collection is called *Writings*.

16. *Mark Twain-Howells Letters, op. cit.*, II, 715–716.

17. Stephen Leacock, *Mark Twain* (New York, 1935), p. 144.

18. *Letters, op. cit.*, II, 695.

19. *Europe and Elsewhere, op. cit.*, p. 220.

20. MTP, P #212, "Margrave of Bayreuth," a thirty-eight-page manuscript.

21. *Ibid.*, Notebook #32b, p. 23.

22. *Writings, op. cit.*, XXIV, 268–285.

23. MTP. Notebook #32b, p. 52.

24. *Mark Twain's Notebook,* ed. Albert B. Paine (New York, 1935), p. 368. Hereafter, this work is called *Notebook.*

25. *What Is Man? And Other Essays, op. cit.*, p. 172. For some reason Mark Twain recalled this eulogy from publication at the last moment. It is included in his *Autobiography, op. cit.*, 1, 166–171.

26. *Biography, op. cit.*, II, 1070.

27. *London Daily Chronicle,* June 3, 1899.

28. *See* his 1898 article "Dueling" in *Europe and Elsewhere, op. cit.*, pp. 225–232; *see also, Autobiography of Mark Twain,* ed. Charles Neider (New York, 1959), p. 330.

29. "Stirring Times in Austria," *Writings, op. cit.*, XXII, 248. This essay is fifty pages long.

30. MTP, P #58, nineteen pages.

31. *Writings, op. cit.* XXII, 250–275.

32. MTP, DV #236, seventeen pages.

33. "The Austrian Edison Keeping School Again," *Writings, op. cit.*, XXIII, 255–259. This was the same young inventor Sczezepanik with whom Mark Twain stood ready in 1898 to invest any money he could lay his hands on. His financial adviser, fortunately, killed the deal.

34. "At the Appetite Cure," *ibid.*, XXII, 293–310. This appeared in *Cosmopolitan,* August, 1898.

35. *Ibid.,* XXIII, 230–231.

36. "About Play-Acting," *ibid.*, XXIII, 215. This article on the Burg Theater appeared in *Forum,* October, 1898.

37. *Biography, op. cit.*, II, 1062.

38. MTP, Notebook #32, p. 20.

39. MTP, translation from *Volks-Beldungs-Blätter,* XIII, 193 (Krems, 1898).

40. *Letters, op. cit.*, II, 672.

41. Letter of February 17, 1898, to Baroness Bertha von Suttner; now in the Missouri Historical Society, St. Louis.

42. *Letters, op. cit.*, II, 672–674.

43. Chester L. Davis, "Mark Twain and the United Nations," *Twainian* (November-December, 1950), p. 1.

44. Samuel Eliot Morison, *The Oxford History of the American People* (New York, 1965), p. 802.

45. MTP, *see* his letters to J. B. Pond and to Senator Cole of California in 1898.

46. *Letters, op. cit.,* II, 663.

47. "Ye Cuban Patriot: A Calm Inspection of Him," *A Bibliography of Mark Twain,* ed. Merle Johnson (New York, 1955), pp. 168–169.

48. *Europe and Elsewhere, op. cit.,* p. 224.

49. *Notebook, op. cit.* p. 364.

50. *Biography, op. cit.,* II, 1079.

51. MTP, DV #237.

52. *Mark Twain-Howells Letters, op. cit.,* II, 697.

53. MTP, Notebook #32b, p. 56. Paine did not print this or the savage anti-Church portions of *The Mysterious Stranger.* The villain's role was given to the astrologer.

54. *Ibid.,* DV #327, typescript pp. 128–128. Mention of indemnities dates this passage somewhat later than Mark Twain's Vienna period.

55. *Mark Twain-Howells Letters, op. cit.,* II, 691–692.

56. MTP, unpublished letter of July 12, 1899. Part of this letter is in Clara Clemens' *My Father: Mark Twain* (New York, 1931), pp. 214–215.

57. MTP, see typescripts of unpublished letters to Richard Watson Gilder, August 22, and to Laurence Hutton, September 18. *See also,* his letter of September 6 to Joe Twichell, *Letters, op. cit.,* II, 683.

58. "My First Lie and How I Got Out of It," *Writings, op. cit.,* XXIII, 147.

59. MTP, Notebooks #31, #32a, #32b.

60. *Ibid.,* P #46. Today the population of Monaco has more than doubled, whereas its area has been reduced to about one-half of a square mile.

61. *Letters, op. cit.,* II, 697.

62. MTP, DV #239, twenty-eight pages.

63. *Letters, op. cit.,* II, 690.

64. *Ibid.,* II, 700–701, letter to J. Y. M. MacAlister.

NOTES TO CHAPTER 6

1. *Mark Twain's Letters,* ed. Albert B. Paine (New York, 1917), II, 699; letter of August 12, 1900, to Joe Twichell. Hereafter, this collection is called *Letters.*

2. William Dean Howells, *My Mark Twain* (New York, 1910), p. 76.

3. Albert B. Paine, *Mark Twain: A Biography* (New York, 1912), II, 1064. Hereafter, this work is called *Biography*.

4. Samuel Eliot Morison, *Oxford History of the American People* (New York, 1965), p. 806.

5. *Mark Twain's Notebook*, ed. Albert B. Paine (New York, 1935), p. 395. Hereafter, this work is called *Notebook*.

6. *Mark Twain Papers*, DV #25. All material quoted from the Mark Twain Papers is copyright © 1969 by, and used with the permission of, the Mark Twain Company. Hereafter, this collection is called MTP. *See also*, "As Regards Patriotism," *Europe and Elsewhere*, ed. Albert B. Paine (New York, 1923), pp. 301–303.

7. *New York Herald*, October 16, 1900, reprinted in *Life As I Find It*, ed. Charles Neider (Garden City, N.Y., 1961), pp. 334–335.

8. MTP, P #42a, "Book One," p. 18.

9. See my *On the Poetry of Mark Twain: With Selections from His Verse* (Urbana, 1966), p. 34.

10. *Ibid.*, p. 128, where the entire poem is reprinted.

11. *Ibid.*, pp. 129–131, where the entire poem is reprinted.

12. MTP, typescript of unpublished letter to J. Y. M. MacAlister.

13. *Ibid.*, P #89aa, "Aguinaldo."

14. *Ibid.*, P #89aa, "The Great Republic Became the Great Despotism."

15. *Ibid.*, P #52. *See also, ibid.*, DV #128 (12).

16. *Ibid.*, DV #352.

17. *Ibid.*, DV #358, quoted in *Biography, op. cit.*, III, 1164.

18. Quoted in the *Chicago Record*, October 5, 1900, clipping in MTP.

19. MTP, P#267 (DV #101). This differs somewhat from such newspaper accounts as that quoted in *Mark Twain-Howells Letters*, ed. Henry Nash Smith and William Gibson (Cambridge, Mass., 1960), II, 724. Churchill's mother was American.

20. MTP, P #19. Only a small portion of this twenty-five-page typescript is included in the "Tammany and Croker" speech of 1901 in *Mark Twain's Speeches*, ed. Albert B. Paine (New York, 1933), pp. 114–117.

21. *Ibid.*, DV #359a. A Paine note on the manuscript says, "about 1905 on the Russ-Jap War," but the subject seems more like the Boxer Rebellion.

22. *Biography, op. cit.*, III, 1127. This was published in the *New York Herald*, December 30, 1900, and widely reprinted.

23. MTP, in 1900 letter file, together with a covering letter to C. Moberly Bell.

24. *Ibid.*, Notebook #32b, p. 74. References to the MTP Notebooks are to the typescripts whose pages are numbered.

25. *Letters from a Chinese Official: Being an Eastern View of Western Civilization* (New York, 1904), p. 30. Copy in MTP.

26. *Europe and Elsewhere, op. cit.*, p. 261.

27. *Ibid.*, p. 264.

28. Many of these clippings are still among his papers in MTP.

29. *Europe and Elsewhere, op. cit.*, p. 295.

30. MTP, P #249.

31. *Letters, op. cit.*, II, 770, letter to Twichell.

32. MTP, P #83 (DV #203).

33. *Ibid.*, DV #265.

34. *Europe and Elsewhere, op. cit.*, pp. 310–314.

35. *Mark Twain in Eruption*, ed. Bernard De Voto (New York, 1940), pp. 1–34.

36. Not "For God and S——," as quoted in Philip S. Foner, *Mark Twain: Social Critic* (New York, 1958), p. 286. The manuscript and typescript are both clear. In the passage quoted below Foner also gives "sling-shot" for "slung-shot." *See*, MTP, DV #345.

37. *Biography, op. cit.*, III, 1149.

38. *Europe and Elsewhere, op. cit.*, p. 398.

39. *Biography, op. cit.*, III, 1208.

40. MTP, manuscript in letter file. For more about this club, *see*, *Biography, op. cit.*, III, 1153–1154; *Letters, op. cit.*, II, 717–719; *and* the unpublished autobiographical dictation of April 9, 1906, in MTP, which also contain many letters written to the different club members.

41. Paine mistakenly puts this cruise in April or later: *Biography, op. cit.*, III, 1162–1163.

42. *Notebook, op. cit.*, p. 379.

43. MTP, DV #351.

44. Published in *Harper's Weekly* and *Harper's Monthly*, respectively, in 1904.

45. *Notebook, op. cit.*, p. 387.

46. "The Czar's Soliloquy," *North American Review*, CLXXX (March, 1905), p. 323.

47. *Ibid.*, p. 324.

48. *See, Krokodil,* November 20, 1960, *and especially* M. O. Mendelson, "Mark Twain's Unpublished Literary Heritage," *Soviet Review,* II, 9, (September, 1961), pp. 33–53.

49. MTP, from the rough draft of a letter dated May 7 [1899].

50. *Ibid.,* P #28.

51. *Biography, op. cit.,* III, 1242–1243.

52. *Letters, op. cit.,* II, 776.

53. *Mark Twain's Autobiography,* ed. Albert B. Paine (New York, 1924), II, 292, Hereafter, this work is called *Autobiography.*

54. *Biography, op. cit.,* III, 1285. A four-page manuscript, MTP, DV #246, entitled "a Cloud-Burst of Calamities" describes several of these critical days in April, 1906.

55. *Mark Twain in Eruption, op. cit.,* p. 211.

56. Unpublished letter from his secretary Isabel Lyon to W. T. H. Howe, April 2, 1938, in the Berg Collection, New York Public Library.

57. MTP, DV #370.

58. *King Leopold's Soliloquy* (Boston, 1905), p. 9.

59. *Ibid.* (East Berlin, 1961), p. 25.

60. MTP, P #80, "A Thanksgiving Sentiment."

61. *Ibid.,* he describes this episode in an unpublished portion of his autobiography, April 3, 1906. *See also* the correspondence of Mark Twain, Robert Bacon, and Dr. Barbour of the Congo Reform Association, all in MTP.

62. *Ibid.,* DV #370a. Of this sixteen-page manuscript, only one sentence is included in *Biography, op. cit.,* III, 1231.

63. *Autobiography, op. cit.,* II, 190.

64. *Mark Twain-Howells Letters,* ed. Henry Nash Smith and William Gibson (Cambridge, Mass., 1960), II, 804.

65. *Mark Twain in Eruption, op. cit.,* pp. 382–383.

66. *Ibid.,* p. 384.

67. *See especially* MTP, P #105 (DV #31a), "Passage from a Lecture." Roger B. Salomon's *Twain and the Image of History* (New Haven, 1957) is an excellent discussion of this theory.

68. *Mark Twain in Eruption, op. cit.,* p. 68.

69. *Notebook, op. cit.,* p. 393.

70. *Mark Twain in Eruption, op. cit.,* p. 34.

71. *Ibid.,* p. xxvii.

72. MTP, autobiographical dictation of January 9, 1907.

73. *Letters, op. cit.,* II, 806.

74. *The Autobiography of Mark Twain,* ed. Charles Neider (New York, 1959), p. 348.

75. Paine made good use of these in *Biography, op. cit.,* Chapters 257–259, but he did not include most of them in the *Autobiography, op. cit.* The major unpublished portions were dictated July 25, August 23, 26, 29, 30, 31, September 6, 12, and October 1, 2, 5.

76. *Biography, op. cit.,* III, 1398.

77. MTP, P #124.

78. *Ibid.,* dictation of July 25, 1907.

79. *Biography, op. cit.,* III, 1388.

80. *North American Review,* October, 1907.

81. *Biography, op. cit.,* III, 1398.

82. *Ibid.,* III, 1403.

83. MTP, P #204, "Bishop-Speech."

84. *Ibid.,* dictation of October 11, 1907.

85. Elizabeth Wallace, *Mark Twain and the Happy Island* (Chicago, 1913), p. 45.

86. Dorothy Quick, *Enchantment* (Norman, 1961), p. 164.

87. Clara Clemens, *My Father: Mark Twain* (New York, 1931), p. 286.

88. *Mark Twain and the Happy Island, op. cit.,* p. 139.

89. *Biography, op. cit.,* III, 1578.

NOTES TO THE CONCLUSION

1. Van Wyck Brooks, *The Ordeal of Mark Twain* (New York, 1920), p. 256.

2. Rachel M. Varble, *Jane Clemens: The Story of Mark Twain's Mother* (New York, 1964), pp. 59, 326.

3. Letter to George Ade on January 2, 1941, printed in the *Twainian* (April, 1945), p. 4.

4. "Mark Twain: An Inquiry," *North American Review,* CLXII (February, 1901), p. 315.

5. Justin Kaplan, *Mr. Clemens and Mark Twain* (New York, 1966), p. 170.

6. George Hiram Brownell, "Mark Twain on How Wars Start," *Twainian* (January, 1940), p. 4.

7. Paul Carter, "Mark Twain and War," *Twainian* (March, 1942), p. 1.

INDEX

A

"At Homes"; *see* Twain as lecturer
Australasia; *see* Twain on Australia
Australia, Twain on, 188–92
Austria; *see* Twain and
Aziz, Abdul, Twain on, 48
Azores, Twain on, 33

B

Bacon, R., 282
Baetzhold, H., on Twain, 81–82
Bahamas, Twain on, 272
Beard, D., 144
Belgium, Twain on, 280–83
Bell, M., 251, 288
Benjamin, P., 8
Benson, I., on Twain, 19
Berkeley (in *American Claimant*), 157, 158
Bermuda; *see* Twain and
Bigelow, P., 224
Billings, J., 28
Birrell, A., on Twain, 292
Bismarck, O., 51, 95, 242–43
Blackmer, M., 295–96
Blair, W., on Twain, 143
Bliss, E., 27
Bliss, F., 113
Bohemia, Twain on, 246; *see also* Marienbad
Bourget, P., 183, 184; Twain on, 191
Bright, J., 123
British Isles; *see* Twain and England; *see also* England
Brooks, V. W., on Longfellow, 3; on Twain, 72, 303
Brown, Dr. J., 85
Brown, Mr. (a Twain character), 23, 28, 36, 71, 109
Brownell, G. H., on Twain, 306
Browning, R., 169

Buffalo Express, 16, 72, 74, 242
Burlingame, A., 16–17, 72
Burnet, J. G., *The Gods of India,* 271
Burns, R., 179

C

Calverton, V. F., 35
Camelot (in *Conn. Yankee*), 147, 148, 156, 178, 257
Campbell, C., 211
Canby, H. S., 29
Canty, Tom (in *The Prince and the Pauper*), 124–25, 126–27
Carlyle, T., 146
la Carteloise, Alisande (Sandy) (in *Conn. Yankee*), 152
Carter, P., on Twain, 306
Catholic Church; *see* Twain and
Cauchon, Pierre (in *Joan of Arc*), 179
Cervantes, M.; *Don Quixote,* 143, 152; Twain's admiration for, 143, 229; Twain compared to, 270, 306
Ceylon, Twain on, 197
Chamberlain, J., 227, 229, 259, 266
Chatto and Windus, 224, 237, 249
China; *see* Twain and
chivalry, Stedman on, 143; Twain on, 143, 152, 153, 154
Cholmondeley, R., 118
Churchill, W., Twain on, 262–63
Clemens, C., 91, 163, 166, 167, 182, 185, 190, 197, 198, 220, 223, 232, 237, 247, 249, 275, 295, 297, 298, 300
Clemens, Jane, on Twain, 303
Clemens, Jean, 132, 163, 170, 217, 247, 251, 273, 285, 297, 298
Clemens, L., 74

Clemens, Olivia, 17, 28, 57, 62, 67, 72, 73–74, 75, 76, 83, 84, 85, 87, 90, 132, 162, 163, 164, 167, 170, 177, 180, 181, 185, 186, 190, 198, 210, 218, 220, 223, 230, 237, 251, 269, 272, 273, 274, 275, 289; censors Twain's writings, 57, 170, 190, 269; influence on Twain, 57, 72, 185, 220, 230; poor health of, 73–74, 84, 85, 164, 186, 273, 274, 275
Clemens, Orion, 181, 236
Clemens, Samuel L.; see Twain, Mark
Clemens, Susy, 74, 83, 91, 132, 163, 164, 166, 182, 186, 217, 223, 224, 232, 238
Congo; see Twain and
Conway, M., 118
Cooper, J. F., 4, 5, 29, 64, 68, 83, 129, 301, 302, 304
Crane, S., 163, 230
Curzon, Chancellor, 293; on Twain, 292

D

Dahomey, Twain on, 113, 114
Daily San Francisco Alta California, Twain writes for, 23, 25, 26, 51, 54, 57, 62, 64
Darwin, C., 118
Dauphin (in *Joan of Arc*), 179
De Forest, J. W., 30-31
De Mill, J., 31
De Voto, B., 124; on Twain, 287
De Winton, Colonel, 127
Dickens, C., 128
Dickinson, L., 67
Doré, G., Twain on, 79–80
Dreyfus Case, Twain on, 244, 249, 277

E

Eastern Europe, Twain's fear of, 226, 230
Edward VI (in *The Prince and the Pauper*), 125–26, 127

Edward VII, Twain and, 144, 172, 177, 224, 290
Elizabeth, Empress (Austria), Twain on, 233
Elizabeth, Queen (Romania), 234
Emerson, R. W., 4–5, 8, 29, 45, 52, 65, 71, 117, 154, 301, 302
England, Adams on, 9–10, 79, 302; Cooper on, 303; Lowell on, 302; Melville on, 6, 7, 8; see also Twain and

F

Fairbanks, Mrs. A. W. ("Mother"), and Twain, 27, 36, 57, 60, 72, 76, 84, 90, 91, 138, 177
Far East, Twain on, 187
Fiji Islands, Twain on, 188
Finlay, F., 163
Finn, Huck, 176
Fiske, S., 30, 31
Flanders, Twain on, 83
Ford, D. R., 72
France, Adams on, 1, 9; see also Twain and
Franklin, B., 1, 14, 301
Franz Josef, Twain on, 233–34, 243
Freneau, P., 2
Fuller, M., 66
Funston, General F., 261, 284

G

Gabrilowitsch, O., 166, 237, 295, 297, 298
Galaxy, Twain writes for, 16, 74
George I (Greece), Twain on, 48
Germany, Adams on, 9; see also Twain and
Gorky, M., and Twain, 279, 284
Great Britain; see Twain and England; see also England
Gould, J., 144
Grant, U. S., 17, 81, 131, 132, 162
Griffin, G., 91
Gwyn, N., Twain on, 145

H

Hackett, F., 124
Harper and Brothers, 243
Harper's Magazine, 144, 234–35, 236, 269, 278
Harper's Monthly, 269, 280
Harris (a Twain character), 106, 109, 167, 169
Harris, A., Twain on, 244
Harte, B., 92; on Twain, 64
Harvey, G., 278
Hastings, W., Twain on, 198–99, 263
Hawkins, J., Twain on, 139
Hawthorne, N., 5–6, 29, 52, 302
Hay, R., 91
Henderson, A., 289
Henry, Prince (Prussia), 271
Henry VIII (in *The Prince and the Pauper*), 124, 125
Holy Land, De Forest on, 30–31; De Mill on, 31; Melville on, 7, 59; *see also under* Twain and the Middle East
Hotten, J. C. ("Hottentot"), Twain on, 78, 82
Howells, W. D., 9, 10–11, 14, 78, 92, 110, 120, 136, 155, 186, 226, 230, 236, 238, 244, 246, 256, 284–85, 302, 304; on Twain, 75, 82, 94, 144, 147, 171
Hungarians, Twain on, 238

I

imperialism, Adams on, 303; *see also* Twain on
India; *see* Twain and
Ireland, Twain on, 131, 132, 251
Irving, W., 2, 3, 7, 8, 12, 32, 34, 64, 83, 86, 119, 164, 301, 302, 305, 307; *Sketch-Book,* 2, 4, 86
Italy, De Mill on, 31; Fiske on, 30; Hawthorne on, 6; Howells on, 10–11; Melville on, 6; *see also* Twain and

J

James, H., 6, 9, 11–13, 14, 40, 43, 62, 65, 66, 158, 251, 302, 305
James, W., 12
Jameson, Dr. L. S., 197
Jefferson, T., 1, 301
Jews, persecution of; *see* Twain on
Jim (in *Tom Sawyer Abroad*), 176
Joan of Arc, 261; Twain on, 178, 249

K

Kaplan, J., on Twain, 305
Kellgren, H., 247, 249, 251
Kipling, R., 195, 212, 227, 228, 292, 293, 297; on Twain, 270
Kossuth, F., 238
Kossuth, L., 238
Krumpelmann, J. T., on Twain, 170

L

Lang, A., 144, 155, 180, 224
Langdon, C., 62, 72, 73, 241
Langdon, Jervis, 241
Langdon, Mrs. Jervis, 85, 98, 162
Langdon, Julia, 230–31
Langdon, Olivia; *see* Clemens, Olivia
Langtry, L., Twain on, 135
Leacock, S., 32; on Twain, 124, 230, 303
Leary, K., 163, 273
Lecky, W. E. H., *History of European Morals,* 251
Leopold II (Belgium), 280–82, 283, 303
Leschetizky, T., 232, 237
Lewis, R. W. B., 32
Lewisohn, L., on Twain, 305
Liholiho, King (Hawaii), Twain on, 188
Longfellow, H. W., 3, 164, 301, 305, 307
Lorne, Marquis of, 127
Lowell, J. R., 8–9, 31–32, 66, 302
Lucy, Sir H., 251

Lyon, I., 297

M

McClure Syndicate, Twain's travel letters for, 163–66, 172
McKinley, President W., 256, 259, 266
Malory, Sir T., Twain's interest in, 137–38
Mansinghji, T. S., 205
Marienbad, Twain on, 165–66, 173
Mark Twain Papers, 74, 124, 132
Marryat, Captain, 128
Massiglia, Countess, Twain on, 273–74
Mauritius, Twain on, 215
Meisterschaft, 170
Melville, H., 6–7, 8, 10, 29, 37, 59, 64, 301, 302
Merlin (in *Conn. Yankee*), 144, 154
Middle East; *see* Twain and missionaries; *see* Twain and
Missouri, University of, and Twain, 270–71, 288
Monaco, Twain on, 250
monarchy, Jefferson on, 1; *see also* Twain on
Monroe Doctrine, 193–94
Morgan, Hank (Boss) (in *Conn. Yankee*), 145–46, 147, 148–49, 150, 151–52, 153, 154, 158, 163, 178, 257
Morison, S. E., 257n
Morris, W., 143
Morse, S., 1

N

Napoleon I, Twain on, 178
Napoleon III, 45, 46, 50–52, 305
Nast, T., 75
Neal, J., 4, 301
Netherlands, Twain on, 116
Newell, J., 27
New York Herald, Twain writes for, 83–84
New York Sun, Twain's travel let-ters for, 163–66, 172
New York Tribune, Twain writes for, 22, 86
New Zealand, Twain on, 194–95
Nicaragua, Twain on, 24
Nicholas II (Russia), Twain on, 275–76, 277, 278
North American Review, 261, 265–68, 271, 275, 284
Nuhn, F., 2

O

Oxford University, Melville on, 7–8; and Twain, 288, 292–93; Twain on, 87

P

Paine, A. B., 131, 138, 139, 297–98, 299, 300; on Twain, 74, 83, 113, 165, 187
Palestine; *see under* Twain and Middle East
Phelps, W. W., 169
Philippine Islands; *see* Twain and
Pitcairn Island, 117
Punch, 251; on Twain, 293

Q

"Quaker City," Twain sails on, 25, 26, 32–33, 45, 49, 62, 63, 72

R

Reid, W., 86
Rhodes, C., 226; Twain on, 221–22, 228, 231
Riley, J. H., 73
Rogers, H. H., 181, 218, 237, 243, 251, 272, 296, 297
Roosevelt, T., 287; Twain on, 269, 277–78
Rossmore, Earl of (in *American Claimant*), 157
Russo-Japanese War, Twain on, 266, 277–78, 303

S

Sahara Desert, 176

Saint-Simon, H., 134, 146
Sandhurst, Lord, 198
Sandwich Islands; see Twain and
Hawaiian Islands
Saraswati, Swami, Twain on, 208–
209
Savage Club, Twain and, 224, 247,
293
Sawyer, Tom, 176
Sayaji Rao III, 207
Scott, Sir W., 157–58, 161, 176,
178; Twain on, 129, 130, 135,
143, 153
Scotland, Twain on, 84–85, 132,
251
Sellers, Colonel M. (in American
Claimant), 156, 157–58, 159,
232
"Seward's Folly," 50
Shaw, G. B., 178, 179; on Twain,
68–69, 289–90
Sherman, S., on Twain, 36, 68, 161
Singh, Sir S. M., 213
Smythe, C., 185, 217
Smith, General, Twain on, 261
Society Islands, 20
Spaulding, C., 91, 98
Spaulding, P., 224
Staley, Bishop, 20
Standring, G. C., 142
Stanley, H. M., 224
Stedman, E. C., 143
Stoddard, C. W., 86
Stoker, B., 224
Strout, C., 2
Sweden, Twain on, 247, 251
Szchenyi, Count, 295

T

Tasmania, Twain on, 192–93
Tauchnitz Editions, 92
Taylor, B., 8, 9, 29, 112, 236, 302
Taylor, C. B., on Twain, 306
Tchaikovsky, Twain on, 278–79
Tennyson, A., 143, 144; Twain
on, 153

Thakombau, King (Fiji Islands),
188
Thoreau, H. D., 5, 61
Times (London), 251, 264, 288;
on Twain, 294
Trilling L., on Matthew Arnold,
136
Turner, F. J., 65
Twain, Mark, AND ANTIQUITY, 34,
37–40; ON ARISTOCRACY, HE-
REDITARY, 78, 80–81, 82, 135,
136, 137, 139, 141, 148, 149–
50, 152, 153–58, 232–33, 245,
285, 286, 287, 294, 306; see
also under Twain and U.S.; AND
ART, 35–36, 37–38, 79–80, 100:
on the Old Masters, 35–36, 79,
80, 100–101, 111, 167–68; on
opera, 36, 99–100, 111, 164;
AND AUSTRIA: on American
Minister to, 244; on Bismarck,
242–43; on Burg Theater, 238;
on Catholic Church in, 235, 245;
on dueling in, 234; on Empress
Elizabeth of, 233; on Franz
Josef, 233–34, 243; on Jews in,
235–36; in Kaltenleutgeben,
241, 243; on newspapers in, 235;
on parliament of, 234–35, 243;
Vienna, reception in, 237, 238,
243, 246; BECOMES TOO FA-
MILIAR WITH EUROPE: 93–94,
174–75, 183; AND BERMUDA:
on British in, 89–90, 287, 288;
on cleanliness of, 88–89, 287;
love for, 62, 88–90, 288, 299;
on serenity of, 89, 288, 299;
vacations in, 14, 88–90, 287–
88, 295–300; BOOKS OF: The
American Claimant, 156, 157–
59, 160, 164; Captain Stormfield's Visit to Heaven, 268; A
Connecticut Yankee in King Arthur's Court, 41, 48, 138, 142–
56, 157, 158, 159, 163, 178,
245, 256, 280, 286; Eddypus,
258; Following the Equator,

186–222, 224, 227–28, 237, 263; *The Guilded Age*, 22, 80, 81; *Huckleberry Finn*, 87, 90, 122, 130, 149, 162, 209; *The Innocents Abroad*, 3, 7, 23, 28, 29, 31, 32, 35–36, 41, 44, 46, 50, 59, 61, 64, 65, 67, 68, 69, 71, 74, 79, 82–83, 86, 94, 104, 120, 304; *The Innocents Adrift*, 167–69; *King Leopold's Soliloquy*, 280, 281–82, 283; *Life on the Mississippi*, 87, 128, 129, 130; *The Mysterious Stranger*, 142, 244–46, 269; *Personal Recollections of Joan of Arc*, 177–80, 182; *The Prince and the Pauper*, 90, 122, 123, 124–27, 130, 147, 150, 182; *Roughing It*, 16, 17, 74; *Tom Sawyer*, 87; *Tom Sawyer Abroad*, 176; *A Tramp Abroad*, 93, 94–95, 99, 100, 103, 106, 109, 110, 113, 120, 121, 222, 237; *What Is Man?*, 230, 263, 284; BUSINESS VENTURES OF: *Buffalo Express*, 72, 74; financial difficulties from, 90, 92, 130, 137, 162, 180–81, 185, 230, 237, 238; Paige typesetter, 147, 162, 175, 180; publishing house, 146, 162, 175, 180; AND THE CATHOLIC CHURCH: in Austria, 235, 245; contempt for, 33, 48, 52–53, 54; in England, 151, 154; in Hawaii, 33; in Holy Land, 53, 54; in Italy, 33, 48, 52, 53–54, 110, 302; AND CHINA: and American Minister to, 16–17; on Boxer Rebellion in, 17, 262, 264, 265; on imperialism in, 245–46, 255, 263, 264, 265–66; interest in ambassadorship to, 17; on missionaries in, 246, 264, 265; and students from, 17; ON CHRISTENDOM, 59–60, 263–64, 269: on progress of, 246, 258; ON COMMUNISTS,

276–77; AND THE CONGO: on Belgium in, 280–83; and Congo Reform Association, 280; on U.S. role in, 281, 282–83; ON COPYRIGHT, INTERNATIONAL, 135, 160, 251; ON CUBA, 22, 239, 241–42, 256, 259; *see also* Twain on Spanish-American War; AND ENGLAND: on the Anglican Church, 135, 225; on Anglo-American alliance, 226–27, 230, 262–63, 277, 302; on the aristocracy in, 78, 80–81, 135, 136, 137, 139, 141, 148, 149–50, 152, 156; on arrogance of, 117–19, 132, 225; on the British Museum, 78–79; on British tourists in U.S. 128–29; at Brown's Hotel, 252, 253, 290, 293; on Catholic Church in, 151, 154; on Chamberlain's foreign policy, 227, 229, 259, 266; on Churchill, 262–63; defends America to, 122–23; difficulty in writing to, 75, 76–78, 119–20; honored by Oxford, 288, 292–93; love for, 75, 76, 81–82, 249, 292; on monarchy in, 135, 136, 137, 139, 140, 141, 148, 156; on newspapers in, 119, 140; on penal code of, 123, 124, 125–27, 150, 192, 225, 226; on people of, 78, 79, 117; planned book on, 74–75, 76, 118; praise for, 75, 76, 78–79, 82, 89–90, 116–19, 247, 302; and Prince of Wales (Edward VII), 144, 172, 177, 224, 290, 293; on the Queen's Jubilee, 225–26, 230; reception in, 75, 83, 87, 247, 249, 251, 288–90, 291–94; on Stonehenge, 87; on superiority to America of, 81–82, 84, 87–88, 291–94; on Westminster Abbey, 80; AND FRANCE: on Bois de Boulogne, 37, disillusionment with, 51–52;

dislike for people of, 113–15, 133–34, 249–50, 301; on Dreyfus Case in, 244, 249, 269, 277; on dueling in, 97–98, 234; on French view of U.S., 183–84; on Grand Prix, 114; on hotels of, 45; on immorality in, 113, 114, 115, 132, 134, 184, 249–50; on lack of modernity in, 44–45; learns French language, 52; on literature of, 134, 168; on Napoleon III, 45, 46, 50–52; on Notre Dame, 38; on prostitution in, 41, 114; on railroads in, 44–45, 46; on Saint-Simon, 134, 146; on Versailles, 47; on Zola, 168, 269; AND GERMANY: on Berlin, 169, 170, 172–73; on customs of, 98, 101, 102, 104–106; on dueling in, 97; on government of, 96; in Heidelberg, 91–92, 166; and language of, 52, 91, 102–103, 104, 132, 169, 170; on newspapers in, 103, 170, 176; praises people of, 98–99; reception in, 92, 169, 171; on student life, 97, 102; on Wilhelm I, 96; on Wilhelm II, 171; AS GOODWILL AMBASSADOR, ix, x, 240, 243, 294, 307; AND THE HAWAIIAN ISLANDS: ambivalence toward, 18, 23; on Americans in, 18–19, 21, 22; on British in, 21; on Chinese in, 16; on French in, 20, 21; on hospitality of natives, 18–19; on imperialism in, 18, 19, 20–21; on missionaries in, 18, 19–21, 23; on monarchy in, 21, 48, 188; planned book on, 130–31; on serenity of, 18–19, 187–88; on slavery in, 16; on U.S. annexation of, 21, 22, 23, 86; AND HEADS OF STATE: Alexander II, 46, 49, 50, 141; Alexander III, 141, 147, 159–60, 303, 305; Abdul Aziz, 48; Edward VII, 144, 172, 177, 224, 290, 293; Elizabeth (Austria), 233; Franz Josef, 233–34; George I, 48; Paul Kruger, 217, 227; Leopold II, 280–82, 283; Liholiho, 188; Prince of Montenegro, 286; Napoleon III, 45, 46, 50–52; Nicholas II, 275–76, 277, 278; Shah of Persia, 83–84; King of Sweden, 251; Wilhelm I, 96; Wilhelm II, 171; HONORARY DEGREES OF, 270–71, 288, 292–93; AS HUMANITARIAN, 35, 39–40, 46, 47–48, 54, 55, 142, 147, 150, 151, 160–61, 191, 255–56, 303–304; ILLNESSES OF: bronchitis, 198, 273; carbuncles, 185, 186, 189, 190–91, 194; cholera, 58, 63; dysentery, 113; heart trouble, 298, 299–300; rheumatism, 93, 113, 164, 175, 247; ON IMPERIALISM, 18, 19, 20–21, 89–90, 188, 189, 192–93, 195, 198–99, 207, 215–16, 220–21, 227–28, 229–30, 231, 245–46, 255, 256–59, 261–65, 266–67, 268–70, 303; see also under Twain and U.S.; AND INDIA, 195–214: on Agra, 212; on Baroda, 205–207; on Benares, 201, 202; on Bombay, 197–98; on Calcutta, 209; on caste system in, 202–203, 214; on Darjeeling, 210–11; on English in, 198–99, 207, 214; on Warren Hastings in, 198–99, 263; on Jaipur, 212–13; love of exotic in, 195, 197, 199, 200, 206, 213; on missionaries in, 201–202; on the Parsees of, 204, 205; reception in, 198, 204, 205–206; on religious atmosphere of, 200–201, 208, 209; on Suttee in, 200; on Thuggee in, 200; on the Taj Mahal, 203–204, 208, 212; INTEREST IN HISTORY OF, 34, 37–

40, 124, 127–28, 167, 178, 191–92, 302; AS INTERNATIONALIST, 226–27, 240–41, 302–303, 306; AND ITALY: on Catholic Church in, 33, 48, 52, 53–54, 110, 302; first trip to, 26; and Florence, 47, 52, 175, 177, 273–75; on Milan, 47; on Naples, 43, 55–56; on officials in, 55; on peasants in, 55, 56, 274; on people of, 55–56, 110; on Pompeii, 37–38, 39; on Rome, 38, 46, 56, 110; on St. Mark's, 47, 110; on St. Peter's, 47, 65; on Turin, 109–10; on upper class in, 55; on Venice, 43; on women of, 56; ON JEWS, persecution of, 235–36, 249, 275, 278; AS LECTURER, 17, 24, 74, 86, 162, 185, 186, 189, 190, 191, 194, 195, 205, 206, 210, 212, 214, 215, 218, 222, 223, 230, 238, 243; AND THE MIDDLE EAST, 32–34, 39, 40, 41, 42, 43, 46: on the Bedouins, 43–44; disillusionment with the Holy Land, 42, 43–44, 56–61; on the Ottoman Empire, 48–49; on Palestine, 46, 53, 54, 57–61; on Tangier, 33–34; AND MISSIONARIES: on Rev. Ament, 265–66, 267; on American Board of Foreign Missions, 265, 267; in China, 246, 264, 265; in the Congo, 281; in Hawaii, 18, 19–21, 23, 263–64; in India, 201–202; in New Guinea, 202; in the Philippines, 264; in South Africa, 202; as tools of imperialism, 19, 20–21, 263–64, 265, 267, 269; AS MODERNIST, 44–46, 64–65, 69, 111, 154, 173, 304–305; ON MONARCHY, 21, 48, 50, 52, 73, 84, 96–97, 104, 127, 135, 137, 139–41, 148, 150, 151, 155, 156–57, 164–65, 166, 188, 234, 245,

286–87, 305; ON NEWSPAPERS ABROAD, 103, 119, 140, 170, 176, 235; AND NOBILITY, ASSOCIATION WITH, 171–72, 232, 251, 305; see also under Twain and heads of state; ON PATRIOTISM, 69–70, 144–45, 227, 257, 261, 268, 275–76, 285; PESSIMISM OF, 149, 154, 224, 246, 258–59, 296, 304, 306–307; AND PHILIPPINE ISLANDS: on Aguinaldo, 259, 261; on U.S. in, 256–58, 259, 261–62, 263, 266–67, 284; see also Twain on the Spanish-American War; AS PROPHET, 9–10, 245–46, 306; ON RAILROADS ABROAD, 44–45, 46, 119, 173–74, 190, 194, 205, 208; ON REVOLUTION, 149, 159, 278–79; AND ROMANTIC SENTIMENTALISM, 129, 152, 301–302, 306: of guidebooks, 41–43, 68, 79; AS ROMANTICIST, 129–30, 180; AND RUSSIA: on Alexander II, 46, 49, 50, 141; on Alexander III, 141, 147, 159–60, 303, 305; early admiration for, 49–50; and Maxim Gorky, 279, 284; on Jews in, 275, 278; on Nicholas II, 275–76, 277, 278; and Ottoman Empire, 48–49; on Russo-Japanese War, 266, 277–78, 303; on Siberia, 159, 160; supports revolution in, 159, 278, 279; on Tchaikovsky, 278–79; on U.S. purchase of Alaska from, 50; AS SELF-CENSOR, 57, 67, 82–83, 95, 110–11, 113, 119, 155, 190, 230, 268, 287; ON SLAVERY, 16, 139, 154, 221; AND SOUTH AFRICA: on the Boers, 197, 220–21, 227, 228, 229, 230; on Boer War, 217, 220, 227–30, 302; on British in, 226–28, 229–30, 263, 266; on Jameson

Raid, 17, 228; on Cecil Rhodes, 221–22, 228, 231, 269; on Zulus in, 114, 117, 197; ON THE SPANISH-AMERICAN WAR, 229, 241–42, 256–58, 259, 261–62, 263, 269, 284, 303; AND SWITZERLAND: on Alps of, 37, 107–108; dislike for people of, 108, 109, 232; praise for, 166; on St. Nicholas, 107, 109; on Weggis, 231, 232; TIRES OF TRAVEL, 63, 93–94, 111, 120–21, 122, 162, 185, 186, 187, 191, 211, 251; ON TRANQUIL-ITY OF EUROPE, 61–62, 65, 302; TRAVEL LETTERS OF, 17–18, 19, 20, 22–23, 24, 26–27, 33, 64, 72–73, 83–84, 163–66, 172; AND U.S.: on Americans abroad, 68, 128–29; on Chinese in, 15–16, 17, 187; on diplo-mats of, 236–37, 244; disillu-sionment with, 81–82, 87–88, 96–97, 112, 117, 147, 155, 257–59, 301; entertains visitors to, 284–85; home in Hartford, Conn., 74, 90, 181; on imperial-ism of, 21, 22, 23, 86, 242, 256–59, 261–63, 264–67, 268–70, 276, 284, 285; on Indians in, 34, 113, 114, 118, 152; on Irish in, 16, 116, 131; news-paper career in, 14–15, 17, 303; on New York City, 25; on police corruption in, 15, 16; predicts hereditary aristocracy in, 141–42, 158, 285, 286, 287, 294; on racial prejudice in, 21; on slavery in, 154, 221; on Tammany Hall, 263, 269; VIC-TORIANISM OF, 18, 100, 115, 182
Twainian, 240

Twichell, D., 241
Twitchell, J., 86, 87, 88, 89, 91, 92, 95, 107, 108, 167, 230, 233, 241, 251, 252, 255, 267, 268, 287–88; *see also* Harris

V

Vanderbilt, G., Twain on marriage of, 295
Van Doren, C., 178
Very, J., 108, 166–67
Victoria, Queen (England), 205, 226
Virgin Islands, 22

W

Wales, Prince of; *see* Edward VII
Wallace, E., on Twain, 296–97, 299
Ward, A., 28, 86
Warner, C. D., 135
Webb, C. H., 24
Webster, N., 2
Wells, H. G., 284
Whitman, W., 9, 35, 67, 135, 256
Wilberforce, Archdeacon, and Twain, 291
Wilhelm I (Germany), 96
Wilhelm II (Germany), 97, 144, 171, 172, 229
Willis, N. P., 3, 8, 76
Wilson, W., 299
Witmer, T., 29–30, 31
Wood, General L., 261, 284
Woodress, J., 10

Y

Yale University, and Twain, 270–71, 288

Z

Zola, E., 168, 269